"I GAVE THEM A SWORD"

BEHIND THE SCENES OF THE NIXON INTERVIEWS

"I GAVE THEM A SWORD"

BEHIND THE SCENES OF
THE NIXON INTERVIEWS

By
DAVID FROST

WILLIAM MORROW AND COMPANY, INC.
NEW YORK 1978

Library of Congress Catalog Card Number 77-93662

ISBN 0-688-03279-6

Printed in the United States of America.

First Edition

1   2   3   4   5   6   7   8   9   10

BOOK DESIGN CARL WEISS

PHOTOS BY JOHN BRYSON

To the Memory of My Father,

the Reverend W. J. Paradine Frost,

Whose Example

I Have Tried to Follow

ACKNOWLEDGMENTS

THIS BOOK WILL, I HOPE, MAKE CLEAR THE DEBT I OWE TO JOHN BIRT and to Bob Zelnick, to Jim Reston and to Marv Minoff, and to everybody who took the leap of faith with me in bringing *The Nixon Interviews* to television—the stations and the advertisers, the investors and the networks around the world.

Here, however, I want to express the particular debt of gratitude I feel to Bob Zelnick for the contribution he made to this book. He performed in a sense the same role in *"I Gave Them a Sword"* that he did in the Interviews: he marshaled the research, talking to many of the participants, and he acted as a sounding board throughout the months of prepublication as he and John and their colleagues had throughout the months of preproduction. His advice and his perception were invaluable.

And together with his name, I must add the names of Libby Reeves Purdie, my secretary in London, Liz Sykes, my secretary in New York, and Jenifer Shell, who, having worked on the transcription of the Interviews, then undertook the task of transcribing the 100,000 or so words I wrote for this book.

For all their work on *"I Gave Them a Sword,"* I give them my thanks.

DAVID FROST

Los Angeles, California
November 1977

8

"I GAVE THEM A SWORD"

BEHIND THE SCENES OF THE NIXON INTERVIEWS

CHAPTER

1

Always remember, others may hate you, but those who hate you don't win unless you hate them, and then you destroy yourself.

—RICHARD NIXON, August 9, 1974

EVEN FROM A BLACK-AND-WHITE PICTURE ON A TELEVISION SET IN A hotel room ten thousand miles away in Sydney, Australia, you could feel the tension in the East Room. And that remark—were we really supposed to take it as a lofty and impersonal lesson to the world with no relation to Richard Nixon's own demise? Was there buried somewhere in the remark any unconscious admission, or only an unconscious irony?

Since Sydney is fourteen hours ahead of Washington, both Richard Nixon's resignation statement to the nation and his farewell to his White House staff took place on the same day as far as Australia was concerned. The drama of the moment and the pathos I found inescapable, even at that range. Early in his 1968 quest for the presidency, I had conducted a series of interviews with the nine declared presidential contenders, and when I had asked candidate Nixon how he would most like to be remembered, he had responded, "As having made some contribution to a kind of a world in which we can have peace in the last third of this century." In his first inaugural address he had repeated this theme, noting that "The greatest honor history can bestow is the title of peacemaker," proclaiming his intention to "lead the world at last out of the valley of turmoil and on to that high ground of peace that man has dreamed of since the dawn of civilization." To a nation torn by war and racial bitterness, he had pledged to "bring us together." He had also promised to avoid the sort of inflated, angry and bombastic rhetoric which had so polarized American society during the 1960's, and to "listen in new ways to the voices of quiet anguish, the voices that speak without words, the voices of the heart—to the injured voices, the anxious voices, the voices that have despaired of being heard."

But neither Richard Nixon nor the country would know real peace while he inhabited the White House. He would undertake major initiatives with America's traditional foreign adversaries—the Soviet Union and the People's Republic of China—but would not achieve an armistice in Vietnam until early 1973. He would never win the trust of America's downtrodden, its racial minorities, many of its young people or most of its educated elite, despite statistics on matters like racial integration that look better in retrospect than they seemed at the time. And from the Vietnam Accords and a fierce though one-sided reelection campaign, he would plunge immediately into his Watergate morass, at times appearing to threaten the delicate balance among the executive, legislative and judicial branches of government, using the powers of his office as a shield against his personal political downfall, pushing like a desperate Samson against the pillars of American democracy, inflaming the passions on all sides in a cause that, reduced to basics, was only himself.

Richard Nixon had succeeded in "bringing the country together" only in the belief that he was guilty of high constitutional crimes and misdemeanors, and in fulfilling his pledge of peace and unity only by resigning his office. Hours later, while Nixon was still in the air, en route to California, President Ford would underline that the circumstances leading to the Nixon downfall would not—in the short run at least—continue as a subject of partisan debate.

"Our long national nightmare is over. Our Constitution works: our great Republic is a government of laws and not of men; here the people rule."

The words were strikingly similar to those spoken by Archibald Cox on the evening of the "Saturday-Night Massacre" the previous October, the night President Nixon had fired him as Special Watergate Prosecutor. Spoken again by Nixon's handpicked successor at the very moment of his swearing-in, they emphasized that Nixon's opponents had won the debate as well as the game. Even those who had been among the former President's most zealous supporters were now willing to concede that his forced resignation represented a triumph of the American system of government rather than merely a political victory for his foes.

Yet, even as I watched this unique changing of the American guard, what I felt most was an irresistible sense of fascination with Nixon himself. Having spent the entire postwar period at or near center stage in American politics, he was now leaving the most powerful office in the world in utter disgrace. Only moments before, I had seen him flashing victory signs from the steps of his helicopter as though off on nothing more than a short campaign hop to neighboring Virginia. I knew him to be a proud and private man, yet throughout the Watergate period he had shown an almost infinite capacity to absorb personal humiliation, often apparently self-induced. The paradoxes were everywhere. In each case, which was the "real" Richard Nixon? The unanswered questions about his presidency were almost equaled by the unanswered questions about his personality. For me, he was without doubt the most intriguing man in the world to interview—and in this moment of ignominy, probably the least likely to make himself available.

At least for now. More intriguingly, it seemed to me that Nixon would one day want to talk. His career had been a succession of recoveries from disaster: from the dark early stages of the Alger Hiss investigation, from the Nixon Fund revelations and the Checkers Speech of his 1952 campaign with Eisenhower, from political defeats at the hands of John F. Kennedy in 1960 and California's Governor Pat Brown in 1962, the latter complete with that "last" press conference, and, even as President, from economic and political reverses serious enough to leave him apparently vulnerable as the year 1972 began.

A political comeback was, of course, out of the question to the extent that it implied yet another quest for elective office. But a comeback in the sense that it implied a hoped-for revision of the immediate judgments made about his presidency, a return to political respectability, was something else again.

Having regarded Watergate at first as a "third-rate burglary" and later as a "blip on history" or "the broadest but thinnest scandal in the history of American politics," Nixon would certainly, I felt, be heard to argue in the future that it paled in the light of his other political and international accomplishments. Even *in extremis,* he had conceded nothing. When, on August 5, he had released the "smoking pistol" tape of June 23, 1972, in which he had instructed his chief of staff, H. R. Haldeman, to use the C.I.A. to blunt the F.B.I.'s Watergate probe, he had said this latest evidence "does not justify the extreme step of impeachment and removal of a President." And in his resignation speech, he had sounded more like a Chief Executive who had lost a close vote over dam projects than one being ridden from office because of grave abuses, claiming that while he would like to continue the battle "it has become evident to me that I no longer have a strong enough political base in the Congress to justify continuing that effort."

Richard Nixon, in sum, having lost the battle for his presidency, would, I felt sure, begin another one for his place in history. It would be a battle he could not wage simply through his memoirs and the accounts of his hard-core supporters. Apart from being overwhelmed by the weight of orthodox opinion to the contrary, these would be discredited before even being written, were Nixon not to subject himself to the cut and thrust of informed interrogation. Either in a courtroom or elsewhere, Nixon, to regain any semblance of credibility, would have to subject himself to searching inquiry, to have his account of events tested in something akin to an adversary proceeding.

And, in a moment that would in later months appear at times to have been sheer madness, I decided that I was going to try to make that happen. If at all possible, and as soon as possible, I would interview Richard Nixon.

"Don't waste your time," said an Australian colleague, adding cheerfully, "You've got Buckley's," a piece of Australian vernacular which is intended to make a lost cause seem roseate by comparison.

"In the words of David Schoenbrun during World War II," I replied, "let de Gaulle say no."

I knew from experience that getting a clear response—whether yes or no—would not be easy. The experience came from *The David Frost Show*: following the interview with candidate Nixon in 1968, we would make annual requests for the President to appear on the program. The annual White House response had an almost ritual quality to it. It would be signed by Mr. Nixon's press secretary, Ronald Ziegler. Always Ziegler would begin by saying, "I accept your invitation for the President to appear on a show with you." And, always, after "accepting" the invitation, Ziegler would state that the question of if and when to actually *make* the appearance on the show would be taken up with the President, with further information to be provided should Mr. Nixon actually agree to be interviewed.

This touching little habit of accepting pieces of paper on which invitations were written without responding affirmatively to the invitations themselves, I came to accept as wholly innocent indications of Ziegler's ability to render the English language inoperative, even in matters not involving alleged presidential culpability. Just once, though, I would have liked to have Ziegler reject my invitation and Mr. Nixon agree to be interviewed.

But that, of course, never came to pass. Neither, understandably enough, was there an immediate response to my phone calls now to San Clemente. Indeed, such response as there was seemed intended to convey that now was a perfect moment for biding one's time. I did, however, share my thoughts with Clay Felker, then of *New York* magazine, now of *Esquire,* a friend of many years' standing and the last man on earth to splash cold water on an idea simply because of its unconventional nature or high risk potential. Clay said he would do anything he could to help, one of those vague indications of support which when spoken by most people mean little but which, in Clay's case, is the equivalent of a bond.

September 1974 was an important month for Richard Nixon's new situation—and therefore for my embryonic plans. He received his "full, free and absolute pardon" from President Ford, "for all crimes, which he, Richard Nixon, has committed or may have committed or taken part in during the period from January 20, 1969, through August 9, 1974." That meant Nixon would not himself be standing trial. And his near-fatal bout with phlebitis a few weeks later meant that the Watergate trial of Haldeman, John Ehrlichman, John Mitchell and others would proceed in Washington without his having to appear as a witness. Even as Nixon was recovering, Judge John Sirica refused to postpone the proceedings to enable Nixon to be examined publicly and under oath. Nixon's role in Watergate and other alleged abuses of power would remain for others to speculate about until he chose to speak himself.

And his September 27 contract with Warner Books for the publication of his memoirs, negotiated for two million dollars by his literary agent, Swifty Lazar, indicated that he certainly did intend to speak himself. Which in turn had several implications for my own plans. The fact that Nixon was not about to take a Carmelite vow of silence was clearly all to the good, but in another sense the memoirs could clearly become an obstacle. I was determined that the television interviews, if they took place, would not be merely an adjunct to any book, but would precede the book and make news in their own right. That might now be more difficult to achieve in any negotiation.

But the first thing to be achieved was a negotiation, and that still seemed somewhat less than imminent. In the early months of 1975 I spoke with Herb Klein, formerly director of communications at the Nixon White House, and at the time with Metromedia. I explained my thoughts to him and he said he liked the idea and undertook to speak directly with Nixon about it. He did so more than once, reporting first that Nixon was not necessarily implacably opposed to the idea, and then that he was considering the idea quite seriously. Marv Minoff, my executive vice-president in New York, came away from a May breakfast with Herb Klein quite encouraged.

"Meanwhile," said Marv, "with all the waves of debate following the Haldeman interview on CBS, do you have any second thoughts about doing what we are clearly going to be required to do— namely, pay Richard Nixon for his services?"

The issue of so-called checkbook journalism indeed had to be faced. I had, of course, thought long and hard about it for months before deciding to go ahead. First of all, I felt, we would clearly not be setting a precedent. Lyndon Johnson had already been paid for his television interviews on CBS, and he had not told the full story of Vietnam before leaving office, any more than Richard Nixon had told the full story of Watergate. And, indeed, he had retained some measure of editorial control over the finished product, something that I was determined would not occur. If there was a precedent to be set by the Nixon Interviews, the precedent would be set over the question of complete editorial control.

Secondly, it seemed to me that if our concept of privacy means anything, then a man's life has to be his own to dispose of in any way that he wishes—after he leaves public life. While in office, the time of a public servant belongs to the people he was chosen or elected to serve. It would obviously be unconscionable, for example, for a President or Secretary of State to sell his time exclusively to selected media while in office, or agree to appear at press conferences only under the sponsorship of, say, Geritol. Beyond that, however, I could not for the life of me see why, after leaving office, it was perfectly proper for a member of the executive or legislative branch to accept a position in a Washington law firm, or on the board of directors of a leading corporation, or a chair at a prominent university or a senior position with one of the many national "think tanks"—all of which trade directly on his knowledge and experience gained while on the public payroll—but improper for him to receive payment for a book of memoirs or an exhaustive series of television interviews.

Third, I failed to see any distinction in terms of principle between memoirs that appear in print and electronic memoirs that
are drawn out through the medium of on-camera interrogation.
Both involve intense preparation and the sale of one's private time
and efforts. And both serve to flesh out the record of a particular
period in the political life of the nation. Ulysses S. Grant, whose
administration was hardly free from scandal, had sold his memoirs
to a publisher named Mark Twain, and Dwight D. Eisenhower had
published his White House memoirs for a fee, but if the term "publisher" could have been replaced by that of "television producer"
in their business relationships, it would not have altered the underlying principle of what they did. It would just have substituted one
form of ordeal for another. Instead of the blank page, sitting
ominously waiting to be filled, there would have been continuous
interrogation, the face-to-face testing of their credibility. I knew
many people who found the prospect of being interviewed on television for only two or three minutes nerve-racking. How, I wondered, would they feel about all the hours we were planning with
Richard Nixon?

Except for the pardon and the illness, of course, Richard Nixon
would probably have already had to account publicly for at least
some of his illegal misdeeds. But now we were responding to an
opportunity to undertake a deadly serious journalistic project with
one of the most formidable and historically significant men of mid-
twentieth-century America as the interview subject. The job was
begging to be done. While Richard Nixon may have been unique
in the American political experience, there was nothing unique
about my approaching him with a proposed television contract or
his accepting one. Had I not acted when I did, there were plenty
of potential takers who would have, then or later. And I moved
with the confidence that the project would eventually be judged
on its editorial merit rather than its financial terms.

The potential breakthrough came in late June when Clay Felker,
returning from a weekend in the Hamptons, telephoned to say
that he had encountered Swifty Lazar at a party. Clay said that he

had gained the distinct impression that Swifty was now authorized to act for Nixon in the area of television as well as that of books, and that indeed one of Swifty's purposes in visiting the East Coast was to see what sort of interest in a Nixon interview he could whip up among the three networks. I knew I had to move quickly—and alone. Apart from Clay, Marv, and a few close colleagues, the Nixon Interviews were something I had not spoken to anybody about, partially for fear of being declared certifiable, but more because I didn't want to give the idea to anyone who had not yet had it already. I thought that an existing network outlet was pretty unlikely, but obviously negotiations about any interview with either networks or advertisers could scarcely precede negotiations with the subject. However, I was utterly confident that my interest in the enigma of Richard Nixon would also be reflected by the public's interest in him as well. And, as an independent, I had no corporate bureaucracy to consult. I went ahead and placed the call to Swifty Lazar. I had no corporate bureaucracy to supply any future backup either, of course, but that was not a consideration in my mind at the time—only the overriding thought of being first in the race to question Richard Nixon about his years in the White House.

I was glad that I was dealing with Swifty Lazar. Noted for his legendary ability to enter a revolving door behind you and come out in front, Swifty believed in getting right to the point. He wanted $750,000 for his client for a maximum of four one-hour shows. The main competitors—later revealed to be NBC—were currently at $300,000 and on their way to $400,000 for two hours, and would not guarantee more than two hours. That seemed to me to be a heavy rate per hour—and an underestimate of how much Nixon had to offer, both in terms of information and public interest. Others might not agree, but I was sure there was more—much more—than two hours of potentially riveting television in Richard Nixon. I said I was thinking of a maximum of $500,000 for a minimum of four hours. Before returning to the question of a fee, however, I ticked off the points I regarded as mandatory.

First, the point on which I expected the most trouble: editorial control. I must have sole control of content and editing; Nixon must have none. Given the history of Swifty's client's relations with the media, it was a tall order, I knew, but essential. Indeed, I thought back to my 1968 interview with Nixon when he had admitted that his 1962 press conference was probably his biggest mistake, but only because he had become a public figure again, and not remained a private citizen. "I can also assure you," he had then added somewhat overoptimistically, "that as far as getting into an argument with the press, it won't happen again, as long as I'm a public figure."

On the question of editorial control, Swifty would check with his client.

Second, Watergate. I knew that the Warner Books deal contained no specific reference to Watergate at all. Reports of other approaches suggested that the "Watergate factor" might have been a problem in those negotiations. But, regardless of all that, I had to have a cast-iron contractual assurance that Watergate would be one of the four shows. That was new, and Swifty would investigate.

Third, exclusivity—before and after—was a must. An independent venture ran far greater risks, and we just could not afford to take, say, a two-million-dollar risk and then be undercut at the last moment by some network with a valid-sounding interview pretext. I refer to the networks here not as hooded and villainous enemies, but rather as almost inevitable competitors. Although I was in dialogue with all three of them on other projects, and would leave the network door ajar as long as possible, if my fears were justified then by next spring I would probably be having to erect my own network. That I knew would mean a lot of work. (Although, since it had never been done for something like this before, I was at the time mercifully ignorant about just how much!)

Fourth, time for interviewing. Although Swifty was talking about four hours on the air, I would want the right to many hours more of taping than that, a ratio of at least four to one, in case Nixon should ramble or stern and persistent cross-examination prove necessary. Sixteen hours, Swifty mused. He could see the point, but that was asking a heck of a lot.

Fifth, one other point on hours. I wanted the freedom to make the agreed number of hours to be broadcast in the United States different in content from the agreed number of hours to be broadcast abroad. An idea had been forming in my mind for some time that maybe we could tape special material for some foreign countries that would increase local interest and make the overseas broadcaster in effect a partial co-producer. It was a clause that was to prove crucial in the negotiations that lay ahead.

Finally, I told Swifty there was one other vital point. The book for which he had negotiated such a massive contract—when was it due? Delivery of the whole book, Swifty told me, or one of two books, was due in October 1976, with publication the following year. "Well," I said, "we have to ensure that the television interviews precede the book—and the serialization of the book—by a minimum of three months."

"Are you sure?" asked Swifty. "That might cause me problems with Warner Books, and after all, they have a first option on the television rights too."

"Yes, but they must have passed on those, Swifty."

"True—but they might reconsider."

"Well, that is their right." As far as I was concerned, the television had to come first.

"A lot of these points are new," said Swifty. "I'll be back to you." I gave him my phone numbers in London, and waited.

Within days, the word came back: the response was not unfavorable. Swifty, God bless him, felt "duty-bound" to tell me that the "rival offer" was now $400,000 for two hours, and then returned to his magic figure of $750,000. I said I could not really go beyond my original figure unless I had more time on the air. We compromised at $600,000 plus 20 percent of the profits, if any, for four ninety-minute shows, with $200,000 of that to be paid on signature. The symmetry was pleasing. I had initiated the ninety-minute one-on-one interview format with Westinghouse, much to their early trepidation, though ensuing pleasure, and now it was to be the form for the toughest challenge I had ever taken on.

However, the financial side of our negotiations took the least amount of our time. Now we had to turn to the other points, almost any one of which could break the deal.

First, the *sine qua non*. What was the position on absolute editorial control? I waited for an explosion. "Agreed," barked Swifty. "He does realize that means having no right to know any of the questions in advance?" I asked somewhat incredulously. "Of course," said Swifty, "but I think he also realizes that the *bona fides* of these interviews have to be demonstrable if they're to have any impact at all."

The foreign versions were not a problem. But did I really need all that time for the interviewing? Yes, I said, knowing it was important. (Though not yet knowing just *how* important.) And now, with six hours of programming, that meant a total of twenty-four hours' taping. I gained the impression that the resistance on that point was relatively token.

The former President was worried about the exclusivity. "Other television and radio interviews being out is understandable, but how about one- or two-minute statements for the news bulletins?" asked Swifty. I took a deep breath. I rarely seem to have the time normally to think back to my childhood, but for a second I wanted to pinch myself just to make sure that a Methodist minister's son from Beccles, Suffolk, was really laying down conditions like this for the former President of the Western world. I confirmed to myself that, indeed, I was. "Only by mutual agreement," I told Swifty.

Next, did the former President understand the need for me to be protected from the book? "Yes, he does," said Swifty, to my relief. Though, naturally, the former President felt very strongly that the publishers had to be protected too when it came to the Watergate material. "Watergate," said Swifty, "is the main problem."

And it's all been going so well, I thought. But then Swifty amplified his point. It was not that the former President had any objection to Watergate being part of the contract, it was just that he felt he could not possibly speak out freely on the subject as long as he might affect the appeals of Mitchell and Haldeman and Ehrlichman, which were still in progress. It seemed a fair point and we wrestled with the principles over the telephone, reaching a broad agreement which was eventually to be enshrined in a cautious and complex clause:

> You and I agree that in the interests of justice, you are unable and unwilling to write, discuss or participate in any way in the publication or dissemination of any information affecting the so-called Watergate appeals (the appeals) which will be included in the last of the programs referred to in paragraph 2. Therefore, you agree that, simultaneously with the commencement of your writing of any material relating to the appeals, you will make yourself available to me for three 2-hour interview sessions covering that subject, and I agree that I will not exhibit or distribute the program involving that subject matter until the first to occur of: 10 weeks prior to the publication of any book or serialization in hard or soft cover, written directly or indirectly by you, and containing the aforesaid material; or 8 months after the disposition of the appeals; provided, however, in the event I determine, in my sole discretion, that the publication of such material or its serialization will be made prior to the 10-week period described above, I shall be free to exhibit and distribute the program involving the appeals without any restrictions or limitations.

The clause seemed to cover most of the eventualities we could think of. Nixon wanted to wait until the disposition of the appeals, but, on the other hand, if he changed his mind, whenever he started to write, he had to grant the Watergate interviews. The publishers would only be scooped by television by ten weeks, but if, on the other hand, they decided for some reason never to publish a Watergate postscript, I could still go ahead regardless eight months after the disposition of the appeals, which at that time was expected to occur a good deal earlier than it actually did.

I was delighted with the Watergate clause. It would confound all my friends who had said that I would never get "that S.O.B." to commit to a Watergate provision. It was a real achievement at the time. It was only later that it would come back to haunt us.

Finally, after several more telephone calls between Swifty in Los Angeles and myself in London, I was able to cable him at his cable address, "Lazy Beverly Hills," on July 31 confirming the main points we had agreed. What remained to be done now was to have Paul Ziffren, my California counsel, draft a contract reflecting precisely the terms we had agreed upon, to review it with Swifty and then, of course, to present it to the former President himself. Previous commitments, including a trip to France, prevented my arriving in Los Angeles prior to the morning of Friday, August 8. We decided to convene at Paul's office that afternoon, and to travel to San Clemente to meet with the former President and sign the contract the following day.

August 9 was, of course, the first anniversary of the Nixon resignation. That Nixon would choose that particular day to enter into a contract for his electronic memoirs would be viewed widely as an act of singularly Machiavellian plotting, and indeed noncontrition. But on this charge, at any rate, the ex-President was innocent. August 9 was simply the first day I could get there. Swifty said he would inform NBC so that there could be a graceful withdrawal by the former President and the network from their particular negotiations.

With the timetable set, I had work to do too. The project could cost as much as two million dollars if it was going to be done right. (Eventually it cost more.) That money had to be found. As the negotiations progressed through July, two sources of European finance had come to light, almost by chance: one a European banker, the other an industrialist. We reached verbal agreement that they would provide the risk equity, with bridging loans providing the remainder.

But the immediate problem was the $200,000 check that I was going to have to present to Richard Nixon on August 9. This they agreed to have waiting for me when I arrived from France on August 7. They would obtain all the necessary permissions to transfer the funds. They reconfirmed it to my colleague in London, Michael Rosenberg, who called me in France with the added reassurance that all was well.

Knowing that a banker's word, and indeed an industrialist's word, is as good as his bond, I flew to New York with relish and with total confidence. That confidence was marginally shaken by a Telex from the banker that was waiting for me saying, "Having failed to speak to you before your departure, have discussed changes we wish to see with my partner who is authorized to act on our behalf."

"Having failed to speak to you . . . ?" He had my telephone numbers in France. It sounded odd. My telephone call to him was worse than odd. The "changes" to the proposed agreement with the ex-President were totally impractical, would, as he well knew, strike to the heart of what had been agreed, and would destroy the deal. Surely, the banker could not be withdrawing weeks after he had committed, and two days before the check he had promised had to be presented? And long after it was too late for me to obtain the necessary permission to transmit any other funds from England?

When I met with the banker's New York partner, it rapidly became clear that that was exactly what was happening. During the most rancorous meeting I can ever recall, when I said that I had spoken to the banker since he had sent his Telex, his partner yelled, "Impossible! In any case, it does not matter what you say. You are not going to get your check." Finally he screamed, "That's it. The deal is over." And, almost as loudly, I asked him to leave.

"Well," I said to Monte Morris, my New York lawyer, "what the hell do you make of that?"

"Either he came here with orders to kill the deal at all costs, or I imagine he will be dismissed in the morning."

Of course, he was not dismissed in the morning. And eighteen months later, when I ran into him again on a Concorde flight, he summed up his role succinctly. "Oh, come on. You know it was quite simple," he shrugged. "I was employed to welsh on a commitment."

Despite the resounding clarity of their words and deeds, I still could not bring myself to believe that "men of honor" would really behave like that. Neither could Jim Wolfensohn, then president of J. Henry Schroder Banking Corporation, now a leading investment banker, when I told him the story later that night.

"But if they really do back out, can I come to you for help?"

25

"Yes, just call," said Jim, "but I still can't believe that it will be necessary."

I had to fly to California early the next morning. But while waiting for an eleventh-hour reprieve from the banker, I had to have a check for $200,000 immediately for delivery in thirty-six hours' time. And British citizens do not retain, even at the best of times, large cash sums abroad, waiting for emergencies like this. Surplus funds must be repatriated. But there was a temporary way out. My company did have a little over $200,000 we had earmarked for another project just seven days later. I would use that, and if the elusive duo in Europe did not honor their word, then if and when we got the contract signed, I would have five days to find the money and save the other project.

But for the next thirty-six hours, that little problem had to be put to one side. When I met with Paul Ziffren and Swifty Lazar on Friday afternoon, there were a few details to be ironed out. Swifty needed a clause declaring that the interviews would not be aired until after the 1976 election. "The President does not want to be accused of affecting the result of the election," he explained. Or to become any more of an issue, I thought. There was also a provision in the draft contract which could, in certain circumstances, have reduced the former President's fee by $50,000. That clause caught Swifty's eye like an unsightly wart. My position with respect to Nixon was eminently reasonable, he conceded. But why should he, Irving Paul Lazar, lose commission on the efforts of his negotiating genius simply because of conditions beyond his control?

It is a tribute to the force of Swifty's personality that I agreed to pay him his $5000 commission regardless, even if Nixon's fee were reduced by $50,000. It is even more of a tribute to the force of Swifty's personality that the following day, Nixon himself uttered not a word of complaint about the vigor with which Swifty had protected his own position. I guess the ex-President must have felt that it was my $5000 to donate to whatever deserving cause I chose.

On that Saturday morning, the four of us—Paul Ziffren, Swifty, Marv Minoff and myself—set out at ten thirty for San Clemente in Swifty's rented limousine. On later visits, I would be struck by the serenity and beauty of the area, with its brown cliffs and white beaches, its Spanish-style clusters of adobe haciendas with multi-colored slate roofs, flowers of every shade and gentle palm trees providing a setting of perfect tranquillity for a man whose soul remained far from tranquil, far from the Quaker sense of peace at the center he had so often defiantly—and unconvincingly—claimed for himself even during the final days. At that moment, however, I was completely engulfed in the personal experience, not quite believing that the draft contract I had in my hand was real, and wondering in what sort of physical and mental shape I would find the former President.

We were met at the compound, familiar to millions as the Western White House, by Nixon's chief of staff, Jack Brennan, the black-haired, athletically trim former Marine Corps colonel who had resigned his commission in order to serve his former Commander-in-Chief. Fun-loving and tough-minded, with a disarming man-to-man integrity, Brennan would become a firm adversary and a good friend, and my principal contact with the Nixon team. Like his colleagues Frank Gannon, Diane Sawyer and Ken Khachigian and former speech writer Ray Price, Jack would come to represent to us the kind of right-of-center deeply patriotic type who could accept the complexities and contradictions in the Nixon character, understand full well the darker side of the man and still respect him deeply while waiting for the day when the happier side of the Nixon record would achieve the recognition they felt it deserved.

That, at least, was the way we came to see them almost two years later, though not, I must say, during the interim period. We were so conditioned by years of the Nixon White House that when Richard Nixon or one of his staff said "Good evening" our first thought was always, "What does he mean by that?" They, in their turn, felt the same way about the media and therefore us. The potential for mistrust on both sides was considerable, and at times overwhelming. However, none of that was readily visible on August 9.

Nixon, dressed in his familiar dark blue suit, was waiting for us in his office. His handshake was firm, his gaze steady, his voice relaxed and confident. He had gained weight. His hair had grayed. His face was tanned. He bore little or no resemblance to the haggard photographs that had been appearing over the past few months. He looked good—reassuringly good—to someone who was about to have to start a worldwide search for life insurance.

We exchanged pleasantries. Small talk. Always the most difficult part of any conversation with Richard Nixon. But today there was news in the papers of Brezhnev. I mentioned it.

"I would not like to be a Russian leader," said Nixon, shaking his head. "They never know when they're being taped."

Not a hint of a smile. Was he unaware of the irony? Or just keeping the straightest face in the business?

"Communism stifles art," he said a moment or two later. "There is little important art you can cite from Communist countries. Solzhenitsyn is not nearly as impressive as Tolstoy."

But the purpose of the meeting was business. And for close to six hours—interrupted only by crab salad—Nixon paid attention to the task in hand. He reviewed the contract paragraph by paragraph. He discussed its terms with Swifty, quibbling over one provision or another as though he had not previously heard about it, in the end accepting most of it very nearly as written. As pages were approved, they were ferried in and out of the office for retyping. The options for two specific further shows seemed in particular to come as complete news to Nixon. They seemed to worry him. After prolonged discussion, they became a general first-option, first-refusal arrangement, which in turn made the "before and after" exclusivity provisions more speedily acceptable. My "sole right to determine the content of and to edit each program" went through unscathed. "No holds barred," muttered Nixon, "no holds barred."

He asked his secretary to call in a tax attorney who had apparently been waiting in the wings to review the final document. As he entered, Nixon half smiled. "If I'd used this man four years ago, I wouldn't have gotten into all that trouble with the I.R.S.!"

The moment came for signatures. And then, the check. With a firm hand but a slightly trembling mind, I wrote the name,

"Richard M. Nixon," and then the words, "Two hundred thousand dollars." And then the numbers, "$200,000."

To Nixon's "Thank you," I replied, "It's more than a pleasure, Mr. President." I hoped that sounded appropriate in the circumstances. It was not the kind of situation covered in much detail in Emily Post. Actually, the word that sprang to my mind at that moment was *risk*. Personally. Professionally. And, of course, financially. I thought that Nixon, who admired the Puritan work ethic so much, would have approved greatly if he knew how hard I was about to begin working to ensure that the project actually came to pass.

Nixon reached for his billfold, but Swifty cut him short.

"Can I have the check, please?" he demanded.

"It's made out to me," the former President protested. "I'll deposit it."

"No, no, give it to me. That is the customary procedure."

"But what about the bank?"

"I'll take care of it."

"But, but—"

"Will you give it to me . . . *please*?" said Swifty, this time enunciating every word separately and distinctly.

Nixon handed the check to Swifty with the forlorn look of a little boy not allowed to consume the cookie he has swiped from the jar before dinner.

The transaction thus completed, Nixon invited us to climb into his presidential golf cart for the short ride to his house past the pool that had once been a tennis court. "I despise that game," he noted as we passed. Inside the house, his discussion turned to the foreign visitors who had stayed there, most notably Leonid Brezhnev during the June 1973 summit.

I remembered the moment. It was the week John Dean was to have testified before the Ervin committee. But the committee delayed the hearings for seven days in order to spare the Chief Executive and the nation embarrassment. Now, in exile, Nixon's mind was wandering back not to the ordeal, but to the heady moments of statesmanship. He took us to a sitting room on the second floor of Casa Pacifica. "This is where Brezhnev and I met. It was ten thirty. We had already retired when the word came that he wanted to see me. And for three hours we talked. He said we had to lean on Israel for a settlement. I told him we would reason with Israel, but we could not dictate the terms of a settlement. Brezhnev sat there, Dobrynin there. Kissinger sat there." A pause, then: "He didn't say very much."

At first hearing, it sounded like an unnecessary afterthought. But in fact we had just received advance notice of at least one line of approach that Nixon was consistently going to take in the interviews many months later.

The press conference the next day at the Beverly Hilton was naturally an exhilarating experience. I announced that the contract had been signed the previous evening. I declined, as the ex-President had requested, to reveal the size of his fee, something I continued to do even, somewhat fruitlessly, for several months after the correct figures had been disclosed from other sources. I emphasized the point about my editorial control, giving Nixon what I felt was his due on that particular point: "I should make it clear that the former President has *neither requested* nor has he received any editorial control."

What on earth was I going to do about security and possible leaks? I was asked. I had no all-embracing security plan whatever at that particular moment, of course, so I just mentioned lightly in passing that maybe we would use non-English-speaking cameramen, or that perhaps I would shoot the whole thing myself with a Polaroid Land camera, and then moved on to other topics. However, that casual throwaway was picked up and translated in all seriousness into Japanese, and eventually found its way back into English in a London newspaper under the headline FROST TO USE REVOLUTIONARY NEW TECHNIQUE. It was not the only remark to be given a surprising interpretation. Bearing in mind the special foreign versions I was contemplating, I added that I had acquired the exclusive rights "on behalf of an international consortium of broadcasting organizations"—a rousing phrase that still, however, embodied a dream more than a reality, since most of these "broadcasting organizations" had yet to be made aware of what they would hopefully regard as their good fortune.

The phrase, however, triggered off a remarkable comment in a *New York Times* editorial: "Mr. Frost says that he acquired the rights on behalf of 'an international consortium of broadcasting organizations,' a blind phrase that until explained carries the muffled rustle of laundered money." And then a sentence on behalf of all establishments everywhere. "This obscure arrangement is quite different from a project for written or televised memoirs under the auspices of publishers and broadcasters, here or abroad, with known managements."

The piece concluded, "The least that is required is full disclosure of the personnel of the 'international consortium' that is to be Mr. Nixon's financial angel."

Full disclosure to *The New York Times* editorial page be hanged, I thought as I read it. At that moment, I would have settled very happily for "full disclosure" of the existence of such a group to me!

Back in New York on Monday, I called Jim Wolfensohn, who was out of town at a conference in Aspen. I told him what had happened—or not happened—on the $200,000 pledge, which was probably almost as unwelcome news to him as it was to me. However, he was as good as his word. I needed $200,000 by Thursday? He would give it his blessing, and his people and I would meet.

But his people *hated* the idea. A loan in three days to a new client? To someone involved in a project about which *The New York Times* had said what it had said? Jim had clearly taken leave of his senses. The sheer unanimity of their reaction created a situation in which almost any chairman in the world would have felt able to withdraw, citing the fact that his people or his fellow board members were implacably opposed. But not Jim Wolfensohn. The phone lines between Aspen and Schroders in New York must have been red-hot, but eventually, subject to my lodging some British shares with Schroders in London, getting Bank of England permission to do so, and giving my personal guarantee, Jim's executives reluctantly signed on for the loan, limiting it to only twenty-eight days, and making it very clear to me that they had been overruled and that they were going to make sure everyone in the company knew who had done the overruling: Jim Wolfensohn.

"As you know, I've got faith in this whole project," he said, "but, please, for me, don't be late on that twenty-eight days!"

I had the $200,000. The other project was saved. But only for twenty-eight days. I flew back to London, spoke to the Bank of England and then set about replacing the loan with my first equity investor. I spoke first to David Gideon Thomson, of Polygram, the Dutch-German leisure group, with whom I had had warm dealings already. I explained the urgency of the situation and within twenty-four hours Coen Sollafeld, the president of Polygram, had given the go-ahead from Holland for a 100,000-pound investment (then $212,000 before the further travails of the poor beleaguered pound). Papers were drawn up in two days, and the money paid within another two days.

I called Jim Wolfensohn in Aspen. "I hope you don't mind the loss of interest, Jim, but we're repaying Schroders today—after eight days rather than twenty-eight."

There was something approaching ecstasy at the other end of the phone.

"I think I shall sleep well tonight for the first time in a week."

"Was it really that bad?" I asked him.

"It was worse. Much worse. How much worse has to stay privileged within the bank."

The impact was all the greater for being unspoken. By underwriting my loan or guaranteeing my credit rating or whatever, Jim was on the line with his colleagues for more than $200,000. In order to keep his word to me he had staked his reputation—perhaps even, in that Byzantine Freemasonry, his future—on the fact that I would keep my word to him. If the other banker's behavior had been unprecedented, this was ten times more so. I determined at that moment that the quality of the Nixon project was not going to let down Jim Wolfensohn either.

CHAPTER

2

It would be January before I saw Nixon again, and in the meantime there were a lot of plans to be set in motion, and reactions to be explored.

The joys of being an independent are considerable. But I had never felt quite as much of an independent as I did over the next few weeks. By the end of September, it was clear that the initial response from all three networks was no. All the meetings were cordial and highly civilized. "Well," I said to one, "if I know you would never be able to take it, then I won't offer it, and then you won't have to tell people you've rejected it, will you?"

I say "the initial response" because I had decided I could afford to allow an opportunity for second thoughts at least until the middle of 1976. There were indeed some later discussions: Paul Klein would have liked the Interviews for NBC and Roone Arledge for ABC, but the Nixon Interviews had been classified as news and the three network heads of news—Dick Wald of NBC, Dick Salant of CBS and Bill Sheehan of ABC—stuck firmly to their conviction that the combination of Richard Nixon, a freelance interviewer, and an outside production company made the proposition untenable for their departments, and that Richard Nixon speaking for the first time was just too obviously "news" of the first magnitude for them to consent willingly to it being classified as a "special" and thus conveniently removed from their bailiwicks.

"Look here, David," said one network vice-president in the programming division, "we've climbed out on a limb, and we're asking you to show us the way back." But that was clearly going to be easier said than done.

The initial sources of finance that we approached emphasized our sense of independence, or, to be more accurate, loneliness. The name Richard Nixon was understandably the turnoff for some. The thought of controversy in any shape or form was enough for others, but least helpful of all were two successive gatherings where it gradually became apparent that the friendly folk we were meeting had actually come to try to borrow two million dollars from us!

Of course, there was encouragement from friends. "You'll obviously want to try to finance this in America if you possibly can," said Jimmy Goldsmith of Banque Occidentale over lunch, "but if for any reason that proves tough, come back to me and I'll do whatever I can to help." I thanked him warmly, at the same time agreeing with him that the ideal strategy for an American project like this was to find predominantly American backing. Also, I had already ruled out the idea of tax-shelter investment for a project as politically sensitive as this. I soon realized, though, that raising two million dollars for the Nixon Interviews, however historic, was going to be a great deal more difficult than, for instance, had been raising five million dollars for a movie like *The Slipper and the Rose*. It became clear that overseas sales were going to be essential to the success—or even viability—of the venture. Over the next few months I began the delicate process of negotiations in Britain and set off on regular trips to France, Italy and Australia— where there was considerable interest—and to Japan, where I enjoyed the food and achieved absolutely and precisely zero.

Soon *Rolling Stone* reported to my astonishment that my backers were Robert Abplanalp and Bebe Rebozo. I denied it immediately, but the Rebozo suggestion was part of a general skepticism in the press which, maddening though it was at times, I could well understand. A successful Nixon effort at revisionism could have had serious consequences. Had I been his willing accomplice, or (equally dangerous) his helpless victim, as he rewrote history, then abuses of power would have seemed ratified and courageous investigators would have appeared Cassius-like tormentors.

In January I dined with Frank Gannon and Diane Sawyer, who were holidaying in London during a brief break from their labors on the Nixon memoirs, and it became clear that they felt Nixon would be more relaxed recording the Interviews after the election. That seemed O.K. to me. I could well imagine that the ex-President retained his well-known, near pathological fear of leaks—and that a leaked preelection revelation would worry him every bit as much as a broadcast one. Although I had insisted in our negotiations on having the right to broadcast the Interviews on any date I chose once the election was past, I had always wondered if it might be better to wait until February or March, after the State of the Union message. So this was a relatively painless accommodation as far as I was concerned, and fitted in well with my general philosophy—of trying to build on whatever semblance of trust there might be at San Clemente, while remaining unyielding on editorial control in all my statements, a message I had to get across to the public anyway.

I had been told that one of the key factors in Nixon's granting me editorial control so speedily was that he had felt fairly edited in that interview way back in 1968. The other candidates had all felt the same, but it was not a feeling that Richard Nixon had often allowed himself to have as far as the media was concerned. Anything that I could do, without compromising, to condition this extraordinarily private man to open up, I resolved that I would do. In public I simply stressed the ground rules, adding that I felt Nixon wanted to "confront his past," and tried to leave it at that. All of which in any case reflected a lifetime conviction of mine that judgments are for the viewer to make on the basis of the interview, not for the interviewer to spell out for him in advance.

In New York in mid-January, I met for the first time with Bill Sarnoff and Howard Kaminsky, of Warner Books, Nixon's publishers. It was a curiously warm meeting. We knew that in a sense we were rivals, but we also knew in another sense that we were men with a common interest: that of persuading Richard M. Nixon to "tell all." I felt sure that Sarnoff and Kaminsky would have preferred that the interviews had never been invented, but now that they had been, it was probably in their interest that they be as good as possible. That, at any rate, was the burden of my message to them.

Later in January I thought it was time to make a social call on San Clemente in order to keep in touch, and give what I somewhat overoptimistically described on the telephone to Brennan as a "progress report." "So far, no networks and no finance" would have been one version of such a report, but with the aid of some of my tentative overseas understandings and my growing determination to put together an independent network in the United States especially for the Interviews, everything sounded more advanced than in fact it was. Nixon was clearly relieved about the marginal change of date—I assumed it had been his idea in the first place—and was happy to agree to a proposal of mine that, overseas, the four ninety-minute programs could become six one-hour programs at the discretion of the local country.

Nixon then invited my companion, Caroline Cushing, to join us and pose for a photograph. "There," he told Caroline, "you can put that in your apartment in New York, and all your liberal friends can use it as a dart board!" Caroline laughed, and explained that she was at the time living in Monte Carlo.

As we left a few minutes later, the former President leaned over to me almost conspiratorially. "Marry that girl," he said. "She's a resident of Monaco. She lives tax-free."

Actually, I had very nearly made the most important piece of progress of all. I had found and almost signed my producer—or "co-producer," as we were later to call ourselves on this project.

The job definition as I ticked it off was daunting. My producer would not only have to be a first-rate journalist in his own right, but be able to command the respect of other first-rate journalists on the project. And, where necessary, be able to translate their thoughts into television terms. He had to be someone who could deal diplomatically with the Nixon people, who could make wise decisions fast under what might become incredible pressure, and who would constantly test my own instincts and conclusions. He must not be shy about expressing disagreement with me in our private strategy and production sessions. He had to be a conceptual thinker and at the same time know television technique and equipment as if it were second nature to him.

Did such a paragon exist? Fortunately I knew that at least one did. John Birt was the most outstanding current-affairs producer I had ever worked with. I had persuaded him to leave Granada Television, where he had been appointed head of the investigative *World in Action* at the age of twenty-four, in order to come over to London Weekend Television (LWT) to produce the 1972 series of *The Frost Program.*

Within four weeks we had been through four very different experiences together. We had flown to Bangladesh and filmed the first interview with Sheikh Mujib after his release from captivity in West Pakistan, flown back and edited the film together, arriving at the studio from the cutting rooms with the completed film after a wild dash across London just three minutes before air time; we had a remarkable confrontation with the "factually inventive" Ian Smith in Rhodesia, and conducted a passionate debate among striking coal miners live from a smoke-filled workingmen's club in the Rhondda Valley in Wales; and a week after Bloody Sunday, we had done a program from Northern Ireland which had shown John Birt the television professional at his very best. Half the program was to be with an audience of Catholics in the Bogside in Derry; half with an audience of Protestants in Belfast. All members of the Mobile Unit had to be volunteers because of the danger involved. Many of them came from different companies and had never worked together before, and yet the whole operation moved like clockwork, despite a background accompaniment of bomb threats.

John Birt, now controller of current affairs for LWT, was, I knew, the man for the job, and after weeks of discussion he obtained a three-month leave of absence from November to January to devote himself to the project. The quality of the rest of the team could also make or break the project. The journalists on the team would have to be competent not only to research the wealth of factual material associated with Nixon's five and a half years in office, but be able to put those facts into analytical perspective, to develop a "theory of the case" with respect to all aspects of the Nixon presidency. Equally important, the people I assembled would have to be able to help me redefine our strategy as the taping sessions progressed. The sessions would stretch over a period of a month. Certain approaches would work. Others would not. Nixon's line of response had to be anticipated, wherever possible, prior to each session. And our line of attack had to be flexible. So whom to choose? There were top-flight investigative reporters available to serve as consultants and others who could write intelligently about the foreign and domestic initiatives of the Nixon administration. But I needed people ready to work full time on the project, journalists who could combine Birt's demand for diligent reporting with an intuitive sense of theory and strategy.

In June, I contacted columnist Joe Kraft, a longtime friend whose journalistic stature is attested to by the fact that he has been on more presidential hit lists than any other columnist in living memory. Kraft first recommended James Reston, Jr., who had not followed his distinguished father into *The New York Times* but was pursuing his own successful career as a novelist and English instructor at the University of North Carolina. Gentle, sensitive, yet with convictions passionately held, Reston had already collaborated with Frank Mankiewicz on two hard-hitting books about Richard Nixon and his abuses of power. Reston was eager to join us, and I was pleased to welcome him to the team.

A bit later Kraft recommended Bob Zelnick, a veteran reporter and, until recently, National Public Radio bureau chief, hardly known outside Washington but well respected among his colleagues. According to Kraft, Zelnick could write intelligently about almost any issue, domestic or foreign, and was well plugged into the Washington scene. Zelnick had also practiced law, a background I sensed would come in handy once we got to California, if not before. I talked to Zelnick at length on the phone and asked Marv Minoff to meet with him while I was in London and, if he liked him, to hire him. Marv liked Zelnick so much that he asked him to serve as senior member of our journalistic team, to recruit a third reporter when he needed one, and to generally act as the bureau chief with the smallest bureau in Washington.

We set July 1 as the starting date for Bob and Jim. John Birt would fly from London to Washington to meet with them a few days later on July 12. The tempo of events was quickening. During May and June, the BBC in London had said yes, and Pacific Video of Los Angeles had agreed to become the facilities and technical unit for the production, deferring their fee of $290,000 to be recouped out of income. Then they would share in the surplus, if any. This was a plan which I originally devised in order to promote the cause of security: co-venturers would obviously have more of a vested interest in keeping secrets. With no investors other than Polygram anywhere in sight at that point, it now seemed a doubly good idea! But production costs were some way in the future. In the meantime, Bob's salary and Jim's and the cost of the Washington office would have to come from Paradine itself, from my company.

During June we had also found our "network erector": Syndicast Services would organize our network for us, deferring their fee of $175,000 in a similar way to Pacific Video. We set July 12 as the day on which we would announce that the special network was about to come into being. I was confident, but I could not help recalling the recent words of one reluctant noninvestor.

"The networks have said no," he had told me. "The stations won't dare go it alone."

A journalist had echoed the same theme. "Deep down, those

stations are very influenced by the networks. They'll think the
networks are not doing it, there's no smoke without fire, it must
be a bad media buy." I did not believe it. Neither, fortunately for
me, did Syndicast.

July was to be perhaps one of the most unpredictable months in
the whole unpredictable history of the project. It started well, back
again in Sydney, Australia, when Kerry Packer of the National
Nine Network said yes at dinner on the night of July 1. We would
settle the details over the phone before I left for Los Angeles the
next day. The next morning I completed a week's guest stint from
nine till noon on radio—on Sydney's 2SM and networked throughout Australia. There had been some dramatic telephone interviews
during the week with Bing Crosby and Nelson Rockefeller, Neil
Diamond and Elliot Richardson, Billy Graham and Foreign Minister Andrew Peacock, but the call to Kerry's office after the program had of course a particular drama to it for me. Kerry confirmed
that he wanted to take the Nixon Interviews but would not go a
cent above $160,000. I said I would not come down a cent below
$175,000. An impasse like that—particularly between friends—can
always end in disaster.

"Let's toss for it," I said.

"O.K., Frostie," said Kerry, "you call . . ."

"Tails."

"Tails it is, old son."

I set off for the States in good heart, looking forward to a
social dinner and general update with Jack Brennan and Frank
Gannon in Los Angeles en route to New York. On this occasion,
however, the mood of Nixon's two advisers seemed far from care-
free. When they finally explained why, it proved contagious.

The President, Gannon explained, is a man who has difficulty
concentrating on more than a single major endeavor at a given
time. And now he had put his total energy and concentration to
work on his memoirs but had fallen far behind his October 1976
deadline. Indeed, it now appeared that the memoirs would not
be finished until April or May 1977. Breaking off for the months

it would take him to prepare for the Interviews, not to mention the month of arduous taping sessions, was totally unacceptable. There was just no way we could get to that business until May or June of the following year.

June 1977. That, I thought, would be a disaster. We had already accommodated Nixon by pushing the Interview date back until after the 1976 election, and had had to adjust our public statements accordingly. Now agreements and contracts were due to be drawn up with the major networks in Great Britain, France, Italy, and Australia. News stories were already being set in type, ready to appear the week of July 12, announcing the independent network to be erected in February or March 1977. This sort of sudden delay would mean we would have to wait until the following season. And Brennan and Gannon must know that. What the hell did they think they were playing at?

"I'm afraid that's impossible," I snapped. "I have made commitments on the basis of your commitments to me. Even on our current schedule, one of my investors will have had his money tied up for about eighteen months. That sort of delay is out of the question."

Brennan then unveiled his doomsday weapon. "If that's the case, then the President would prefer to return your check and call the whole thing off."

"Fine, Jack," I said, as calmly as I could. "I would say that will cost him between fifteen and twenty million dollars in damages growing out of his breach of contract. There are worldwide rights at stake now, not to mention our whole credibility. And I know what our rights are and what his obligation is. When we drafted the contract, we didn't leave ourselves vulnerable to this sort of game playing."

Brennan had no immediate answer but said he would carry my response back to Mr. Nixon and await further instructions. We parted company, and I flew to New York.

In New York, I immediately wrote to Brennan underlining what I understood to be the realities of the situation. I said that "the schedule we need to observe" was November and December and concluded, "There are certain obligations that are not totally in our power anymore, particularly now that we have come so far and have had to make the commitments consistent with our contract that we have had to make."

I flew on to London, and acquainted John with the new crisis. There was nothing we could do until we got a response from San Clemente, so we turned to the preparatory work we wanted from Zelnick and Reston. We both felt that to test Nixon's account of his presidency, we had to fully develop our own. If we came at Nixon with darts, he would dodge each of them in turn. Working on memoirs about his presidency, he was bound to develop a coherent, mutually reinforcing theme. We needed equally coherent alternative themes supported by as much evidence as we could muster.

In Washington, Birt met first with Zelnick. From their initial handshake, they hit it off immediately. Their ideas of what I wanted the project to be, and their sense of what it ought to be, meshed so completely that John found himself wondering if perhaps Zelnick had been present at our meetings in London without our noticing him.

First of all, there was agreement on the purpose of the next few months' research activity. We were working toward a series of interviews, not preparing a documentary on the Nixon administration, nor an investigative report. All the research was a means to an end. While it would certainly be possible to develop some new information about the Nixon administration, and to spotlight the areas in which Nixon alone had new information to offer, what we would learn would, for the most part, be useful in providing us better information with which to draw Nixon out.

We would, with Nixon and myself as the alchemists, be using our own raw material to provide a better quality of source material for journalists, historians, and political scientists to ponder. Some questions which we knew would produce news stories might never be asked. Others, unless of overriding importance, might be edited out. News *per se* was not our first priority. Insight into the man and his administration was. Further, we would not turn the proceedings into a fishing expedition, a search for spectacular admissions as to improprieties rumored or suspected but which a brilliant battery of lawyers, investigators and journalists had been unable to sustain. For one thing, it would be foolish to demean the quality of our interrogation with items for which no proper foundation could be laid, or indeed existed. For another, why toss soft pitches masquerading as hard ones only to watch Nixon swat them out of the park?

I would remain ever alert, of course, for targets of opportunity, for moments of potential openness, such as would occur months later when Nixon himself introduced the topic of his alleged foreign bank accounts and his rumored love affair with a European countess. But that was different. That was seizing the moment. In our general preparation, the thrust of every line of questioning had to grow out of that which we already knew. A proper foundation for each line of questioning was critical.

Birt told Zelnick we wanted four "program briefing books," each dealing with a separate aspect of the Nixon administration. While the shape of the programs would be defined finally by the material generated from the interview sessions themselves, it was not too early to be thinking in terms of Nixon's foreign and domestic policies, Watergate, and the other abuse areas. There was also Nixon the man himself. John asked Zelnick to prepare scripts on Nixon's foreign and domestic policies.

"We want to see Richard Nixon through the prism of your research and interpretation," Birt told Bob. "In effect, we are asking you to write a book about those areas of the Nixon presidency you study and to see that Jim Reston does the same."

Birt's first session with Reston he found less encouraging. Jim regarded Nixon as the epitome of evil and, despite his resignation, a continuing threat to the American body politic. He felt that Nixon would know more about all areas of his presidency—including Watergate—than we could ever learn, and thought it inevitable that he would win any confrontation between us based upon an evidentiary interrogation. His views were very much influenced by those of his colleagues on the University of North

Carolina faculty. Indeed, he arrived for his session with Birt with several cassettes recorded at a round-table discussion prior to his leaving Chapel Hill. The academics were adamant. "In the adversary position, Nixon is bound to win."

Jim was speaking partly as the novelist. What he seemed to want was a psychohistory of the Nixon presidency which would at once explain the mind of Richard Nixon and the dark forces in American society which had carried him to the pinnacle of political power and which could again provide the driving force behind a comeback. He feared that our project could be the launching pad for this return to respectability, a disaster which could be averted only by a shrewd and informed exposition of his diabolical mind.

Birt was flabbergasted. "I quite agree," he said, "that David must try to use these interviews in part to provide a window on the Nixon mind and personality. He is intrigued by both. But he feels strongly, as do I, that the vehicle must be Nixon's record as President and Commander-in-Chief. Perceptions and motivations are fine, but only in that context."

Reston held firm. He had theories about Nixon's penchant for self-destruction, his view of death as an ally, "survivor guilt" growing from the boyhood deaths of his brothers, the authoritarian mentality that came from stern paternal upbringing during periods of maternal absence, and his "strange" friendship with Bebe Rebozo, all of which begged for on-camera inquiry.

Zelnick joined in the discussion. Like John, he thought that the danger of failure originated from sources poles apart from what Reston feared. "The biggest danger is in failing to do a thorough job, and not putting this man on record on things about his presidency which he has never had to address in a comprehensive way," he argued. "My God, he lost fifteen thousand Americans and a million Indochinese during his administration and all of Indochina fell less than a year after he left office. Ford's pardon spared him the need to testify about Watergate, and his three top associates have since been convicted pleading many of the same explanations Nixon offered while in the White House. How could you not interrogate him about those things?

"And the second biggest danger, in my judgment," Zelnick went on, "is going at him in a knee-jerk way, assuming that he is a terrible guy and that everybody knows it and then asking him a batch of questions as to how he got to be that way. That sort of thing would create more sympathy than anything else."

I arrived in Washington on the fifteenth to find the argument still going on, with Birt by now harboring serious doubts as to whether he and Jim could ever work fruitfully together. The team lunched at the Federal City Club, with the discussion continuing there and afterward at our temporary suite at the Madison Hotel.

I could not accept Reston's approach to the Interviews, yet I knew his position was well thought out, articulately expressed and representative of a considerable body of opinion in both the academic and journalistic communities. Indeed, at lunch with Bob Woodward two months earlier, he too had made the case that the full story of the Nixon administration was pretty well known and that the principal value of our project would be in providing such insight into the Nixon character as we could.

I was all for providing insight into the Nixon character, if at all possible. But to make that the be-all and end-all was setting the sights far too low. I believed we had to confront all the major issues, as John and I had discussed in London. On the other hand, I felt that the vigor with which Jim had pressed his position might be obscuring for a moment his credentials for the job. Jim had an intelligent mind and a very solid background as a researcher and was, perhaps, the finest pure writer associated with the project. In my view if he lacked Birt's combination of intellect and television professionalism or Zelnick's logic and tactical intuition, he added a dimension of passion and creativity which could prove exceedingly valuable.

Reston would stay on the team, I decided. Zelnick would recruit the third reporter to handle the "abuse of power" research, and Jim would focus on Watergate and, to a lesser extent, Nixon the man. It was a decision I would never regret. While Reston would continue to press doggedly with his lonely plea for a quasi-psychiatric interrogation of Nixon, he not only did a masterful job researching and organizing the Watergate material but also came up with a number of journalistic exclusives that would, as it turned out, keep us on the front pages of every newspaper in the country during the crucial week preceding the initial broadcast.

Friday, July 16, started superbly. I met with Syndicast at eight fifteen. They told me that in the previous four days since July 12, two of the nation's most respected station groups—Scripps-Howard, whose markets were Cleveland, Cincinnati, Memphis and West Palm Beach, and Corinthian, with stations in Houston, Indianapolis, Sacramento, Fort Wayne and Tulsa—had both committed to the Nixon Interviews. At eight forty-five, Syndicast had arranged a meeting with George Moynihan and Pat Polillo of Group W Westinghouse Broadcasting, whose markets were Boston, Philadelphia, Pittsburgh, San Francisco and Baltimore, and at ten o'clock with Larry Fraiberg of Channel 5 in New York, who was representing the Metromedia group of stations in New York, Los Angeles, Washington, Kansas City and Minneapolis.

At both of these meetings I reiterated our basic message. We had the first crack at Richard Nixon, before anyone else in the world. We would be on the air well before his book hit the stands. We had complete control of the editorial content. My sense moreover was that Nixon was anxious to confront his past, since only by admitting what he had done wrong would he get anyone to pay attention to what he had done right. The Nixon Interviews were certainly going to make news. If we had anything to do with it, they would make some history as well.

By lunchtime, both station groups had said yes. We had 40 percent of the nation in one week! I picked up the phone to *Variety*, called Bill Greeley and invited him to come over to the Plaza after lunch for a cup of coffee. I had something to tell him. By next Wednesday, the industry would know that every major market in the country would eventually be able to watch the Nixon Interviews.

We had the stations. We still had to find the advertisers, and there for the moment we left our options open. As Greeley said in his article, "The interviews will be open for the standard amount of prime-time commercial sale, but just how they will be sold apparently has not been fully decided. Most probable at this time is a straight barter deal, with the stations getting the programs at no cost in return for 50 percent of the available commercial time going to Syndicast for sale to national advertisers."

Greeley left at 4 P.M. My euphoria lasted less than an hour. At four forty-five the call came from San Clemente. It was Jack Brennan and Frank Gannon. Brennan spoke first.

"We've had discussions with the President and he's very anxious that you don't get screwed. He wants you to know that."

That was nice.

"And you were quite correct about the contract. It is your right to start taping after the election. That's fine. But obviously, also as per the contract, we won't be able to discuss Watergate yet. The Court of Appeals has yet to rule."

That was certainly no surprise. We had discussed the possible legal timetable in Washington, and Zelnick had predicted it would be late autumn at the earliest before the circuit court decided the case, and late in the following term before the Supreme Court handed down its decision. Perhaps as far ahead as June 1977, Bob had added. Later, as I had flown to New York, I had viewed the Capitol Hill area from my aircraft, my eyes finally settling on the nation's supreme tribunal, where the Watergate appeals would finally be weighed. And I had murmured to myself, "God speed this honorable court."

"Well, that's a great relief, Jack," I said. "I look forward to going in November and December then with everything except Watergate."

"Yes," said Jack. "Everything except Watergate. Which as we define it, covers the break-in and the cover-up, and also the resignation, the pardon and the final days. Because obviously they all bring up the whole question of guilt, which you can't discuss without discussing Watergate."

Before I could express my vehement disagreement with that interpretation, Gannon chimed in. "It also rules out the mind-set leading to Watergate, of course," he added. "All the security leaks whether of a national security or a political security nature."

"Because that might well involve excesses indulged in by, or the psychology of, individuals in the appeals," said Brennan.

Needless to say, I could scarcely believe what I was hearing. But I might as well hear it all. What exactly did they feel "the mind-set" would exclude?

"Oh, the installation of the taping system, the Pentagon Papers, the early wiretaps, the Plumbers and Ellsberg, of course. And anything from June '72 is difficult."

I am not quite sure how I managed to end the call in a civil fashion, but I murmured something to the effect that we would have to discuss all this further. I said John Birt would go over it with them when he visited San Clemente; but that this wasn't the sort of matter that was going to be resolved now.

I put down the phone. The bastards, I thought. That interpretation is sheer and unadulterated rubbish, and they must know it. We had chosen that wording very specifically: "affecting the so-called Watergate appeals." By any standard, that was a very narrow definition. Indeed, Phillip Lacovara, formerly counsel to the Special Prosecutor's Office, had gone further and told us that he felt that the legal process had now progressed to the point where nothing that the ex-President could say would "affect the so-called Watergate appeals."

Whichever way you looked at it, this was a pure wrecking operation. No Pentagon Papers. No Ellsberg. No Plumbers. No wiretaps. No taping system. No mind-set leading to Watergate. What did they expect me to talk about for eighteen hours? The bloody Postal Reform Act and the 1969 Ohio State–Purdue football game?

This is precisely the sort of Nixonian move you were warned against, Frost, I thought. You're dealing with the best poker player in the business; that's what they had all said.

O.K., Frost, now that it's happened, how are you going to deal with it?

The first thing was to call John Birt in Washington, who flew up for lunch the next day before I left for six weeks of filming for

The Crossroads of Civilization in Iran and the Near East. If anything, the news felt worse the next day than it had the night before. Because with Watergate already scheduled to be delayed, we had been relying on a lot of these other abuses of power to demonstrate our *bona fides* to the skeptics.

We did not find a solution at lunch that day. John's "good-will trip" to San Clemente had clearly become an intelligence-gathering mission of the first importance. In the meantime, we decided that in the last resort, if necessary, we would go ahead with what—despite the absence of any Plan A—we called Plan B: domestic policy, foreign policy and the abuses of power; and if Nixon tried to walk away then America would get the confrontation, the accusations of bad faith and the counteraccusations all in living color in their living rooms.

On that unhappy note, I left for Iran, and John left for Washington and California. A week later he called me at the Shah Abbas Hotel in Isfahan to report. He had spent almost a whole day at San Clemente. Apart from a tour of possible locations—the ex-President's office, the conference room—all of that time had been spent in Brennan's office, slowly feeling each other out. John thought the conversation had gone on for about six hours.

"I wasn't offered any refreshment whatsoever. I didn't say anything, but I was rather thirsty," he said with slightly plaintive English understatement.

However, the main thrust of the day had been positive. Firstly, to John's and my surprise he had decided that Brennan and Gannon were probably not trying to castrate or destroy the Interviews by confining them to discussing China, revenue sharing and King Timahoe. They were indeed genuinely behind with Nixon's memoirs. They convinced John that Nixon could really only concentrate on one project at a time, five and a half years of the presidency notwithstanding, and they also convinced John that their desire to finish the book first was a genuine one, motivated partly by financial reasons and a fear that any further delays would send their research budget sky-high, and partly simply by concern for "the boss."

"He can't write a book and do the Interviews simultaneously," they told John. "We plan to prepare him for the Interviews in much the same way we are preparing him for the book. In much the same detail. But when he's finished the book in April or May then he can do the Interviews . . ."

That was the catastrophic part again, of course, but there was one other piece to the jigsaw. .

"Having realized that they were probably telling the truth about the book," said John, "I gingerly approached the question of Watergate and taking them into my confidence—'I'm alone on this, David doesn't agree with me, etc.'—I said that I thought that the Watergate program should not be delayed, but should even go out first if possible—to clear the air. And to my surprise, Gannon and Brennan did not disagree. They did not agree either— well, we were not negotiating anyway—but in short, David, I don't think that their whole strategy is designed to stop at nothing to stop us from doing Watergate or dirty tricks. They're just panicked about the book."

I was confident that John would have read both the situation and their characters accurately. If all this was so, maybe we could achieve a compromise: only delay until, perhaps, March and broadcast in May, still in the same season and still in a peak viewing month. But on one condition: that Watergate became one of four consecutive shows. That would hopefully protect our credibility in the face of another delay. Without knowing of our new problem, Gary Deeb in the *Chicago Tribune* was already remarking about our existing Watergate timetable. "Terrific. By that time Julie Nixon Eisenhower will be the grand old woman of the *Today Show* and her husband David will be baseball commissioner. Thus the Nixon-Frost sessions represent another typical Nixon deal. The deck is stacked and the cards are marked."

John would call San Clemente and make a date for me for the first available day after Labor Day, which turned out to be September 9. Both of us felt we had something more than a sporting chance. If their genuine desire was for a delay rather than disguised censorship, they would give something for that. If not, Plan B would still apply. The horror for me was that for the next four or five weeks, every time I picked up *The Final Days* or Anthony Lukas's *Nightmare*, I would be reminded that I had no way of knowing which contingency I was preparing for.

Marv Minoff and I arrived at San Clemente on September 9 by helicopter. I explained to the ex-President that I had to be back at Los Angeles Airport to catch the 1 P.M. flight to Chicago for a lecture at the University of Northern Illinois.

"Are you getting paid?"

"Certainly."

"Just make sure you pay your taxes," he warned. "Otherwise you can get yourself in trouble . . ."

Thanking him for the advice, I turned to the subject at hand. The prospect of waiting until May or June was devastating, I argued. That would mean we couldn't complete the editing until July and it would be August at the earliest before the shows would be aired. And no stations or advertisers would be confident of getting a large audience in August.

"I don't know about that," said Nixon. "We got a hell of an audience on August 9, 1974."

"Yes," I said, "but what do you do for an encore?"

Waiting until May or June, I said. was out of the question. Even a lesser delay could hurt. Pacific Video had organized its schedule for November and December 1976. And I did not yet know how Syndicast thought the stations would react, as I had not wanted to alarm them unduly. Nixon began to see the point. He and Brennan agreed to move back from May to March, for airing in May. I then said that in order to combat the credibility issue, Watergate had to be one of the four consecutive shows. Nixon needed time to think about that. O.K., I needed time to consult with my partners.

It soon became clear that we had to have Watergate. Syndicast felt we needed it for credibility with the stations. During a social drink with Bill Sarnoff, I sought to predispose him favorably to the idea too. Pacific Video (P.V.I.) felt we needed everything we could possibly get in return for a delay to which they were in fact very much opposed. They would have to find new business to cover the days they had reserved in November and December. And some of those dates were only two months away. Just to make sure everyone got the point, Jack Meyer spelled out his objections to any postponement in a three-page letter. "Unfortunately, however, P.V.I. is not in a position to be able to respond to President Nixon's request for such postponement without considering the possible negative reactions to such postponement on others who are intimately involved in this project from both a legal and practical standpoint." Etc., etc.

Clearly a new meeting had to take place. It was fixed for Thursday, September 14. Again, Nixon began our session by inquiring about my lecture in Chicago and making sure I had been paid.

I came straight to the point. The proposed delay had been received far worse than I had feared. There were two distinct and separate problems. First, credibility. Syndicast said that we had to have the Watergate show as one of the four shows in order to come through this new delay unscathed. Second, cost. The delay was probably going to cost me a hundred thousand dollars one way or another, and Pacific Video in particular was going to have problems quite apart from their investment in the project. For them, and for the rest of the investors, I had to find at least an extra hundred thousand dollars of revenue, and I therefore needed to have a seventh hour that we could broadcast. We could recoup our losses from that.

"Oh, well," said Nixon, "if it's money that you're worried about, I'll reduce my fee by a hundred thousand dollars."

I didn't like that idea at all. Paying less than our original contract called for might create a sense of obligation running from me to him, something I dearly wanted to avoid.

"No, I don't think that's a good idea. Why should you reduce your fee? I don't think that's fair. If you just give us the extra hour, we will bear the cost."

At that point, Jack Brennan intervened. "Don't commit yourself now, Mr. President. I think you should have time to think about which alternative you would prefer."

The principle of some financial concession seemed to have been agreed. I was happy to leave that point there for the moment, and return to Watergate.

"Do you agree, Mr. President, to Watergate becoming consecutive, becoming the fourth show?" I quoted Phillip Lacovara again—though not by name!—on the question of not affecting the Watergate appeals.

"I don't mind, but I do have a responsibility to the publishers. After all, the contract as it is now drawn does protect them somewhat on the subject of Watergate. I would not want to agree to do this without their O.K."

"But just so that we're absolutely clear on this, Mr. President. If we get the publisher's O.K., then you are saying you agree to Watergate becoming one of the four consecutive shows?"

Nixon agreed that that was indeed the case. We took our leave, and Marv and I met up with Jack Brennan for a drink at the San Clemente Inn. "Oh, God," he said, "I hope this delay does go through. The President's been like a man with a weight lifted off his mind for the past week, since he thought it was going to happen."

Bill Sarnoff had told me he would be traveling through Germany until Thursday or Friday, when I could reach him at the Frankfurt Book Fair, at the Warner Books booth. We finally made contact on the Friday evening at eight forty-five, when he called me back at the Plaza. I explained the situation to him.

"Yes, I know," he replied. "I've heard all about it from the people at San Clemente."

"And is that O.K. with you, Bill?"

"Well, I've thought a lot about it," he said. An agonizing pause. "And I can't think of a logical reason for saying no."

I arranged to thank him in person as he passed through London. The crisis was over. We could make all our new plans. Pacific Video could try to get some new bookings for November and December. John Birt would have to try to get his LWT sabbatical moved into the spring of next year. Bob Zelnick would stay with us continuously through until California. Jim Reston and Phil Stanford, Bob's excellent choice as our Third Man, would work through to the end of their current contracts at the end of December, and then come to California for the actual taping if they could. Jim thought that he could; Phil thought that other commitments might make it impossible.

And that, I would like to say, was the end of that. But the crisis was not in fact over. On September 30 Marv Minoff sent off a two-page letter detailing the changes the ex-President had agreed to, with the emphasis on the new dates and above all the new Watergate clause:

> The taping or filming will include all the subject matters covered by the agreement with none of the restrictions contained in Paragraph 8 of the agreement; and all the programs referred to in the agreement including, without limitation, the so-called "Watergate appeals" program referred to in Paragraph 8, will be distributed and exhibited without regard to any limitations contained in said Paragraph 8.

Two weeks later, another bombshell. A letter from John V. Brennan.

> Dear Marv,
>
> Your letter of September 30 is enclosed unsigned. There was not an agreement to ignore or alter the provisions of Paragraph 8 of the basic contract, nor can there be.

Marv spoke with Brennan. "Jack, there isn't a comma in that document that we didn't agree to at San Clemente," he said. "And there's simply no way we can start renegotiating things we've already negotiated and conveyed to our staff, our stations, our backers and our potential advertisers." During a flurry of phone calls between Marv and Jack Brennan, and between the respective lawyers, it became clear that San Clemente's main concern was the possibility of a court order precluding Nixon from discussing Watergate pending the appeals. But of course that was not what Brennan's letter had said, and as one limited proviso it presented no particular problem. If a court issued a specific order restricting or precluding Nixon from talking about Watergate, then of course we would not—indeed could not—treat it as a breach of the agreement.

A new clause was drafted, to everyone's general approval. It took note of the point that had been raised:

> The Interviews shall cover all subjects. The program containing the so-called "Watergate appeals" may be taped, filmed, distributed and exhibited without regard to any limitation or restriction contained in Paragraph 8 of the agreement. Notwithstanding the foregoing, you shall not be required to discuss the Watergate appeals in any interview so long as you are specifically precluded from doing so by a restraining order or injunction issued by a court of competent jurisdiction.

I sent off this letter on November 3, and expected a signature as a matter of course more or less by return mail. We carried on with our planning, but there was no reply, no signed document. The month of November passed. On December 7, I had to return to California to address the Hollywood Radio and Television Society. I arranged to meet Frank Gannon for a drink and some hard discussion later.

I began by reviewing point by point the terms that had been derived from both the September 9 meeting, at which he had been present, and the September 14 meeting, which he had missed. Clearly I was reciting nothing he hadn't seen with his own eyes or heard about at the time.

"Frank," I said finally, "the thing that puzzles me is that when we have these problems, always in the end the President acts honorably and helpfully. But for the life of me I can't understand why it is done in such a way as to invariably deprive him of any credit he might otherwise earn by being cooperative. I don't know if it's the advice he's getting or what, but why are we getting f---ed around like this?"

Gannon said he would look into it. The next day we received word that the letter of understanding had been signed in the form submitted. A day or two after, Marv collected it from Jack Brennan at Los Angeles Airport. There were scratch marks near the Watergate clause. Someone had begun obliterating it and then changed his mind.

I now had my contract, barely more than three months before the first Interview session. A vast weight had been lifted from my mind, but the brinksmanship along the way had obviated any sense of gratitude I might otherwise have felt toward Mr. Nixon. And to this day, I can't begin to explain why it took so long to implement something that had been agreed upon so much earlier.

But it was a lesson we took to heart. Clearly, to put it at its mildest, throughout the Nixon Interviews we were going to have to be ready for anything.

CHAPTER

3

SEPTEMBER HAD BEEN AN ACTIVE MONTH FOR THE PROJECT ALL around.

In Washington, Jim Reston's combination of original research and consultation with experts provided us with an enormous dividend: fresh evidence in the most thoroughly raked over case in the history of the United States.

It began in mid-September with Reston perusing the Watergate trial transcript at the Federal Courthouse on John Marshall Place. Leafing through the prosecution exhibits, he came upon a conversation between Nixon and Charles Colson dated June 20, 1972, just three days after the break-in and only hours after the Nixon-Haldeman conversation that was later subjected to eighteen and a half minutes of manual erasure.

Early in the conversation, Nixon tells Colson, "If we didn't know better, we would have thought it was deliberately botched."

Moments later, Colson remarks, "Bob is pulling it all together. Thus far I think we've done the right things to date." A page or so later, this exchange occurs:

Nixon: Basically, they're all pretty hard-line guys.

Colson: You mean, Hunt?

Nixon: Of course, we're just going to leave this where it is, with the Cubans . . . at times I just stonewall it.

Finally the President concludes, "We've got to have lawyers smart enough to have our people delay, avoiding depositions . . . that's one possibility."

On its face, Reston thought, the transcript is damning. Three full days before the so-called "smoking pistol" tape, here is Nixon showing considerable familiarity with the operation, knowing about the involvement of Hunt and already talking of "stonewalling," leaving it with the Cubans, delaying, thankful that those arrested were "hard-line guys." Strange that the tape had not figured more prominently in the public case against Nixon.

Reston read on, past the more familiar transcripts of June 23, September 15, January 8 and others. Then another Nixon-Colson exhibit, February 13, 1973. And here is Nixon speaking: "When I'm speaking about Watergate, that's the whole point of . . . of the election; this tremendous investigation rests unless one of the seven begins to talk; that's the problem."

Again Reston stared at the transcript. Here again was Nixon prior to his much trumpeted March 21 conversation with John Dean, talking like the veritable mastermind of the cover-up. And again, no one had seen fit to cite the conversation as evidence of his role in the conspiracy.

But for Reston, a February 14 Nixon-Colson conversation was the clincher. Jim had become something of an Alger Hiss buff through his work on earlier Nixon books and our own project. Now here was Nixon recalling that case with his political crony Colson.

Nixon: Hiss was a traitor. It was a cover-up.

Colson: Yeah.

Nixon: A cover-up is the main ingredient.

Colson: That's the problem . . .

Nixon: That's where we gotta cut our losses. My losses are to be cut. The President's losses gotta be cut on the cover-up deal.

Reston knew he might have overlooked or forgotten the earlier material. But the Hiss reference, the incredible Nixon propensity for rationally recognizing one minute that, like Hiss, his own vulnerabilities lay with the cover-up rather than with any initial culpability, and then proceeding like an addict with more of the cover-up—this Reston would not have forgotten. Not if it had ever been published before. No. This evidence had to be new.

Reston's intuitions were quickly confirmed by sources on the old Special Prosecutor's staff. Yes, the transcripts he had seen had been among the sixty-four subpoenaed by Leon Jaworski. Since Nixon was not himself a defendant, the legal justification for the subpoena was that the tapes were needed to prepare for the prosecution of those under indictment, including Colson. But subsequent to the subpoena, Colson had "copped a plea," pleading guilty to a felony growing out of his role in the Ellsberg case. In exchange, the Watergate charges against him were dropped. And while marked as exhibits and circulated among the various lawyers for the accused, the tapes were never introduced at the cover-up trial. In fact, it was only through oversight that they had been preserved as part of the public record. Reston's was the best kind of scoop— developed not through a leak or a breach of ethics on anyone's part, but through his own sheer shoe-leather diligence. We could only hope that no one else would follow in Reston's footsteps before we could confront Nixon with his discoveries.

Jim, incidentally, also managed to do some productive digging over at the National Archives. It seemed that on August 8, 1974, his last full day in office, Nixon had had the presence of mind to write Chief Archivist Arthur J. Sampson, revoking a provision in his earlier bequest of vice-presidential papers which would have opened them to public inspection three years after his leaving office, and providing instead that prior to 1985 no one was to gain access without Nixon's personal approval. At the same time, Jim discovered that Nixon aides were busily visiting the Republican National Committee, and taking away every bit of Nixon film footage that the Committee Library had on hand. Alas, we never found a pertinent time to raise these historical footnotes with the former President himself, but a copy of the Nixon-Sampson letter discovered by Reston remained in our files.

Meanwhile, back in London, I had lunched with Jimmy Goldsmith. I did not need to raise the subject of the Nixon Interviews since Jimmy always asked about them, but on this occasion I said I would like to take him up on his kind offer of a year earlier. His response was immediate.

"We don't want to do the whole thing, but we will match anybody else. For instance, if you can find half of what you need from somebody else, we will automatically come in with the other half. Just so long as we know the project has the funds to get completed. Since it's Banque Occidentale, it will have to be done as a banking transaction, with some of your foreign contracts serving as security and so on, but then I think it will be no problem."

It was a handsome gesture. The Nixon Interviews were scarcely in the main line of the bank's business, but Jimmy had said he would help, and now he was being as good as his word. Not that finding the matching investor was going to be all that easy. Marv Minoff still has nightmares about an evening he spent arm wrestling in a rather bleary macho fashion until 3 A.M. in a series of bars all over New York with a leader of a Southern consortium that had shown some interest. It turned out that their interest in arm wrestling was considerably greater than their interest in the project.

The search went on. And the search for advertisers began. As a first move, Mickey Johnson, the president of Syndicast, wrote to thirty major institutions to see if they would be interested in sole sponsorship of all four programs. "The opportunity exists for . . . to perform an unprecedented public service and to reach at the same time a very large and intense audience."

If it had not been so serious, the response would have been hilarious. The thirty companies were unanimous. "We would have no interest whatever in programs of this type," said one. "It does not fit our communication needs at the present time," said another. "I'm sorry to tell you that our television strategy over the next several years does not include this kind of program." And one distinguished advertiser thought so little of the whole idea that he scribbled "Thank you but we're not interested" on the bottom of Mickey Johnson's actual letter and sent that back to him again. Though, to be fair, he did splash out on a new envelope.

One advertiser's letter seemed to have two distinct authors: "While we agree with you about the outstanding historic nature of these broadcasts, I am sure you can see it would be dangerous for us to be associated with an enterprise like that."

No sole sponsors then, that was clear. The commercial spots would have to be offered separately, one by one. The advertising fraternity, like the financial community, was obviously going to need some more attention, but important—nay, essential—though they all were, the priority was the research coming out of Washington. And both John Birt and I were delighted by its quality and its depth. Months later, as we would gather in my suite at the Beverly Hilton to prepare for each Interview session, Bob Zelnick would play Nixon to my Frost as we engaged in the sort of give-and-take anticipated the following day, but these were no ad hoc performances, no sudden little impersonations extemporized on the spot. From the moment our research team had begun to form, I had discussed with Birt and Zelnick the importance of trying to understand the Nixon administration as Nixon's closest remaining supporters would view it; of interpreting events as they would interpret them; of seeing the Nixon presidency in its most favorable light rather than its worst. For, as many a successful barrister has told me, it is difficult if not impossible to argue successfully your own case unless you fully understand your adversary's. Where Nixon deserved to score points, let him score them. While it was essential to develop our own theory of the Nixon presidency, I would be an advocate for the fair-minded viewer, not for any particular point of view. Where his account proved less than credible, then I would become his opponent. But in any case, I had to know what his perspective would be.

Zelnick began his research by asking himself the question that was basic to his task: What would have been the view of the Nixon administration had Watergate not intervened to abbreviate it? Like both Jim and Phil, he sought answers not only from the big-name advisers who had served in the Nixon White House and at Cabinet-level jobs, but from the apparatchiks—the people who wrote speeches, worked on bureaucratic reorganization, tracked the economy, lobbied on Capitol Hill, searched for a formula to end the fighting in Vietnam, wrote anticrime bills and argued the administration's positions in the courts. And, also like his colleagues on the team, he read virtually every piece of substantial literature published by and about the Nixon administration, including Nixon's own White House public papers and articles in foreign affairs and academic journals.

Nixon, Zelnick concluded, could argue credibly, if not convincingly, that he had presided over an important transitional period in the American postwar experience, steering the country out of a dangerous era of confrontation with the Soviet Union, establishing a relationship better suited to the relative parity that existed between the two nuclear superpowers and, in the domestic sphere, closing out the era of *de jure* racial segregation in the South without further alienating the white Southern establishment, and establishing a political climate which made it possible for a Southerner to run successfully for the presidency in 1976. ("We were responsible for Jimmy Carter," Nixon said to me in one of our meetings.)

Nixon would surely point out that he ended U.S. combat involvement in Vietnam. He concluded the first significant arms-control agreement with a major adversary in modern times. He built bridges to the People's Republic of China with its population of almost 800 million. Through his National Security Adviser, later Secretary of State, Henry Kissinger, he proved brilliantly opportunistic in the Middle East, restoring relations with the key Arab powers without reneging on American commitments to Israel. Domestically, he might claim, he had provided the Republican Party with a progressive ideology—the New Federalism which was neither a pale replica of the Democrats' New Deal nor the reactionary negativism of a Barry Goldwater.

What was also made clear from Zelnick's discussion with former Nixon policy aides was that, to the extent most of them had dealt personally with him, the man they knew was a well-informed, civil, clear-thinking human being with a fantastically analytic mind and a decent desire to do what was right. It will not, I am sure, be violating any confidences to share Zelnick's recollection of Nixon's chief economic adviser, Herbert Stein. Stein spoke of many personal moments when Nixon had shown genuine human concern for him. Finally, sipping nervously on a beer and touched by his own recollections, Stein said simply, "He was very good to me. I have nothing but pleasant memories of him. I wept when he left. I regard him as a friend. I see him when I visit California."

And there was Fred Malek, a tough, efficient, scrupulously honest graduate of the Harvard Business School, who patiently explained how he had attempted to reshape the bureaucracy for Nixon and how many of those he worked with had ended up in jail, concluding, "I thank God they didn't ask me to lie. I can't say what I would have done."

As I read that, I was reminded of the words of Herbert (Bart) Porter, a C.R.P. official who committed perjury and eventually went to jail for it: "I did not do it for a position, I did not do it to hide anything because I did not think I had done anything . . . my vanity was appealed to . . . when I was told my name had come up in the highest council. They said I was an honest man, and that I made a good appearance. That sort of thing. My loyalty to the President was appealed to. Those things coupled with what I had found to be a weakness in my character, quite frankly—to succumb to that pressure."

Another longtime presidential associate told Zelnick: "You're never going to believe this, but I dealt with Richard Nixon more than any other public figure and in all the years we worked together I never heard him utter a profane word." But after a pause he added, "The memory of Nixon tortures me now. I feel raped, betrayed. I have had nightmares—screaming nightmares—about him."

A second domestic policy adviser theorized that there were really two Nixons: the one who was fascinated with both great international issues and the mechanics of governing, and the frighteningly insecure political thug. Each Nixon surrounded himself with a predictable set of colleagues. Depending upon the proximity of an election campaign, one or the other set would gain preeminence in the Nixon White House. In the end, the thugs prevailed and were responsible for bringing down the Nixon presidency. But both Nixons existed. Like the poor hero in Hesse's *Steppenwolf*, Nixon could well complain, "Alas, two souls beat within my breast." Or, as Dr. Johnson said of one of his contemporaries, "He may do very well, as long as he can outrun his character; but, the moment his character gets up with him, he is all over."

Still another close associate, who staked his reputation as a decent and principled liberal in service with the Nixon administration and lost a good part of it, stared at his desk and pondered aloud, "How did he become President? How did he become President? The sentry really fell asleep."

"A democracy has many sentries," Zelnick replied. "A couple were shot, a couple were coopted. Maybe a few fell asleep. But there were a hell of a lot still around in 1973 and 1974."

Zelnick's foreign-policy paper tied together the many seemingly contradictory themes of the Nixon foreign policy. "Détente with the Soviet Union, Nixon will say, does not assume the two countries will agree with each other's system of government. It does not mean that they will refrain from competition in one area of the world or another. What it does mean is that the United States and the Soviets attempt to build a structure of cooperation so that in a crunch they will be more prone to negotiate than to fight. Certain vital interests of each power are recognized as sacrosanct by the other, and where the two sides compete, as in the Middle East or Africa, they do so in defined, or at least, understood areas and pursue defined, or at least understood, ground rules."

But the Soviets would continue to seek targets of opportunity where they perceived the United States as unable or unwilling to stand firm. Thus, in the lexicon of Nixon and Kissinger, "seeing it through in Vietnam" was justified as an important ingredient in the new relations between Washington and the Kremlin. But our questioning must be punctuated with references to the enormous costs of the war in terms of money and human lives—both Asian and American—and the horrible ruptures it produced within the United States. Even assuming that refusing to "cut and run" in Indochina was of marginal assistance to our dealing with the Soviets, was the gain worth a thousand American lives? How about ten thousand? Or the fifteen thousand that were actually lost during the Nixon administration? And the million or more Asian lives that were lost? Was it worth Kent State and Jackson State? Did it justify unleashing Spiro Agnew and polarizing the United States? And, most tantalizingly, was it worth the stockade mentality that developed inside the Nixon White House, and the abuses that sprang from it?

Meanwhile, Phil Stanford was outlining concisely the nub of the abuse of power issues included in the second Article of Impeachment framed against Mr. Nixon by the House Judiciary Committee. His career as a free-lance investigative reporter with *I. F. Stone, The New York Times Magazine, Saturday Review* and many more, suited him ideally to the task. Stanford's research included the abuse of the I.R.S., the formation of the Plumbers, the anti-Ellsberg campaign, the Huston Plan, the enemies lists and the seventeen national security wiretaps instituted by the White House. Together with Reston's exploration of the former President's personal taxes and Zelnick's analysis of the secret bombing of Cambodia, we would have a complete exposition of all non-Watergate areas of alleged wrongdoing in which there was credible evidence of involvement by Mr. Nixon himself.

This research was essential also in deciding the topics we would *not* pursue, either because the evidence of Nixonian involvement was too sparse, or because the relative smallness of the alleged abuse ruled it out in terms of our time priorities. Illegal campaign contributions in general, ITT's $400,000 pledge to defray expenses for the Republican Convention in San Diego, and the sale of ambassadorships had all remained elusive in terms of proving a direct involvement by the ex-President. Exhaust fans at San Clemente seemed somehow on a different scale to some of the other abuses we were considering, as did the wiretap that Richard Nixon had the Secret Service install on his own brother, Donald. "Indeed," noted Zelnick, "my own inclination runs against asking the former President about his brother. If Donald Nixon were my brother, I would wiretap him too."

Stanford also reviewed the findings of the Rockefeller commission and the Church committee for evidence of similar abuse by previous administrations. From the beginning we had anticipated that two of Nixon's main lines of defense would be, first, that the allegations of constitutional abuse against him had ample precedent, and, second, that Watergate itself was—reduced to basics—little more than a campaign prank or the "third-rate burglary" Ziegler had described days after the break-in. Understanding what previous administrations had done was thus one of the crucial elements in our effort to place Nixon's own conduct in perspective.

Stanford's summaries showed clearly that Nixon would not want for ammunition. Just a few examples:

For about twenty years the C.I.A. and, for a lesser period, the F.B.I. had conducted mail covers and inspection of letters addressed to or by U.S. citizens.

Wiretaps of U.S. citizens without court warrants had been commonplace at least since the 1930's. Indeed, the number of national-security wiretaps conducted during Nixon's administration was lower than under any president since Franklin Roosevelt.

Warrantless room bugging—the so-called black-bag jobs—had been conducted by the F.B.I. and C.I.A. since World War II. Burglaries had also been commonplace.

Embarrassing personal information on political foes had been sent by the F.B.I. to a number of presidents, again beginning with F.D.R.

C.I.A. and F.B.I. infiltration into domestic political groups was extensive under Johnson. The infamous F.B.I. Cointelpro effort, involving the surveillance, harassment and slander of New Left groups and individuals, was also born under Johnson.

C.I.A. excesses against foreign nations and leaders were also well documented in earlier administrations.

The list went on. As Stanford indicated in an introductory

memorandum, one of Nixon's key defenses might be, "I didn't do it, but if I did, others did it worse."

On my regular trips to Washington to meet with the team, we would begin the process of anticipating the Nixon strategy and, equally important, search for gaps in our material. The thought that a major area might have escaped us nagged at me. I asked Phil Stanford to reexamine the evidence on Nixon and organized crime, and to take a second look at the alleged C.I.A. involvement in Watergate. I wanted a separate paper on that. Also, I wanted Reston's views on the Alger Hiss case and on the Nixon psychology, organized and presented in narrative form. And I felt we needed a separate paper on the Agnew affair, another on the sequence of key events in Nixon's postresignation life and a complete chronology of all the important events of his presidency—including Watergate matters. I asked my secretary in New York, Liz Sykes, to obtain blank diaries for the years 1969 to 1974, and then I asked Bob to fill them, so that we had side by side the events we knew about at the time they happened, and the events that may have happened on the same day that we only found out about much later.

On December 12 the *London Sunday Times* added to our store of research. In a brilliantly documented account entitled "Cambodia: The Blame," William Shawcross detailed one of the most terrible episodes in the Nixon presidency: the destruction of Cambodia. I read and reread his words. They linked in my mind with the chilling figures in the House Judiciary Committee Impeachment Report, which demonstrated that the United States had dropped about twice the bomb tonnage on Cambodia as on North Vietnam during the Nixon presidency.

And they linked with Zelnick's own findings, after conversations with one former top N.S.C. staff analyst. N.S.C. papers had discounted the military effectiveness of a) strategic bombing conducted for purposes of interdicting enemy supply routes and denying vast areas to North Vietnamese troops, and b) the Cambodian incursion. (The N.S.C. not only discounted the disruptive impact of the invasion but warned that the forces used in the operation would be diverted from areas of higher priority in South Vietnam, which would in turn make it infinitely more difficult to contain enemy activity in the South Vietnamese provinces.) Indeed, in regard to the Cambodian invasion, what had changed between Nixon's statement on April 20, 1970, that things were going well and that the "just peace" we had long sought was then "in sight" and his decision only days later to invade? Zelnick was informed that there was no sudden buildup of enemy troops, and no credible evidence that an invasion of South Vietnam was contemplated through the Parrot's Beak area.

Shawcross seemed to have summarized it very well: "Cambodia was taken to war more to serve a concept of global American 'credibility' than a response to the facts on the ground. The fate of Cambodia itself was never of concern."

If progress in the vital area of program preparation was proceeding according to schedule, progress in the other areas that we had to worry about was considerably less speedy.

Marv's patient presentations to advertising agencies were no more fruitful than mine or those of Len Koch, Bill Koblenzer and their colleagues at Syndicast.

As one ad man explained to me, "Look, you've got a big problem. Out of the companies you're approaching, 50 percent wouldn't have wanted to be seen having anything to do with Nixon even when he was President, and the other 50 percent are trying to make people forget that they did."

"But this is not an endorsement, or anything of the kind," I would argue. "This is, potentially, at any rate, history."

"Sure, David, sure."

Clearly their advertising budget for history for the year had already been spent.

There had been a ray of light after the Hollywood Radio and Television luncheon on December 7. Datsun had made the first verbal commitment for four thirty-second spots. The first signed agreement came on January 7, from Weed Eater in Houston. They obtained their reward in *60 Minutes* four months later, when they became a subject of national debate on that outstanding news magazine:

"Weed Eater," said Mike Wallace. "I don't know what Weed Eater is, but they have bought one spot, two spots?" I was not, I must confess, totally equipped to answer him.

> FROST: Weed Eater is a product that you're going to come to know and love and understand, but first I hope that I come to understand it. Let's be clear about this. We're seeking advertisers who realize it is history, but it's controversial history. So, we are seeking advertisers with courage, and these people have courage. But we are—
> WALLACE: Weed Eater has courage?
> FROST: Weed Eater has courage.

There was still no sign of the additional finance, but the message about the seriousness of our editorial intentions was beginning to seep through. Jack Anderson had written on November 22: "When Richard Nixon faces the television cameras for his first interview since he abandoned the White House, he'll be cross-examined as if he were on the witness stand. TV interviewer David Frost, in the strictest of secrecy, has drawn up a set of questions that would satisfy a Watergate prosecutor."

And on December 15, Henry Grunwald and Dick Duncan of *Time* magazine sat down with Marv and me at "21" to discuss possible special coverage of the Nixon Interviews for *Time.* Their interest was encouraging, even though the ground rules would take a further two months to prepare.

On January 5 I met with Dick Gelb, the president of Bristol-Myers. His observations were acute, and his awareness of other advertisers' reluctance to take a risk on the Interviews was total, but he nevertheless clearly shared my belief in their potential and in the virtues of diversity within the broadcast media. I was impressed by the man, and encouraged by his initial response. Then on January 6 I explained the project in depth to Merrill Panitt, editorial director of *TV Guide,* in the hope that they would deem the Interviews worthy of a cover.

By the beginning of January, Jim Reston had completed his Watergate briefing book. His last paragraph read:

Watergate is fundamentally an antidemocratic event: it's an assault on democracy and democratic institutions. It was an effort to undermine free choice, free competition in an election and to undermine governmental institutions that operate only through the trust in them by the American people. And it can be argued that Richard Nixon is a fundamentally antidemocratic personality, that his political statements over twenty-five years were never rooted in any deeply held political beliefs, that he is the classic "main-line politician" who adopts positions which mirror, rather than educate, the mood of the electorate and, worse, panders to and inflames the prejudices of the time. That such a figure without belief, for whom "winning" was everything, could for a quarter of a century so dominate the political life of a country that prides itself as the greatest democracy in the world, is a stunning phenomenon of the twentieth century.

Jim was also continuing his personal crusade on behalf of the Nixon psychohistory school of approach. I shared Jim's fascination with Richard Nixon the man. Indeed, over the months it had grown rather than diminished. But while I was not averse to trying, I was convinced that we would not strike gold if we put Nixon on his guard by sounding like psychiatrists ourselves. I simply could not see him responding enthusiastically to inquiries about "survivor guilt" or the significance of his penchant for mashing potatoes upon later visits to his mother's home.

But Jim was right in wanting to bring us back to the question, What makes Richard Nixon tick? Jim had written of "winning" being everything, and yet there were descriptions like Stewart Alsop's about "the look of a man who rather expects to lose." There were the general remarks Nixon had made or written that one so much wanted to make personal and particular. That quote in *Six Crises,* for example: "A leader is one who has the emotional, mental, and physical strength to withstand the pressures and tensions created by necessary doubts and then, at the critical moment, to make a choice and to act decisively. The men who fail are those who are so overcome by doubts that they either crack under strain or flee to avoid meeting the problem at all." How would Richard Nixon feel he measured up to that?

And then there were the tapes and the transcripts. In sheer evidentiary terms, of course, the transcripts of June 1972 and March and April 1973 were particularly rich. But as I read them, I found the conversations with Henry Petersen, for example, increasingly distasteful. Was ever a man quite so used and manipulated? And that earlier conversation of September 15 with John Dean stuck in my mind: "I want the most comprehensive notes on all those who tried to do us in. They didn't have to do it . . . They are asking for it, and they are going to get it . . . We have not used the Bureau, and we have not used the Justice Department, but things are going to change now . . ."

Of course, Nixon was talking there about doing something that he said his administration had not done previously, but in terms of what Richard Nixon actually did, John and I had given a crucial task to Bob Zelnick: that of distinguishing between Nixon's abuse of power and the activities of his predecessors as set forth in the Stanford paper. These were some of his headings:

First, Nixon attempted to institutionalize what had been the disparate and seemingly random activities of the agencies and sub-agencies prior to his administration. Further, while former Chief Executives had winked at such agency conduct, or looked the other way, Nixon took personal control of the goings-on. The Huston Plan, for example, was prepared at the urging of Nixon . . .

Second, Nixon's establishment of the Special Investigations Unit (Plumbers) and the resultant power and activities of the group took investigative activities outside the orbit of those provided by law and created what was in fact a private quasi police force accountable solely to the President . . .

Third, Nixon actively participated in a conspiracy to deny a criminal defendant (Daniel Ellsberg) his constitutional rights . . .

Fourth, Nixon's abuse of the I.R.S. was in a class by itself. The taped transcripts and testimony of John Dean alone are replete with evidence of Nixon having authorized the compilations of both "enemies lists" and rosters of McGovern campaign contributors, with the purpose being to have the I.R.S. harass these individuals with tax audits. Nixon, moreover, received reports from Dean and Haldeman of the unwillingness of I.R.S. Commissioner Jamie Walters and

Treasury Secretary George Schulz to apply the desired heat, and responded by instructions to top aides to go back and insist that the agency officials cooperate . . .

Fifth, Nixon, at the very least, was a willing and active early participant in the Watergate cover-up which involves such crimes as the conspiracy to obstruct justice, perjury, and the payment and receipt of blackmail money, as well as the use of the C.I.A. for purely domestic political purposes . . .

Sixth, Nixon publicly lied about his own roles in the various scandals throughout the final two years of his presidency . . .

Seventh, Nixon interposed his office between his own misdeed and those lawfully charged with the responsibility to obtain the truth. Had the courts not enforced the Cox and Jaworski subpoenas, the tripartite form of government in the United States would have been effectively scuttled with the executive branch made dominant and the courts subservient . . .

Zelnick added two or three more points and then wrote:

Finally, Nixon himself thrived on the politics of polarization throughout his public career . . . Having for years sought the raw political nerve and the political jugular, he could hardly have accepted those whom he branded 'enemies' to forbear when, after a generation of frustration, they at last had him weakened and vulnerable.

Or, as Nixon himself would later put it, "I gave them a sword. And they stuck it in. And they twisted it with relish. And, I guess, if I'd been in their position I'd have done the same thing."

CHAPTER

4

As N-day approached, and preparations were begun to move our base from Washington to California, all of our emotions—both apprehensions and expectations—began to quicken and intensify. Our concern for security, for instance. We were amateurs in the cloak-and-dagger business, but we did our best. We had strict confidentiality clauses for everyone in sight. We had kept a locked safe for all files in our Georgetown office, as "inside" stories appearing based on our research documents or our private discussions could have destroyed the spontaneity of my sessions with the ex-President. We knew the name "Nixon" immediately attracted attention, so in Telexes we had referred to "the Subject." And in restaurants, whenever waiters or captains approached, Richard Nixon would become "William Holden," or "Charlton Heston," but I would be hard pressed to claim that we ever fooled anyone with our little moments of melodrama.

Leaving the table briefly during one of our sessions at the Rive Gauche in Washington, Zelnick encountered one of our regular waiters. "Mr. Zelnick," he said, "I hate to interfere, but I have waited on William Holden dozens of times, and he just doesn't seem like the sort of fellow who would tell witnesses to lie to juries."

Before Zelnick could think of a response, the waiter went on: "But Richard Nixon does, and I hope Mr. Frost gives him hell."

Although the content of the programs was naturally my overriding concern, there were one or two items of unfinished business that required some attention as well. I was eager to increase the number of advertisers to a figure somewhat greater than two, and common sense—not to mention peace of mind—dictated that it was time to resolve if possible the question of financing once and for all. In February I decided to go back to Polygram, who had earlier decided to stick with their original investment, and to ask again if they would invest further in the project. They said yes to a further $400,000, to be secured on various contracts we were in the process of signing, and which were not provisionally earmarked for Banque Occidentale! That in turn would activate the promised investment from the bank, but still left us at least $250,000 short. I then turned reluctantly to the only other potential investor that I knew for sure shared my faith in the project: a company called David Paradine Productions, Inc. All along I had felt we at Paradine were investing enough of ourselves in the project in terms of time and effort without investing cash as well. But it was February, and if $250,000 was needed to activate the Polygram investment, which in turn was needed to activate the Banque Occidentale investment, there was not really very much choice. The step had to be taken. The money we had advanced over the past few months, pending the arrival of our elusive investor, would stay in the project.

The cast of investors was therefore complete: Polygram, Banque Occidentale, Pacific Video, Syndicast and Paradine. No laundered money, no Bebe Rebozo or Robert Abplanalp, no mystery at all— just five companies and a whole lot of praying.

Also in February, I revisited San Clemente in order to check out the offices with the technical team from Pacific Video that Jack Meyer had selected.

"Ah," said Nixon as I entered his office. "The Grand Inquisitor."

"No, no," I said, "just your friendly neighborhood confidant."

In fact, of course, I knew I would probably have to play both those roles, and several more besides. But then that's one of the things that interviewing is all about. We discussed makeup and how his office could be effectively lit.

"It's the way you look that I'm really worried about," Nixon said almost playfully. Then he added, "After all, *you've* got a whole career ahead of you . . ."

The words hung poignantly in the air for a second that felt like an hour, to be followed by the familiar embarrassed hubbub of everybody in the room all trying to change the subject at once.

It was Randy Blim of P.V.I. who casually introduced a new complication from completely out of left field. "What about the LARAN?" he asked, referring to the radar transmitting station for ships at sea, which was apparently operated from the nearby San Clemente Coast Guard station. "When we did any presidential broadcasts from down here, they always turned it off, because otherwise you get a buzz on your audio and a rolling glitch. And you don't want a rolling glitch, do you?"

I was fairly sure that I didn't, though I could not have sworn to it. Randy explained that a rolling glitch was a jagged line that rolled continually through the picture.

"Well," said Jack Brennan, "I will write to the local Coast Guard station and do my best. But it may be slightly more difficult now than it used to be!"

I decided to sound out Brennan and Gannon on one other point while I was there. "Psychologically, when would you recommend taping the Watergate sessions—at the beginning or the end?"

There were obviously arguments both ways. Doing it first might clear the air—or poison it. John and I leaned toward the idea of leaving the major domestic confrontation areas until the end, until after Easter. But if Nixon positively hated the idea, it might help to be flexible.

As it happened, the decision never had to be made. The ex-President welcomed the idea of delaying Watergate until after Easter, and said he would like as long a break before it as possible, ideally seven days in order to prepare himself.

Our own research preparations seemed to be proceeding well, but I brought our conversations back to a nagging fear of mine. Was it possible that, for all our efforts, we had missed some sensational episode of the Nixon presidency, something that dwarfed all the other alleged abuses of power?

Birt and Zelnick did their best to alleviate my concern. This was the most thoroughly researched administration in the history of the United States. Every bright young investigative reporter had wanted to take a crack at Nixon. So had the hundreds of brilliant young lawyers affiliated with the Ervin committee, the House Judiciary Committee, and the Special Prosecutor's Office. They had found nothing they could prove beyond the material already on public record. After all, there were also the dozens of defendants who had copped pleas and still ended up in jail. They were white-collar offenders, for whom so much as a moment behind bars was a particularly terrifying prospect. Wouldn't they have traded the sort of evidence I was looking for in exchange for their freedom, if in fact such clear evidence existed? Birt then mentioned the White House transcripts that we had been reviewing so religiously. Hundreds of hours of them already public, and hundreds of others privately reviewed by prosecutors and counsel. Surely in some unguarded moment Nixon would have let slip that he had accepted an offer from the Mafia he couldn't refuse, or had ceded Alaska back to the Soviets in exchange for a little *dacha* on the Black Sea, if any of that had been true?

I did not disagree with either of them, but nevertheless I felt we must persist. I reread the material the Washington staff had submitted, underlining key passages again in a different color, writing even more illegible notes in the margin. I started plowing again through the thousands of pages of tape and testimony transcripts, and I never said no to the chance to talk to anybody who might conceivably add to our store of knowledge. All the reading, of course, was invaluable. The meetings were fun, but not notably productive.

When I first met with Tony Ulasewicz, for example, in a dark corner of Trader Vic's at the Plaza, I decided to play the old investigative game of pretending I knew a great deal more than I did.

"Why didn't Nixon destroy the tapes?" I asked early in our discussion.

"What good would it have done?" the good-natured Ulasewicz replied. "You know the C.I.A. had copies of all the tapes."

"Yes, of course, I knew that," I nodded. "What about all the money abroad? How much would you say it adds up to?"

"There's a hell of a lot of it," said Ulasewicz. "But it's not Nixon's. It's the Air Force generals', and a couple of large corporations'. You remember the sampan in the Mekong Delta with the gold in, that they were dragging out? That's where Dean was coming back from when the June 17 break-in occurred."

"Now that I hadn't realized," I conceded. "I thought Dean was returning from a drug-abuse symposium in Manila."

"That was the cover story," said Ulasewicz matter-of-factly.

"Fascinating, fascinating," I continued. "Now about the money you gave the defendants for Kalmbach—the $189,000. We know where all of that came from, but what about the rest of it?"

"You mean the other two million dollars?" Ulasewicz asked.

"Exactly."

"Well, that's another story entirely, which we'll have to discuss at some later date."

"How about now?"

"No, I'm thinking of writing a book. Do you think you can help me get it published?"

"I'm not certain, Tony," I replied. "But we'll talk about that later too."

We decided there was not a great deal that we could do with Tony's very entertaining contribution, though if one day the story of the sampan is validated by a congressional committee, then the joke will be on us. We had also decided by now that the whole theory of Watergate as a C.I.A. frame-up should take up as little of our twenty-four hours with Richard Nixon as possible.

As Zelnick had noted, "It seems preposterous to me that if Mc-Cord wanted to entrap his fellow burglars he would have done so by taking more men than necessary into the Watergate complex or leaving tape on the outside of a garage door hoping that some third-rate security guard would notice it and react promptly enough to catch the felons in the act. An anonymous phone tip to police would have been far more certain to accomplish the purpose. Remember too that the June 17 entry was the second Watergate break-in. The first, which occurred over the Memorial Day weekend in 1972, came off without a hitch, save for the fact that the bug on Larry O'Brien's phone did not function properly. Whatever Nixon and his apologists may say about the C.I.A., the fact remains that the Watergate scheme was hatched by Liddy and approved by Mitchell and Magruder—with Dean present for two of the three preliminary meetings and with the CREEP people under pressure from Colson and others at the White House (mainly Haldeman and Strachan) to get the intelligence operation going. And the cover-up was entirely a White House operation."

We decided that it would be a strategic error to introduce the subject in any of the Interviews with Nixon or to do more than note the improbability and irrelevance of the theory should Nixon raise it himself.

A chance encounter with Spiro Agnew provided no new information, though it certainly gave me an angle on the Vice-President's resignation that I hadn't thought of.

"Would you believe that Nixon did not even consult me on the choice of a successor?" Agnew inquired in a tone that could only be described as one of righteous indignation. "Not that I have anything against Jerry Ford," he added. "But, do you know, at that big swearing-in ceremony in the East Room, my name was not even mentioned once? It was like the Soviet Union, where the deposed leaders become nonpersons. It was just as though the previous five years had simply ceased to exist."

"Incredible," I said, meaning it entirely, though perhaps not as the former Vice-President thought I did.

Before I left New York at the beginning of March for two and a half months in California, Dick Duncan and I laboriously sorted out the understanding between *Time* magazine and ourselves. *Time* would obviously have to have some access to the content of the programs in order to ensure itself of the validity of the enterprise. Its integrity had to be protected without compromising our own product by giving too much of it away. I wanted *Time* to proceed, but not at the expense of preempting all the drama from the event itself. With a conviction born of experience, I knew that if people were told the entire contents list of a program, then they forgot that they had read it in a preview and felt, "There's nothing new in this, Grannie," as they watched the program. However, as I pondered the matter, it seemed that a few excerpts from our first program would probably not hurt. After all, Watergate would be our fourth program, and a few quotes from our first could protect *Time* while rewarding it for its enterprise and protecting our own.

Time would have total access to the contents of the first program in order to satisfy itself of the editorial merit of the broadcast, but it could quote liberally from only two important sequences. It could "allude" to two others, but not "characterize" them, and the other sequences would remain a total surprise.

That only left us with the problem of differentiating between the two verbs. As I wrote to Dick Duncan on March 3: "Our highly learned definitions of 'allude' and 'characterize' were summarized by the difference between:

> ALLUDE: "*Time* has also learned exclusively that Richard Nixon discussed, for the first time, the Canadian crisis," and
>
> CHARACTERIZE: "*Time* has also learned exclusively that Richard Nixon reveals for the first time the fact that the Canadian crisis was caused by his visit to Trader Vic's."

Apart from *TV Guide*, *Time* would be first with John Bryson's color photographs from the taping, and we would have a May 2 cover story, unless an earth-shattering event intervened or either party felt the agreement wasn't going to work and terminated it, which both of us had the right to do.

Without the publicity machine of a network behind us, I felt that *Time* magazine and *TV Guide* could give us the sort of launch that we needed, assuming of course that our words and our deeds matched up to their criteria.

By the time I checked in at the Beverly Hilton, Zelnick was already installed and had begun a long series of meetings and telephone calls with Ken Khachigian which would continue throughout our stay. The principal purpose of their sessions was to inform the Nixon staff of the broad subject matters we were going to discuss with the former President in order to enable him to prepare for the tapings. He would never know any of the questions in advance, but this was not a general-knowledge quiz show: we did not want him to spend hours preparing to explain détente, and then catch him out with a surprise question on the date of the Rehnquist nomination. We wanted to surprise him, sometimes to shock him, or confront him, but when we did so we wanted him to have the raw material at his mental fingertips. We wanted him to be at his best.

Khachigian and Zelnick worked well together and Bob soon found that Ken could happily take or even participate in a little bench jockeying at his boss's expense. Needless to say, the White House transcripts and testimony from the Watergate trial furnished a veritable gold mine for these Khachigian-Zelnick conversations. One not untypical example:

KHACHIGIAN: Is the press on your back?

ZELNICK: Mainly the Eastern establishment radic-libs. You know, *Time, Newsweek, The New York Times,* the *Washington Post,* the *L.A. Times.*

KHACHIGIAN: How are you dealing with it?

ZELNICK: I don't give a shit. At times I just stonewall it. Cover it up. Anything that will save the plan.

KHACHIGIAN: That's fine. Once the toothpaste is out of the tube, it's very hard to get it back in.

Later, during one of the Cambodia interrogation sessions, Nixon criticized the work of my "highly paid" staff of researchers.

"Honestly, Ken," Zelnick complained later, "That was a cheap shot. We just don't earn that much money."

"That's not what your income tax returns show," Khachigian responded.

All of our pre-Interview contacts with the Nixon staff had a psychological element to them as well. Beginning with my earliest discussions with Frank Gannon and Jack Brennan and continuing through Birt's San Clemente visit and Zelnick's exchanges with Khachigian, we never let pass the opportunity to suggest the importance of candor on Mr. Nixon's part regarding those areas of alleged wrongdoing by himself and his administration. Time and again we stressed our commitment to fairness and balance. Eighteen of the twenty-four Interview hours had been set aside for foreign and domestic policy: only six for Watergate. But who would pay attention to any of this if there was not a clean breast of the most serious allegations of wrongdoing? Let him put his actions in whatever context he deemed proper. Let him cite the unpublished—indeed the uninvestigated—misdeeds of his predecessors, but for God's sake, don't let him waste this last opportunity to regain personal credibility.

After such encounters we would compare notes and wonder whether we had struck the right sort of vibes with the Nixon staff. Usually we felt we had. But how much clout did they have with the Old Man? And was Nixon himself psychologically capable of confronting the hard truth? On this score, there was considerable doubt. Had Nixon the capacity to take good advice, we felt we would now be preparing to interview a distinguished elder statesman who had only recently turned the reins of government over to his chosen successor, President John Connally.

On March 7, my conversations with Brennan went deeper than they ever had before. After a still photograph session with the ex-President at San Clemente, Jack and I adjourned to the Quiet Cannon a few miles up the coast for what turned out to be a four-hour lunch. The conversation soon became fierce, so much so that our photographer, John Bryson, who had joined us for a prelunch drink did not even bother to finish it before hurriedly making his excuses and leaving. He told me later that he thought that if we had actually come to blows, we would probably not have wanted to have the moment recorded for posterity. As it was, the only photograph he took of the occasion was of the calm before the storm.

"How do we know," resumed Brennan when we were alone, "that you are not going to screw us with the editing?"

I demurred and quickly put the question that was on my mind. "How do we know that you are not going to screw us with the stonewalling?"

We had both stated as baldly as possible our basic fears. We had not put each other's mind at rest, but at least it did make dialogue easier. Brennan went on.

"You know, 60 percent of what this guy did in office was right," he said. "And 30 percent may have been wrong, but he thought it was right at the time."

I stared at Brennan without having to say a word. Both of us had passed arithmetic in elementary school. Ten percent of what Nixon did was wrong, and he knew it was wrong.

Brennan finally broke the silence. "If you screw us on the 60 percent, I'm going to ruin you if it takes the rest of my life."

I did not want to quibble over the exact percentages. Putting my arm around him, I replied, "And if you stonewall us on the 10 percent, I'm going to ruin you if it takes the rest of my life."

It was a curious compact, born of belligerence, but I found it oddly encouraging.

On the drive back from the Quiet Cannon to the Hilton I was horrified to realize that I had left my briefcase behind at San Clemente, containing at least one of our four basic briefing books.

I hastened to find Zelnick, only to discover that he had already learned about the missing item from Ken Khachigian. "Ken just called to extend his thanks for your leaving the briefcase there," he told me. "He says it saved them a fire bombing."

Over a working dinner in the hotel's L'Escoffier Restaurant, I told Bob about lunch. So Brennan's intentions were honorable, we concluded. Khachigian's were too. But again the daunting reality of whom we were dealing with struck home. John Dean's intentions had also been honorable on March 21, 1973. Henry Petersen's had been honorable on April 15. We could only hope, but the precedents were decidedly not encouraging. We had to expect the stonewall, or at best (that phrase we had already come to know and love) the "modified limited hangout."

The quotes of the Nixon era in general were in fact a welcome continuing source of light relief. In particular, his singular propensity for savagely attacking his foes' conduct and then munificently backing off from condemnation. Nixon had not blamed the press in his 1962 Farewell Press Conference for "giving . . . the shaft" to a politician they disliked because, after all, they had a "responsibility" to do that. Indeed, as far back as his 1952 Checkers Speech he had noted the presence of Senator John Sparkman's wife on the Democratic vice-presidential candidate's office payroll, only to add, "I don't criticize him for that."

Thus when some commentator made a particularly negative prediction about the project, it seemed natural to respond, "Of course, that's his right. If he hates me he has the responsibility to give me the shaft, and I don't blame him for that."

Nixon, Bob and I were agreed, had to be examined on the basis of his own statements. We could not quote what other witnesses had said, or other authors had written. I could not be put in the position of arguing John Dean's case or even Woodward and Bernstein's, thereby providing Nixon with the opportunity to rebut the thrust of his own conduct by seizing upon odd inaccuracies, major or minor, in the accounts of others. And we had to be ready on the law as well as the facts—a matter of critical importance in abuse areas beyond Watergate as well as Watergate itself—in the event that Nixon advanced preposterous but high-sounding legal theories to explain away incriminating evidence.

"How much help do you think Bob Haldeman could be to us?" I asked Zelnick over the coffee. The matter had been discussed some months earlier, but it was worth at least raising it again.

"I still feel the same way," Zelnick said. "In theory a lot, in practice very little. Clearly he knows a hell of a lot about Watergate and the other abuse areas, and he was well plugged into everything else that was happening in the White House, too. But, assessing it realistically, I don't think he'd tell us a goddamned thing. For one thing, he's got to stick with his trial story on the off chance that his conviction is reversed and he goes to trial again. So he's locked in. Second, he's supposed to be working away on his memoirs, so I doubt if he'll be giving any gems away on that ground, even in the nonabuse areas. And, third, like Nixon, I'm not sure he has the capacity to face the truth.'"

I agreed with everything Zelnick had said. Trying to get a Christian Scientist to talk about a cancer on the presidency was probably a nonstarter. But on the one chance in a hundred that Haldeman could help us, it was worth exploring.

"Bob," I suggested, "why don't you draw up a list of ten or twenty questions I can put to Haldeman as a litmus test. I'll invite him to lunch. If he can help us, we'll proceed further. If not, I'll turn it off."

I finally made contact with Haldeman later that week, and made a date for lunch on the sixteenth, after I got back from a four-day long weekend trip to Hawaii, which I had decided to take in order to reread all the transcripts in our possession in one fell swoop. There was one other new item on the agenda first, however. On March 8, Brennan called to say he had received a final no from the Coast Guard station with regard to the possibility of switching off the LARAN transmitter. That meant we had to find a new location for the Interviews in a hurry. Marv Minoff and Don Clark, our associate producer, spent the rest of the week scouting possible buildings within easy driving range of San Clemente.

On Friday the eleventh, we took a look at the three most promising prospects they could find. The first was the Casa Romantica old people's home, where the only possible location would be the main dining room. Very touchingly, the residents had already held a meeting and voted unanimously to forgo a hot lunch for the period of the Interviews in order to enable the taping to continue. It was the sort of gesture that we would have felt almost guilty to accept; in any case, we could just see the headlines: NIXON INTERVIEWS

STARVE THE ELDERLY: FROST DRIVES VETERANS FROM THEIR RIGHTFUL HOMES. The second location was depressing to a degree: I am not a fan of dental surgeries when they are bustling with human life, but a deserted dental surgery makes Forest Lawn look like a fun fair by comparison.

That left the home of Mr. and Mrs. Harold Smith in Monarch Bay, about ten miles north of San Clemente. The real-estate agent turned to me and said in a reverential whisper, "He is the head of Smith International," as if this would be self-explanatory, and then we went inside. The large main room, when made to look like a den, would be perfect. There were enough spare rooms for the two staffs, as well as for Nixon and myself. We said we would take it, subject to the approval of the Secret Service, who would check it out the next day.

On returning from my intensive session in Hawaii, I welcomed the tall, brilliantly tanned, apparently relaxed Bob Haldeman to my suite. I needed only a few minutes, however, to conclude that he would be of little substantial help to the project. He told me he knew little about Watergate, because the entire cover-up, if there was one, had been conducted by others. And he repeatedly re-iterated the thrust of his trial testimony, stating again, for example, that the purpose of the June 23 C.I.A. gambit had only been to shield legal though politically embarrassing campaign contributions from public disclosure.

We agreed to talk again on the telephone in a day or so. Since there was already considerable press activity around the hotel, and I had not yet learned from experience how splendidly discreet the hotel operators were, I thought it a good idea for Haldeman to use some other name in any calls to my suite. (That cloak and dagger again!)

"What is your wife's maiden name?" I asked.

"Horton."

"Why don't you use that name in telephoning me?"

"Fine . . . Oh, and one other thing . . . "

"What's that?"

"If we go ahead with this thing before your taping sessions start,

I'm available all day Saturday and then Sunday afternoon."

"Why not Sunday morning?"

"I teach Bible class at my church."

The call came the next day. The hotel operator informed me that "a Mr. Haldeman" was on the line. Somewhat surprised, I asked her to put him through.

"I'm terribly sorry," he said, "but I've forgotten my alias."

I said that I thought the sheer pressures on our time—only six days to go now to the first taping session—would render the long sessions together that we would obviously need, given the difference in our approaches to the subject matter, virtually impossible. Haldeman had probably been having second thoughts about consulting with us too, and both parties agreed not to proceed.

"Well, if you happen to be talking to him again," said Zelnick when I recounted the incident to him, "just tell him your name is 'Rivers' and call him 'The Brush,' and your communication problems will be over."

By now, our troupe had fully assembled at the Beverly Hilton. John Birt had arrived from London, followed a day or two later by Libby Reeves-Purdie, my London secretary and Girl Friday. Marv Minoff, Bob Zelnick, and Jim Reston were commuting between the hotel and our offices in Century City, where Don and Sue Clark and Stew Hillner were handling the awesome logistics associated with the project, poring over airline schedules and trying to work out in advance how you dispatch tapes to Denmark to meet a deadline and get them transferred from 525 lines to 625 lines on the way. Over at Don Stern Productions, Jørn Winther, our director, Don Stern himself, who was to be our editor, and Tony Hudz had been reviewing thousands of feet of newsreel film and tape supplied by our film researcher in New York, Ann Dean. John had brought Bernard Lodge's titles and Dudley Simpson's music theme from London, and he and Jørn were busy checking out the final technical arrangements with Pacific Video. It was a team, small and ad hoc though it may have been, good enough to fill any executive producer with confidence. And, as I write their names again now, gratitude.

The surprises and emergencies were by no means over, however, the next one having to do with dentistry, of all things—a subject on which, as I have mentioned, I am at all times wary, not to say unenthusiastic. On Friday, March 18, with just five days to go, one of my teeth was hurting like hell and Dr. Dudley Glick, a distinguished endodontist, told me he had to operate. I knew that I had an abscess and a temporary filling in that particular tooth, but now Glick told me two things had happened: first, the tooth had been open dangerously long already and might do something extraordinary if left that way for another four weeks and second, one of my previous dentists, while digging away, had taken a wrong turning, perforated the tooth, and trotted off into the bone.

Glick did operate splendidly. The only problem was that there was "an acute exacerbative response" and some "chronic inflammatory tissue" which had to be "curetted." Or in layman's language, the left side of my face swelled up like a balloon, and Dr. Glick had to scrape the gum and cut a bit off for good measure.

All of which would have been thirty-six hours of nobody's business but mine, if medical factors were all that were involved. However, much more relevant was the "visual" factor. I would not have cared in the least for the entire world to know that I had been to the dentist. But we had long since concluded that the programs would be organized thematically rather than chronologically. That meant the material from, say, the tenth taping session could well wind up on the same program as material from the first or second. It meant further that both Mr. Nixon and I would have to wear the same suits, shirts and ties for each session, with our hair forbidden to grow. Appearing with a lump on my face one minute and none the next simply wouldn't work.

With three days to go, the lump was still out of the question. If it stayed that way, postponement would be the only solution. But postponement was impossible. There was Nixon's schedule. There was our editing schedule, almost impossibly tight already. And there was Pacific Video's schedule, booked from the day after we were due to finish. There were our stations in the States who had preempted their networks, and the countries around the world who had announced their broadcasts in the twenty-four hours following the U.S. screening. Surely one idiotic tooth was not going to interfere with all of that? With two days to go, it still was. With one day to go, the swelling was still visible, though encouragingly less so.

On the scheduled first day of taping I woke at six forty-five and raced straight for the mirror—not, I hasten to say, normally my first act of the day! Without leaving even a few hours' leeway, the swelling had finally disappeared. I was getting used to financiers and broadcasters coming through at the last minute, but having deadlines for *teeth* was ridiculous.

On Tuesday, when John, Bob and I met in my suite, we felt we needed to talk particularly about the crucial first few minutes of Wednesday's taping. John and I had always thought that if the first exchanges we recorded could be the first that we broadcast, that would be ideal. At least it was worth trying. And we believed we had to pick up where the audience had last seen Richard Nixon, at the time of his resignation. That was the last experience they had shared. We felt it would be a mistake in any case to attempt to launch directly into the major issues of his presidency. We had to get him talking, and talking about things that were interesting and personal.

"But then we have to move along," said John. "So I would suggest that after having him recall the moments prior to his departure from office, we move right on to a short discussion regarding how he believes history will view his presidency and then launch right into Vietnam."

"I have no disagreement in principle with that strategy," Zelnick said. "In practice, I think it will be difficult to pull off. When you ask him how he felt leaving the White House, you're going to get a deluge of self-serving and emotional homilies. And when you ask him to assess his presidency, you're going to get the last five chapters of his memoirs."

"What's your alternative?" I asked.

"Get into substance right away. Tell him you'll deal with the final days after the Watergate discussion, and begin with Vietnam."

"Now that is exactly what I think won't work," I replied. "He hasn't faced a microphone in nearly three years. He is a chronically suspicious man, uncertain of our intentions. I can't very well come in and say, 'Good morning, outcast. Let's commence with the holocaust your policies produced in Indochina.' Impossible."

"I can only interpret those remarks as indicating disagreement with my recommended approach," replied Zelnick, adding in best Nixon fashion, complete with disclaimer, "Go ahead. Ruin the project. That is your responsibility. I don't condemn you for that."

After more discussion, we decided that out of the first two hours, perhaps the first thirty to forty-five minutes should be spent on the resignation and the final days, and then the bulk of the time on Vietnam, which we had already discussed together at length.

One possible way to get him thinking, and perhaps talking, would be to play on a monitor excerpts from that emotional farewell address to his staff the morning of his resignation, and, later, the actual footage of the walk to the helicopter. With Birt I had discussed that possibility earlier and we had made sure that the appropriate footage would be available on the set. It might also make Nixon feel a little more comfortable about sharing with me painful and difficult events. I did not think that we would win Nixon's trust, but anything that would begin to allay his mistrust could serve a double purpose.

"All right, Bob," I said. "When we come to the assessment of his presidency, we know it will be somewhat more generous than, say, Anthony Lewis's, but will he give any nod at all to his critics?"

"Only a fleeting and general one," Zelnick projected. "Yes, he did some things wrong. Mistakes and misjudgments. The old shibboleth that concedes everything and nothing. But there were ample precedents for anything he was alleged to have done wrong. And in any event, it pales in the light of his massive accomplishments. Then the familiar litany."

"And that," I said, "is where we have a major choice to make. Do we engage him there, or do we let his assessment stand for the moment?"

"The latter by all means," said Birt. "We simply tell him that his account of his years in office is disputed by many and that we are about to begin testing it in one of the areas of greatest controversy—Vietnam. Then get to Vietnam. Get to Vietnam."

Our debate continued for another hour. Then Bob and John retired to begin dictating the questions we had discussed, while I gathered up the books, articles and briefing papers assembled by the staff together with my own notes for a further concentrated session on my own. Libby then typed up the questions on sheets of blue paper, suitable for taking on the set, leaving the left half of each page blank, waiting to be filled with my further messages to myself.

I had completed that task by about midnight. For some years I had liked to approach any interview with a clipboard or a manila folder that combined three categories of notes. First, specific questions that I knew must be asked. Second, more general areas I knew I would like to experiment with. And third, the verbatim quotes—usually from the interviewee—that I knew I might want to call upon. But they were all only road maps, not blueprints. Always, in any interview, the most important thing was to listen, to follow up. The purpose of preparation was lost if it merely shackled the questioner to an inflexible plan, learned more or less by rote. The purpose of preparation was to liberate him to be able to go with any promising new angle that emerged, and that in his instantaneous judgment merited the attention.

I felt that our preparation had been such as to give me that flexibility. And I had the added support of our daily "seminars" as we debated back and forth in order to reach a jointly derived strategy. Were they having similar seminars down the coast? I wondered. We knew that Richard Nixon had been preparing as intensively as we had. But preparing to say what? Was he indeed ready to "confront his past" as I had said so often that he was? Or would I have to confront him first?

Tomorrow we would start to know the answer.

CHAPTER

5

Next morning we met in the hotel lobby at seven forty-five for the one-and-a-half-hour drive to Monarch Bay. John was at the wheel of the blue Mercedes 450 I had leased for our California stay, with Jim Reston riding shotgun. I sat in the back, clipboard on knee, with Bob alongside, ready to restate the Nixon case for us in any area we felt necessary. That first morning, however, I was preoccupied with the best way to get the ex-President talking.

"Why don't we start with the question everybody talks about?" I asked. "Why didn't he burn the tapes?"

Bob didn't like the idea. "It could open up the entire Watergate matter long before we're ready to delve into it. And if he regards it as a breach of our understanding to discuss Watergate after Easter, it's more likely to set exactly the sort of negative tone you're worried about."

Birt was less apprehensive.

"Apart from Bob's point about the breach of understanding, I can't see any real harm in it," he said. "It's not likely to take him by surprise. My goodness, if he's thought of nothing else about Watergate, he's surely thought of that. Provided we don't stay too

long on the subject, I don't feel strongly one way or the other."
We made no final decision in the car, though I said I would certainly check out the matter with Brennan beforehand to cover the
breach-of-understanding point, and see if he thought the idea of
a "surprise question" on the tapes was a good one.

Camera crews from the networks, photographers, and members
of both the national and the local press were waiting as we pulled
past the guardhouse entering the Monarch Bay estate. I paused
for a moment and then hurried into the house to change and get
made up. It was nine thirty-five. Nixon would be arriving at ten
ten, having already changed and only needing makeup. We would
begin taping at ten thirty.

At precisely the appointed moment, Nixon's white Lincoln
Continental pulled to the curb. He emerged smiling and waving
as he had in so many thousands of those public moments during
his long political career. For me it was a moment to savor, the
culmination of a two-year dream. We shook hands at curbside,
commented discreetly upon each other's robust appearance and
went inside. I took Brennan to one side and asked him what he
thought of opening with the tapes. He said he thought it might
work, then went off to join Khachigian and Price in the bedroom
downstairs which served as the Nixon staff's closed-circuit viewing
room.

Fifteen minutes later, Nixon and I both left our respective
bedrooms and walked along the passage and through the kitchen
into the living room where the cameras were waiting. We took
our places in the chairs on the set and Jørn Winther recorded a
special minute of tape that would be used on all future taping
days to ensure that everything matched and nothing had moved.
Then the mike tests, and for the life of me I can't recall what either
of us said. I was studying Nixon for any sign of nervousness or
foreboding. I could detect none. Instead his face seemed set, determined; his gaze firm. Rather than the almost doddering political
and emotional cripple of the final days, I saw again the man who
boasted early in 1973 that he was tough enough to withstand
any strains of office, the man who proudly reminded his inter-

viewer that up to then he hadn't missed a single day for illness, that he prepared for each day's combat by running in place for two hundred paces in his bedroom.

"Thirty seconds," called Don Clark, our floor manager as well as our associate producer, and the only man who would be allowed into the Smiths' living room for the next two hours apart from Richard Nixon, our three cameramen, Mike Keeler, Hank Geving and Mark Meyer, and myself.

"Ten seconds." I'll begin with the tapes.

"Five, four, three, two, one . . . anytime." Here goes.

"Mr. President, we are going to be covering a lot of subjects in a great deal of detail over the course of the next six hours, but I must begin completely out of context by asking you one question, more than any other, almost every American and people all over the world want me to ask. They all have their questions, but one of them in every case is: 'Why didn't you burn the tapes?' "

In our bedroom at the far end of the hall, where Zelnick, Reston, Minoff, Peter Pagnamenta of the BBC, and David Gideon Thomson were watching on a twelve-inch monitor, Zelnick tapped the table with his fist and murmured a quiet "Damn." A methodical strategist, he would prove a somewhat volatile viewer. In the production trailer, Birt smiled resignedly at the thought of an exploratory first day's session.

Nixon seemed numbed by the question. He paused and then began to ramble as if waiting for his thoughts to clarify themselves in his mind. "Mr. Frost, as you know, we agreed that we would cover the Watergate aspects of these various programs, the White House years and the early life as well, in our last taping session, but since you have that as a major concern among your listeners, and viewers, there is no reason why I at least can't respond briefly to it now, and you can explore it at greater length later if you like."

Edit, edit, edit, I thought to myself. I agreed that Watergate was indeed the subject of the fourth program, then went on: "But everybody says, why didn't you burn the tapes, and in a word, I wondered what your answer was."

The "word" would take some twenty minutes for Nixon to articulate, scarcely punctuated by a few passing utterances from myself. He began by telling of an "extensive" taping system which he said had existed in the Johnson White House, one which permitted the former President to tape "hundreds" of conversations both on the phones and in the various rooms of the house. He said he had ordered the entire system to be dismantled. But he claimed that in February 1971 Haldeman had told him that members of the Nixon Foundation Committee had visited Johnson at his Texas ranch to discuss the establishment of a Nixon library. Johnson, Nixon claimed, said he had been "stupid" to remove the system which he argued would be the best way to preserve for history important White House transactions. The Nixon taping system was then installed "very quickly."

In April 1973, Nixon continued, he instructed Haldeman to take the taping system out. Well, not exactly to take it out, but "to make the search that would be necessary to retain all those that had historical value and to destroy those that had no historical value . . ." This came after a "moving" heart-to-heart with two former prisoners of war which Nixon felt should be preserved for posterity.

Then on June 4, 1973, after "Mr. Dean had made some charges that I knew were untrue," he decided that Haldeman had been wise not to remove the system "because the tapes in many respects contradicted the charges that had been made by Mr. Dean . . ."

Again he considered destroying the tapes after Alexander Butterfield revealed the existence of the taping system to the Ervin committee, and before either the committee or the Special Prosecutor, Archibald Cox, had subpoenaed them. He didn't because "it would have been an indication that I felt there were conversations on there that demonstrated that I was guilty."

Then Nixon described another "point of decision," this one after the Court of Appeals ruled in October 1973 that Cox was entitled to the nine taped conversations he had subpoenaed. Here Nixon considered turning over those tapes and destroying all the others, but again "it would have been an open admission, or at least appeared to be an admission, of 'I am trying to cover something up.' " Also, he had to "admit in all candor" that he had not believed "that they were going to come out." At this point I was faced with a choice. Drop the subject or, having come this far, go one step further. I took the next step.

"But, looking back on it now, don't you wish you'd destroyed them?"

Nixon now went on a lengthy detour, suggesting that perhaps he should have destroyed the tapes, not for personal reasons, but because they would affect the quality of advice future Presidents receive, since the best advice is of a confidential variety. "Indeed," said Nixon, "that's why I always assured all the people that came in to see me, 'Look here, you tell me what you think and I'll take the blame if it should fail and I'll give you the credit and take a little of it myself if it succeeds,' and I got very good advice as a result of that tactic."

What an utterly selfless attitude, I thought. Nixon went on to add, "As a matter of fact, if the tapes had been destroyed, I believe it is likely I would not have had to go through the agony of the resignation." Unfortunately, he went on to explain, the discussions, particularly those in which he had been considering "options" or "being the devil's advocate" were taken "out of context." And, of course, what came out—his expressing himself "in a very volatile way"—was embarrassing. "It disappointed a lot of my friends, although I must say, it is not the first time that it's occurred."

Well, that was not the world's most succinct opening exchange, I thought as Nixon concluded his response. But if my last-minute addition had not worked very startlingly, the next question—the one with which we had always planned to begin—led us into even more of a labyrinth.

"When did you actually decide, when did you make the decision to resign?" There followed one of the more convoluted responses in my career as an interviewer. Nixon said he was certain of the date. It was July 23, 1974. And it occurred because the earlier "rosy reports we had received" from those keeping tabs on the House Judiciary Committee were proving unduly optimistic because "the very shrewd and ruthless O'Neill, now Speaker of the House, had put the screws to those Democrats who were leaning toward voting against impeachment."

On July 23, Joe Waggonner, leader of "about fifty" Southern Democrats in the House, passed the word that the three Southern Democrats on the Committee—Walter Flowers, James Mann, and Ray Thornton—were "lost."

This, Nixon said, contradicted advice he had gotten from Vice-President Ford, who had told him on July 12, "We're going to win by at least fifty votes in the House. We've got it made."

Nixon had felt that his one hope was to have his old nemesis, Governor George Wallace of Alabama, intervene with Flowers, who was from his home state. Indeed, his chief of staff, General Alexander Haig, had received a phone call from Charles Snyder, Wallace's 1972 campaign manager, suggesting that Wallace would be receptive to such a call.

The call was placed. But, alas, Wallace "seemed not to understand why I was calling. He said, 'Well this is the first I've ever heard about this.' He said, 'I don't believe that there is anything I can do to be helpful.' He was very kind, however. He said, 'I'm praying for you.' He says, 'I wish this didn't have to be visited upon you, but I think that if I were to call, it might be misinterpreted.' "

"Haig had been in the room as I was talking," Nixon continued. "And I said, and he recalls this very vividly, I said, 'Well, Al, there goes the presidency.' "

There was more, and by the time Nixon completed his account, my head was almost as muddled as his narrative had been. Reduced to basics, I could believe he had in fact concluded on or about the twenty-third of July that he was unlikely to win his battle in the House. But that is a far cry from deciding on that date to resign, come what may. Suppose for example he had won his tapes battle with Leon Jaworski in the Supreme Court, where a decision was announced the following day. Then the "smoking pistol tape" would never have had to be released. Would that have affected his "decision"? And all those fighting statements between July 23 and August 8. What earthly purpose did they serve other than to place his desperate allies even further out on a limb, given the decision he said he reached on July 23?

Should I pursue the matter further now, or let it drop?

"Move in, tear the son of a bitch to pieces," Zelnick was imploring in the monitor room.

"Move along. Move along, David," Birt whispered in the production trailer.

I decided to let Nixon's statements stand for the time being. We were already almost forty-five minutes into the session, and we had not really touched on the final days. I asked about "that heart-to-heart that you had with Henry Kissinger. Was that perhaps the emotional—"

"Yes, it was perhaps as an emotional moment as I have had, except, well it's hard to say what is the most emotional moment, because each is different," Nixon began. "I remember the day I heard that Eisenhower had died . . ."

"Don't do it, please," I murmured under my breath.

But do it he did, about seven minutes on his relationship with Ike and the tears he shed on that day in 1969 when the general died. Ike cursed a lot, Nixon managed to remind us. He had said the same thing earlier about Lyndon Johnson. He wasn't missing many opportunities to score a point.

I brought the conversation back to Kissinger.

But Nixon was not quite ready yet to talk about praying with Henry. Instead, he discussed the moments with his family leading up to the resignation: How "Mrs. Nixon with her rare sense of intuition had started to pack on Tuesday morning"; how Julie had left a little note on his pillow in the Lincoln Room saying, "Daddy, whatever you do I will support you, but wait a week or ten days. Just go through the fire a little longer. I love you. Julie." How on a walk with Tricia following dinner on Wednesday he noticed that "she was just as beautiful and just as controlled as we stood there for Ollie Atkins to take the pictures as she was in her wedding gown when I, you know like the proud father, strutted her down the aisle."

Finally, at long last, Henry made his entrance, summoned to discuss how to prepare other nations for the transition to Ford. Together they reminisced about the great foreign-policy decisions of the Nixon presidency—China, the Soviet Union, the Middle East. "The time of Cambodia, the December bombing of 1972 which was essential and indispensable in order to get the peace settlement we got a month later."

Oh, God, what a job it is going to be to edit all this self-serving material into some sort of coherent shape, I thought.

The reminiscence continued. They had once drunk Courvoisier together after Kissinger had told Nixon that Chou En-lai had invited him to send a representative to Peking to arrange for the visit of the President of the United States. According to Nixon, Kissinger had termed it the "most important message that a President has received since World War II."

And now on the eve of another historic though infinitely less joyous occasion, they sipped from the same Courvoisier bottle, Kissinger pledging himself to resign "if they harass you." Nixon gave the first of several not unimpressive impersonations of Kissinger's accent. "And his voice broke and I said, 'Henry, you're not going to resign. Don't ever talk that way again,' I said, 'the country needs you.'"

Months later, Kissinger would critique Nixon's account of their encounter and tell me, "From the way he described it, you would think the purpose of meeting had been to discuss *my* resignation rather than his!"

Soon, Nixon recounted, Kissinger was weeping and then he too shed tears because "I just can't stand to see somebody else with tears in their eyes."

But Nixon had initiated the praying, silently, on bended knee, and, as he thought, confidentially. And he confirmed calling Kissinger immediately afterwards to ask that their "mountaintop moment" remain an intimate secret between the two.

Nixon recalled how he had spent his last night in the White House reading about Theodore Roosevelt and how T.R. had plunged into the emotional depths when his first wife died, "when he said 'the light has gone out of my life . . .' "

For some time, it had been clear that this session was not going as we had planned. Everything was taking longer than we had expected. The answers were much more rambling than we had anticipated. But we were learning a great deal about his "line" on almost every subject. And his instinctive response to almost every sort of question. On our general approach, we would want to regroup. But now was the time to explore.

"Did you feel in part that the light had gone out of your life forever?"

"No, I didn't feel that way," Nixon replied almost nonchalantly. "I couldn't see what lay ahead . . . but I felt that as time passed, that I might be able, in a field that is closest to my heart, working for peace in the world . . ."

As the answer rambled along, Nixon took an almost defiant tone toward those who wanted him to "just disappear and be a nonperson" after leaving office.

"Well, it's not my nature. I don't intend to."

Weeks later, during our last sessions, the Nixon tone would be quite different, much more real, as he talked of his life in exile. Then his promise to "still be fighting" would sound more like a self-composed epitaph than a statement of intent. It would be a measure of how far we had traveled. Right now his words were a measure of how far we had to travel.

I asked Jørn to play the clip we had taken from Nixon's farewell speech in the East Room. It was the President talking emotionally first about his father, and then his mother who lost two sons to tuberculosis and then nursed four other sufferers in Arizona only to see them die too. "Yes, she will have no books written about her. But she was a saint." The clip ended. I had been watching Nixon closely. His eyes were glued to the monitor. They became red. He was clearly stirred, moved. "That was very much you speaking there, wasn't it?" I asked, hoping that Nixon would now share some of his deeper thoughts and emotions.

"Yes, it was," he answered. "Yes, and very unusual." His countenance suddenly grew stern. I could almost see the emotion being systematically removed. He was back in control. Whatever the film had touched was being hidden again. "I remember . . . ah, Tricia afterward said, 'You know, I'm so glad you mentioned Grandpa . . .'"

I let him complete the answer and followed with another question, this one unmistakably psychiatric in thrust, concerning whether his mother was really stronger in a way than his father "beneath all the bluster."

Nixon would have none of it. Feeling his way for a moment or two he eventually picked up: "My father could be belligerent, but that did not mean that the belligerence was covering up any—any of the—the psychiatrists say 'sense of insecurity' or anything like that . . ."

Nixon clearly knew what the psychohistorians would be looking for almost as well as they did. I went on to paraphrase the thought I had had while watching the East Room speech in Sydney. "At the end of your speech, you said, 'Always remember others may hate you, but those who hate you don't win unless you hate them, and then you destroy yourself.' When you said that, were you saying that as a lesson for other people, or a lesson that you ought to have observed yourself?"

Nixon's response somehow managed to include a passing shot at the media, a reference to his having handled Watergate much more poorly than other far more difficult areas of his presidency, and a tribute to his college football coach, "Chief" Newman. It did not, however, include so much as a syllable's worth of introspection.

I assumed that at first he might have misunderstood the question and then later in his answer sought to evade it. So I attempted to bring the point back to his specific attitude toward political foes. I mentioned the White House enemies list, the administration consuming itself "in a sense with revenge" and doing "exactly what you're warning people against in this quote."

Nixon's reply was daunting: "Well, no, you're drawing conclusions there, that when we get into this other taping I will demolish. So let's give our listeners something to tune in number four."

We could not claim we had not been warned, I thought. Here he was baldly predicting how he was going to deal with the allegations of impropriety growing out of the White House Enemies List. Those would include the abuse of executive agencies, perhaps the work of the Plumbers, maybe even Watergate itself. He was not just going to "deal with" the allegations. He would not be content merely to "answer" them. He was going to "demolish" them.

I next asked Jørn to roll the footage of Nixon's departure from the White House. Even if he was not ready to share the inner man with us, perhaps recalling his thoughts at that awesome moment would at least provide some reflections on his years as President.

Not at once it wouldn't. He began by discussing the novelty of watching himself on television, something he said he never did. Of course, he went on, with me it was different. "I know that in your profession . . . certainly when you were at the Blue Angel, you must have had to feel that you were an actor, and *That Was the Week That Was.* You must surely have looked at the tapes and said, 'Now how could I have done this better?' "

The Blue Angel! Nixon had clearly been doing his homework too.

"Can you remember, however, what your feelings were as that helicopter took off from Washington? What were you thinking?"

I was bringing him back to the subject again. Or at least I thought I was. But Nixon again proved himself a master of circumlocution. For some ten minutes he told of family and servants weeping in public and in private, loudly and faintly, with words or in silence, but always with total sincerity. Nor was he ever the first to cry.

A sentence or two would have to survive editing, simply because the occasion itself was of stunning importance. But 95 percent of it would have to be edited out. At last I asked Nixon directly to assess his presidency, at least as he would hope a historian would.

His answer, as we had suspected, dealt with the contribution of his presidency "to the goal of building peace in the world." He was not speaking naïvely or simplistically. He knew the areas of tension and confrontation. But the potential for a great power clash had been diminished. The War in Vietnam had been ended "in an honorable way, which would discourage aggression." The dialogue with the Soviet Union had been improved. And a start had been made in building relations with the People's Republic of China, which "twenty years from now, maybe fifteen, maybe twenty-five" would be a great nuclear power. And to have it then "outside the community of nations and with no communication with the United States, particularly, would be a deadly peril to the peace of the world."

"Those were some of the positive things. What about the negative ones?" I asked Nixon.

"The primary negative will be that the Nixon administration engaged in political activities which led to the resignation," he began. It was a sentence that admitted nothing. Not "criminal" activities. Not "questionable" activities. But just "political" activities. He mentioned the bugging of the Democratic Headquarters in passing, but rather than further elucidation, he turned abruptly to the "double standard" which had been applied to his administration. After all, Harry Truman had pardoned fifteen people found guilty of stealing votes in Missouri, including the state's political boss, Tom Pendergast.

Two of the anticipated weapons in his arsenal, I thought: the double standard and the activities of prior administrations. Nixon then reiterated his foreign achievements. And, almost as an afterthought, he turned to the domestic issues of racial desegregation, citing statistics on school desegregation to prove more progress was made under his presidency than under any other administration since Dwight D. Eisenhower. "Not through threatening, but through firm, strong, presidential leadership and persuasion." He mentioned George Wallace and then added, "Incidentally, one of my sternest critics in this whole area of desegregation was Sam Ervin of North Carolina."

I smiled to myself. He was not missing a trick. There were many other Southerners besides Ervin whose commitment to civil liberties had also not extended to any of the post-Civil War constitutional amendments, but he had chosen to cite Senator Sam. Just a coincidence, of course.

Not that Nixon himself had led any civil rights charges during his administration. Indeed, the contrary was more often the case. But this was not the moment to engage Nixon in a new area of debate. He had made the case for his presidency. Fine. I would let it stand. At least for the time being; at least until Friday.

So I thanked Nixon for the morning's work, accompanied him to his waiting limousine, and uttered a few somewhat overoptimistic words to the press. I made a quick tour of the crew to thank them for their first morning's work, making some equally enthusiastic noises to them about the quality of the content, and then it was time for the ride home.

I knew we had a lot to talk about. And a lot to think about in the next two days. The morning could best be described as a mitigated disaster.

We had some nuggets, of course. There were moments during the discussion of the tapes. And while giving it his own peculiar slant, Nixon had confirmed the Woodward and Bernstein account of the Kissinger prayer meeting. Parts had been, as Jim said, "visually stunning." And then there had been the main bonus of the morning, the learning process.

But we concentrated on the "disaster" part first.

"He had his way far too much," said Bob. "I know this is not what you were intending today, but you are going to have to challenge him much more."

"Yes, much more than I thought," I added.

"He had his way on almost every issue," Zelnick went on. "He offered some preposterous accounts of events. He was mawkish. And he monopolized the time. When he rambles, you're going to have to tell him he's rambling. You can't go in there and be as polite as you were today."

"Of course, that's right," said John. "But David does not intend to. He never intended to. Today was always going to be somewhat different."

"Quite, but I guess it's the degree that's the surprise," I said. "I mean I wanted to explore today. I wanted to find out how he responded to all sorts of questions and approaches. And I think we did that." That indeed was why the disaster had been "mitigated." "We paid a hell of a price—two hours and ten minutes. And it's one we can't afford to pay again. But he paid a bigger one."

"Yes," said John. "He showed us every card in his hand and we showed him none in ours. There's hardly a thing we're going to be discussing during the next month where we don't have some indication of what he's going to say."

"That's true," said Bob. "Vietnam, détente, segregation, even Watergate."

Richard Nixon had without doubt the most varied repertoire of parrying devices I had ever encountered. We had given him a soapbox—partly deliberately, partly productively. But he was the one who had built it into a platform. And somehow we had to be able to prevent him from doing that.

Next morning at nine we gathered in John Birt's suite to view the previous day's proceedings, which had been transferred onto half-inch tape from the normal broadcast two-inch tape. We invited Joe Kraft, who had flown out to brainstorm with us for two or three days, to join us. For more than two hours he watched the monitor in John's room, his frequent grimaces revealing an antipathy toward the session as well as the subject.

"Well, he's tough," said Kraft. "He's very, very well prepared. Many of his answers seemed to have been studied. And a couple of times it appears as though he actually rehearsed his style of delivery, his gestures. He also looks a lot stronger than I expected him to be."

"What modifications do you recommend?" I asked.

"You were far too tolerant. You've got to take control. You know how well prepared you are for these Interviews. I know it. And your staff knows it. But it didn't come through in this session. Look," he continued, holding the first day's eighty-page transcript in one hand and thumbing through it with the other.

"You have a line or two of Frost and then four or five pages of Nixon. A paragraph by Frost and a three-page response. I'm not saying it has to be precisely even. After all, he is the interviewee, but I feel there has to be more give-and-take. And remember, as things worked out, you weren't even dealing with particularly controversial material. When you get to the tough areas, you're certain to see a real full-blooded filibuster."

The meeting adjourned. Kraft left for Washington. Zelnick went off to return a call from Ken Khachigian, and took the opportunity to talk about the virtues of Nixon keeping his answers shorter, and making them more responsive and to the point. Zelnick emphasized that we had no desire to be unfair to the former President. There would be ample time, for example, for him to attack the work of the Ervin committee or the House Judiciary Committee, or indeed the media. But if he did so during self-created detours totally irrelevant to the subject under discussion, it would almost inevitably end up on the cutting-room floor. Khachigian said he understood the point and would try to convey it to the President. He cautioned, however, that, once on the set, Nixon was his own adviser and had to respond as he saw fit.

Zelnick rejoined Birt and myself. Khachigian was obviously right. He had no magic panacea. This was basically a problem that we had to solve for ourselves. We began to talk about our own view of Vietnam and gradually we began to glimpse what we had to do. We had talked about developing our own coherent themes in order to deepen our research. If Nixon was to be truly tested, to become more disciplined, that process had to happen on the air as well. In answer to an ordinary question, Nixon had the ability to weave such an intricate web—as he had about July 23—that it would take hours to unravel. But if we advanced an alternative hypothesis, a case within a question, it would focus his reply. He would not be answering in a vacuum. As he spoke, he would be conditioned by knowing the context in which his words were being judged, the effect that they would be having.

The alternative hypothesis . . . Which it was up to me to advance. It was contrary to almost every interview I had ever worked on. I believed that the interviewer was the catalyst, drawing out his subject. He became a principal only when facts were being done a disservice. He was in the information business, not the opinion business. The airwaves were not for declaring his own opinions, but for discovering and defining other people's.

But now this was a change of approach: I was going to have to enunciate my opinion, not just as an afterthought but often as the very springboard of the dialogue. Well, not just *my* opinion as such, but the opinion embodied in the alternative hypothesis— sometimes a particular conviction of mine, certainly, sometimes a thinking man's alternative scenario, as it were.

It might work.

Correction. It would work.

Correction. It had to work.

We met again that evening to review the interrogation on Indochina one more time before the following day. Even from Nixon's passing references to the subject the day before, it was clear we had anticipated correctly his broad line of response— from "inheriting" the war to leaving a South Vietnamese government with a "reasonable" chance to survive.

"If Nixon emphasizes again the situation that he had inherited," I said, "and then goes on to argue with some credibility, as I think he can, that simply 'cutting and running' at the time he took office would have produced as much carnage in Vietnam and as much domestic turmoil as his decision to wind the American effort down in the way that he did, what is the ultimate point you both feel we should be making?"

"The moral point," said John.

"Absolutely," said Bob. "If at the time Nixon became President and recognized the calamity our policies were producing, he had devoted all of his negotiating skills to sparing the Vietnamese the sort of bloodbath that might have occurred had the Americans simply picked up and left, to minimizing their future pain and suffering, his position would be defensible. But he didn't do that at all. Because he wanted to have it both ways. He wanted to withdraw and still dictate the terms of the peace. But that was impossible because the military and political realities in the area denied his victory by whatever name it was called. So he settled for the trappings of success. All Nixon ever got out of Vietnam was what we knew at the time to be a fig leaf to cover the defeat that was obvious at the time he took office. And when a million people die in the process of accomplishing that, that is morally repugnant."

"What it all comes down to," added Birt, "is that the substance of the deal he struck in October 1972 and January 1973 could have been obtained years earlier. The language would have been different, but the actual outcome would have been almost identical."

Birt and Zelnick left. I agreed totally with the moral emphasis they wanted to place on our discussion of Indochina. But in a sense I thought they had made it all sound too clear-cut, too open-and-shut. The adversary case would sound better than they gave it credit for, would blur and obfuscate the moral issues they were trying to communicate. Particularly when that adversary case was being put by the man who had had Vietnam as the linchpin of his foreign policy. He would be better prepared on that, even more formidable, than he had been the first day.

I went back to my files and pulled out the Shawcross article from the *London Sunday Times*. Cambodia. That was a problem Nixon had *created*, not inherited. The Khmers had, under Prince Sihanouk, managed to stay out of the war, until Nixon had brought them into it. He had propped up the inept Lon Nol against almost all the sound advice going at the time. He had torn his own country apart by what was little more than a grandiose search-and-destroy mission in April and May 1970. He and Kissinger had repeatedly ignored warnings from the field that the situation was hopeless and that any peace he could obtain was preferable to the bloodletting that was taking place. He had, through America's intervention, been responsible for the growth of a brutal revolu-

107

tionary movement that had previously amounted to only some six thousand highway bandits. One out of every seven Cambodians had died, and for what? Nothing.

I thought of my adversary in San Clemente. I wondered what effect Cambodia had had on him. Had he ever been haunted by the thought of peasants pulled from their ancestral lands, their sons conscripted, perhaps killed, in a cause incapable of being expressed in terms that meant anything to them? Had he ever imagined himself under attack from a misdirected squadron of B-52's? Or was he, like so many leaders, able to depersonalize the life-and-death decisions he made, placing a *cordon sanitaire* between each decision and the human anguish it produced?

CHAPTER

6

THE RIDE DOWN THE COAST THE NEXT MORNING WAS SLOW. THE weather was slightly inclement, the Los Angeles traffic was thick, and we would arrive late enough for Nixon to rebuke me mildly with a few indirect references to the joys of punctuality.

"It seems to me," I had said in the car, "that we have to realize there is a limit to what we can achieve today, even given a fair wind. Vietnam is not the sort of issue where we can ever land a knockout, whatever we do. Nothing about the Vietnam debate smacks of absolute finality. There is always going to be an argument he can make in response to one of mine."

"I'm not in the least bit worried about that," Zelnick replied. "Lay it all out. Make your points. If we can wind up with Nixon resting his whole case regarding what he achieved in Vietnam on his ability to come back in and bomb if his vaunted agreement became unstuck, then the complete moral bankruptcy of that position will be victory enough."

"You're both right," said John. "You can't judge a debate on policy by the same standards you apply to a whodunit, which I

109

suppose is what parts of Watergate are. And the returns won't be as obvious. But the opportunity here is unprecedented. Political leaders are just not in the habit of being interrogated about their wars. If they win them they're usually in the position to define the history written about them. If they lose, the history is imposed on them. Today, Richard Nixon will be writing history through interrogation . . ."

"Mr. President," I began, "the whole area of foreign policy is such a vast one, but at the moment you took office, America's involvement in Vietnam was regarded by many as a disaster that was splitting American society at home in a very grievous way for what seemed to many an obscure or even a mistaken reason. How did it look to you, though?"

"Well, it looked to me, first that the reason for our being in Vietnam had perhaps not been adequately understood by the American people."

Nixon's answer was lengthy, running perhaps six minutes, but well constructed—unlike many of his ramblings during the first session—and, anecdotes aside, almost to the word as anticipated.

He told of a safe for classified documents built into the wall of the President's bathroom. In that safe on his inauguration day, he found only a single item: the battlefield reports from Vietnam.

We were losing 300 Americans a week there at the time. Altogether 538,000 Americans were in the country. And 14,000 a month were being drafted.

While that had to change, Nixon emphasized that the basic commitment undertaken by Kennedy and Johnson was sound. It was the test of American credibility, not only with respect to the nations in the area and others, like Israel, but to the great adversary powers—the Soviet Union and the People's Republic of China—with whom he was about to undertake major initiatives toward a lasting peace. Also to the major U.S. allies, who would be watching not only America's new dealings with the Communists, but also its actions in Vietnam to see whether the country had the "character" to remain preeminent in world affairs.

And so, while "bugging out, blaming it on my predecessors,"

would have been "the easy political path," Nixon was not about to do that, since it would have been "at an enormous cost, eventually even to America, but particularly to the whole free world."

> FROST: But wasn't staying there, I mean, that was also at a massive cost, wasn't it? In billions of dollars; in 138,000 South Vietnamese killed; half a million Cambodians; half a million North Vietnamese, and so on. That cost—it's a question of weighing one cost against another cost, isn't it? But you thought the cost was worth paying for what you got?
>
> NIXON: Looking at my term in office, yes. I think considering the kind of peace agreement we finally got in January of 1973, one which provided for a cease-fire, ah, one which provided for, of course, the exchange in return of our P.O.W.'s. One which also provided for no violations in the future of South Vietnam's territory by the North Vietnamese, among many other things. I believe that having accomplished that, after those four long tortuous years, was worthwhile. And that held for over two years. The cost, I agree with you, however, was very great. It was a close call, a very difficult call . . .

There was more to the answer. Nixon recalled Johnson complaining to him of the political pressures to stop the bombing of North Vietnam. But with American casualties so high, Johnson had said, "How can I tell that boy that's being shot at in Vietnam, that I'm going to stop the bombing in North Vietnam when they're killing him, or that bullet's gonna kill him?"

Nixon said further that he was not impervious to the effects of continuing the fight. "A President, of course, knows what is happening to the people of South Vietnam, the people of North Vietnam. He knows the cost of the war. And, also, I knew, as a political man, the terrible costs at home." But, "for the reasons I've mentioned," he could not make the decision to get out.

So far, this had been a useful exchange. Nixon had advanced on behalf of his decisions most of the arguments that had seemed so convincing to so many in 1968, but which, with the luxury of hindsight and, in all fairness, to many of the dissenters at the time, appeared products of an earlier, more simplistic era. Moreover, he had conceded that, even in the days following his inaugural, the decision to stay in Vietnam had been "a close call." A judgment which contrasted sharply with his definition of the stakes at the time he entered Cambodia—shall America become a "pitiful helpless giant"? —and with the words he and his Vice-President employed against the dissenters who had come down on the other side of this "close" question.

A little further clarification seemed to be in order, though. I asked Nixon whether in 1968 he still believed in the Domino Theory.

"Oh, I certainly did," he replied with what I thought was disarming candor. And he mentioned his visits with the leaders of the "dominoes"—Thailand, Malaysia, Singapore, the Philippines and Indonesia. They all knew that if North Vietnamese aggression was not stopped in Vietnam, it would then bè visited upon them "and that if the United States bugged out of Vietnam, we wouldn't stand up for them. And I think they were right."

I had now set the stage for the series of questions we would return to after taking Nixon through his conduct of the war. He outlined his series of negotiating proposals, the first several of which involved mutual withdrawal of U.S. and North Vietnamese forces and the last of which involved the so-called leopard-spot formula which permitted North Vietnamese troops to remain in areas inside South Vietnam they already controlled. But according to Nixon, "Whatever we did, mutual withdrawal, unilateral withdrawal, nothing that we offered would they consider unless we agreed on our part to overthrow the government of South Vietnam and allow them to take over. And that we would not agree to." And, of course, the Russians wouldn't help a bit, and the Chinese would not be the first to restrain an ally, given their competition with the Soviets.

As if to emphasize the difficult political period over which he had presided, Nixon recalled a recent Harris poll. The poll showed that only 22 percent of the Americans interviewed said they would favor sending American forces to defend Israel "even if Israel were attacked by all of its neighbors supported by the Soviets." Less than half—41 percent—said they would support intervention in Berlin in the case of attack, "and that, of course, is NATO." The only nation receiving a better than 50 percent response was Canada.

Nixon recited the figures sadly, as if they reflected something lost in this society. I made a mental note to return to the subject later in the session. That Harris poll was a two-edged sword. For it was, I believed, the obdurate pursuit of a flawed policy in Vietnam that was responsible for the increased reluctance of Americans to wage war on behalf of more honorable causes elsewhere.

We had been talking theory so far and, while we had each staked different ground, we had not yet come to those areas of Nixon's war policy which triggered severe reaction in the United States or came to be regarded as borderline abuses of his office.

That was about to change. Operation Menu, the secret bombing of Cambodia, begun in March 1969, was next on my agenda, to be followed by the Cambodian incursion itself. I wondered whether the President's demeanor—controlled until now—would change. I turned to the falsification of records that the administration had employed to mask its Cambodia bombing.

Nixon's response was weak. He compared his own action to Eisenhower's on the eve of Normandy. "And, ah, Eisenhower, and his commanders, ah, of course, had all kinds of stories put out deliberately, ah, which were false, in terms of where we might attack and so forth. And then they went into Normandy. Ah, in this case, the bombing had to be secret for the reasons we did."

Quite a difference between not announcing precisely where you are going to conduct an invasion during World War II so as not to alert the enemy, and falsifying reports about where you have already bombed an enemy so as not to alert Congress. Perhaps wrongly, I felt his words made their own point—much to the dismay of my staff in the monitor room—and pressed on. It sounded as though the true purpose of the secrecy was to keep public support behind his war efforts, to avoid telling the American people "about an expansion of the war."

Here Nixon responded with his first flash of anger: "Mr. Frost, it was much better for the young Americans that weren't killed by the great hoards of ammunition, rockets, and the rest, and the number of civilians that weren't killed. My responsibility was to protect those men . . ."

As his answer continued, the anger began to subside, but Nixon's claims about the operation became more extreme. And, seeing me in a more combative posture than in our first session, he tried to land a few personal blows.

> NIXON: Actually, our casualties went down, and perhaps your researchers didn't point this out to you, because they've missed several things I've found already here, they didn't point out to you, you know there was no Tet Offensive in 1969 . . .
> FROST: Well, there was no Third World War, but that wasn't necessarily the result of bombing.

In the monitor room Zelnick snapped, "Goddamn right, David. How the hell did bombing in March prevent a Tet Offensive in January?"

Now to the crux of the Cambodia policy, the incursion of April 30, 1970. Just ten days earlier Nixon had given a nationally televised address on Vietnam presenting a rosy picture of progress. That, plus the fact that our research had failed to unearth anyone at the N.S.C. or indeed the C.I.A. who had recommended in favor of the operation at the time, made me want to know why it was launched.

Nixon stoutly defended the incursion. Next to the May 8, 1972, bombing of Hanoi and mining of Haiphong Harbor and the December 18, 1972, bombing "which brought about the final negotiation," he claimed, "the Cambodian sanctuary operation was the most successful military operation of the war. And they [our sources] know that. And they had to eat their words . . ."

What could Nixon possibly advance now to support that preposterous claim, I wondered, particularly in the light of what occurred in Cambodia during his administration and the awesome dénouement subsequent to his departure?

Very little. Just some old regurgitated statistics on the 22,000 rifles captured, the 15 million rounds of ammunition, the 150,000 rockets and mortars and, of course, the supplies of rice whose capture always seemed to be putting the enemy on the brink of starvation.

But what had changed during the ten days previous to the operation? Nixon talked of major buildups and threats to Allied positions. Apparently convinced, though, of the need for more specific documentation, he added, "And, incidentally, just, just for your historical purposes, I'll—I will furnish you the intelligence materials that I did receive on this, because it's quite a story as to what happened between April 20th and April 30th. And I'm really—you mean to tell me that your researchers, as many as you have, didn't know about what was happening in Cambodia? Do they—do—do—do they know—"

FROST: We—

NIXON: —how many provincial capitals fell? Do they know what movement of troops had taken place? Didn't they know about what the concentration of massive artillery forces, as well as men, ah, in the sanctuary areas? Because I'd—I'd be very surprised because you pay those fellows a lot of money.

FROST: Well, they, it's generally—

NIXON: Or are they just trying to find out something that's on the other side?

FROST: No, no, I don't think so. I don't think that's been our experience. I think we're trying to show all sides.

He's really being a bit of a bugger, I thought, and not paying much heed to the facts. I felt certain that if the situation with respect to the South Vietnamese being directly imperiled had changed materially between April 20 and April 30, not only would we have found out about it, but Nixon would have been able to cite the information by rote, rather than relying upon a promise to share intelligence reports of the period.

My doubts in that regard proved correct. Prior to the next session, Khachigian handed Zelnick the "documentation" Nixon had promised. It proved to be several draft pages from his still incomplete memoirs which listed only a number of enemy operations inside Cambodia—including the capture of a number of provincial capitals—relating exclusively to the civil war then raging in that country rather than to any massive new threat to the South Vietnamese.

Meanwhile, I could not resist Nixon's challenge to the quality of my researchers' work. "It's generous of you to refer to the researchers so fully. In fact, talking to as many people as they could . . . the only thing that they could find between April the 20th and April the 30th was that you'd seen *Patton* twice, so they thought that might be the reason."

> NIXON: Yes, yes.
> FROST: Did that have an influence on you?
> NIXON: Well, I've seen *The Sound of Music* twice, and it hasn't made me a writer either . . .

He then gave a short, curiously stilted "review" of the film, concluding with a Jack Benny-type wave of the hand, saying, "Ah, as far as that was concerned, it had no effect whatever on my decisions."

I determined to continue on the same topic. Nixon had, during his emotional 1970 speech announcing the incursion, indicated that this "decisive" thrust was aimed at the capture of the Communist headquarters for all South Vietnam, which, I reminded him, "made it sound like a sort of Dr. No's Palace, or a Bamboo Pentagon somewhere in Cambodia. We were to discover that there was no such place as that." Nixon said, "That's correct," and then went on to blame that little *faux pas* on the failure of the C.I.A. intelligence, adding that they hadn't even predicted the Lon Nol coup in the first place.

This was to prove a recurrent Nixon theme, knocking the agency at every turn. They had failed in Cambodia; they had failed to predict the 1973 war in the Middle East; they had failed to anticipate Salvador Allende's 1970 victory in Chile. In fact, the agency had needed a good shaking up throughout his presidency. Somewhat surprisingly to us, he always stopped short of blaming them for Watergate, but the invitation for others to draw their own conclusion about the C.I.A. acting in self-defense was clearly there.

We were coming now to the culmination of our discussion about Cambodia. With as much conviction as I would feel at any point in the Interviews, I tried to summarize the facts of the country's anguish within the framework of a question:

"On the subject of Cambodia, let me put a philosophical thought to you, which I put to you particularly, in a sense, as a Quaker. In the sense that a lot of the philosophical studies that I've read of Cambodia and this little nation that started with perhaps six thousand members of the Khmer Rouge and a population of seven million, in neutrality, albeit as we've discussed, flawed neutrality. That, nevertheless, with that flawed neutrality, was somehow surviving in the midst of a holocaust. And the concatenation of events that the administration were involved in, starting with the bombing, the armed incursion, the driving, the driving of people, the North Vietnamese and others, back across Cambodia. The continued bombing and twice the tonnage we dropped on North Vietnam. All of this embroiled this little country in a holocaust that started with this flawed neutrality, and it ended up at the end of this whole saga with, you know, more than half a million dead. There were more dead later, when the Khmer Rouge took over. But that this bringing them up into the holocaust created the Khmer Rouge and destroyed a country that might otherwise have survived, and that therefore, do you have in a Quaker sense, on your conscience, the destruction of this rather pitiful country?"

Nixon's response would establish a pattern of sorts. Often during our sessions, when confronted with a difficult factual question, he would pour forth a highly charged stream of emotional consciousness. When asked a question with a high emotional content, he would offer a cool recitation of what he saw as the facts. Now his response was basically that the Communists were worse than anything that had preceded them, and that they had therefore been worth opposing.

He was missing the point. The Communists were nothing in Cambodia until Richard Nixon's administration, through its policies and its callous, ill-planned use of B-52's and "tactical aircraft," had made the revolution there. In effect, I said, "We created a

117

monster—we created the Khmer Rouge, with all of the bombing that we did . . . much of it indiscriminate . . ."

The exchange would continue for more than half an hour. Nixon pulled out all the stops. It was never the policy of the U.S. to kill civilians. That was the enemy's way. When something like My Lai occurred, we punished the culprit. They pinned medals on their murderers. He listed Communist atrocities throughout Indochina. He cited columnist Ken Crawford's assertion that this was the only war in which the U.S. press had been kinder to the enemy than to its own country. He said that the Communists had intentionally killed or maimed 45,000 civilians when they captured Hue during the 1968 Tet Offensive.

And he was ready with anecdotes. There was the construction worker who visited the White House after the Cambodian incursion and told him, "I have only one criticism of that Cambodia thing. If you had gone in earlier, I wish you had, you might have captured the gun that killed my boy three months ago." There was a "Madonna"-like South Vietnamese girl whom he had visited in a Saigon hospital during a trip to the Far East in 1965. The previous evening the Vietcong had shelled her village. Her parents, two brothers and a sister had died. She had one arm blown off and the other mangled. And all she could say to Nixon was, "Well, Mr. Nixon, thanks for coming, and would you thank the American people the day you get back for helping us in our fight against the Communists." Hours later she died on the operating table.

Some of the stories, I was sure, were apocryphal. I was certain, however, that they were subjectively true as far as Nixon was concerned. He had not only manipulated emotions to rouse political support for his own policies; he had manipulated his own to maintain his bearing, his peace of mind and, quite possibly *in extremis*, his sanity.

One story, documented in part by press reports at the time, stuck with me. Nixon told of attending a judicial conference in Williamsburg, Virginia, late in 1970, "and as I walked up to go into the hall to make a speech, a little girl, I don't think she was more than sixteen, sort of broke through the line of people there, and ah, she just spat in my face, just covered my face with spit, and she said, 'You are a murderer.' Of course, I wiped the spit off, went in and made the speech. As I was walking in, I was thinking, she was such a pretty girl, but at that moment, she was so ugly, and the war made her so. There was nothing I didn't want more than to end the war. Ah, believe me, it was a sore temptation not to just end it, and blame it on Kennedy and Johnson. They got us in, I didn't. They sent men over there, I didn't."

But he didn't because he believed in their cause. Oh, yes, the South Vietnamese were not a perfect ally. Neither were the Cambodians. "But look at the choice, do you want a government with some elections or none? Do you want a government with some free press or none? Do you want a government with some freedom of religion or none?" And, of course, there was always the matter of credibility. Credibility with allies. Credibility with dominoes. Credibility with the major Communist powers.

Some of Nixon's arguments were strong. Others were weak. But to me they all served only to emphasize his incapacity to understand the dictates of the times over which he presided. I respected the sincerity of his emotions as he recalled the spitting incident in Williamsburg. But what that sixteen-year-old beautiful girl whom the war had made ugly could have taught him, he never learned: that the conduct of the war in Indochina had become incompatible with the changing perceptions of a liberal and enlightened Western society. And nothing he did, or could have done, could change that.

We were nearly at the close of our second session. For the third and last time, I tried to stir Nixon with some footage on the monitor, this time a montage of scenes of the war from ravaged villages to the sight of South Vietnamese troops clinging to the skids of American helicopters as the Laos incursion turned into a rout. It made no impact at all. Nixon had obviously been coached by his aides not even to betray any emotion while viewing the film. So he sat chatting amicably and dispassionately while the cameras rolled.

We concluded the morning with his decision to stop the North Vietnamese advance across the DMZ by bombing Hanoi and mining

Haiphong Harbor in May 1972, even as he prepared for the Moscow summit and the consummation of SALT I. At first, Nixon related, both he and Kissinger favored postponing the summit, rather than taking the domestic blame for the Soviets' canceling.

John Connally dissuaded him. Connally argued that Nixon should let the Russians make the first move. He said, "Number one, the President cannot lose this war. Number two, that means he must go forward with this strong action, it should have been done long ago, but now he has got to go forward. Number three, I don't believe the Soviet will cancel, but in any event under no circumstances should the President cancel. Put the monkey on their back for blocking the road to peace because of their involvement in Vietnam."

Connally proved right. Kissinger's original estimation of a 90 percent probability of Soviet cancellation dwindled with each passing day. The Kissinger countenance became brighter and brighter. A Soviet trade minister, visiting the United States days after the bombing began, startled reporters attending an embassy reception by saying that as far as he knew the summit was still on. As a footnote to the way Big Powers communicate with one another, Mrs. Dobrynin was in constant touch with Mrs. Nixon regarding the itinerary, even as the bombs fell and the mines floated.

At last Nixon left for Moscow. The Soviet stake in bettering relations, particularly in light of Nixon's earlier Peking visit, was too great regardless of the situation prevailing in Vietnam.

Still Podgorny, Kosygin and Brezhnev took turns berating Nixon before an 11 P.M. dinner at the *dacha* where the meetings occurred. They told him to stop the bombing, stop the mining, get out of Vietnam. They said they could do nothing with Hanoi to ease his predicament.

But then after the first toast at dinner, Brezhnev told him, "It's an indication of how potentially successful our new relationship will be, that after the kind of frank and sometimes even belligerent discussion we have had for the past three hours, we can now sit down to dinner together, and enjoy each other's company in a friendly way. I hope we can always have this kind of relationship."

In the heady world of Big Power relations, a matter like the 45 million people of Indochina had to be kept in perspective.

John Birt bounded from the production trailer and sprinted to the house so quickly that I hardly had time to exchange amenities with Nixon before he was upon me. He pumped my hand, smiling broadly at the way the morning's proceedings had gone, and repeated "Yes, yes, that was first-rate" several times.

Nixon's people too seemed elated, Brennan, Khachigian and Price joining the three of us in the adjacent kitchen and warmly congratulating Nixon and myself on the cut and thrust of the day's debate. Birt wondered at first how the Nixon staff had been able to muster such enthusiasm, given his sense that their man had not prevailed, but then realized that their reaction was in fact no mystery. As viewed by a "true believer," Nixon had held his own. He had stated his convictions plainly and had not given way, even under thorough interrogation. Moreover—and this, Zelnick later learned from Khachigian, had been a matter of some concern to his staff—he had borne up well physically throughout the long and, at times, heated exchanges on the set. From my own point of view, there was relief that such heated exchanges—and strong allegations —had produced only momentary flashes of anger, without poisoning the air or stunting the dialogue.

Brennan asked the former President whether he would like to be introduced to the team of Frost researchers to which he had referred so scathingly during the questioning.

Nixon obliged, shaking hands first with Reston and asking how his dad and two brothers were doing. Reston murmured his response with equal civility.

"Now, Mr. President, I'd like you to meet Bob Zelnick," I said, "the man whose Vietnam research you so thoughtfully critiqued this morning."

The two shook hands.

"What you said about my research was fair comment, Mr. President," Zelnick said. "But when you complained about how much

Making the arrangements: the former President
talks to David Frost in his office at San Clemente.

"The calm before the storm . . ." Frost and Nixon's chief of staff, Colonel Jack Brennan, at the Quiet Cannon on March 7, 1977.

One of the "seminars" at the Beverly Hilton. Left to right: chief program editor Bob Zelnick, Frost, co-producer John Birt and program editor Jim Reston.

"A moment to savor." Frost welcomes the former President to the home of Mr. and Mrs. Harold Smith on Wednesday, March 23, the first day of taping.

An informal gathering in the Smiths' kitchen. Left to right: Nixon aide Ken Khachigian, press representative John Springer, Frost, Frost's executive vice-president, Marv Minoff, John Birt and (back to the camera) Jack Brennan.

The Nixon staff in their monitor room at Monarch Bay. In the foreground, former speech writer Ray Price; in the background, left to right: Jack Brennan, Ken Khachigian and Bob Dunne, who was recording the proceedings.

The Frost team's monitor room. Left to right: Frost's managing director, Ian Gordon, Marv Minoff, Jim Reston and a visiting investor, Sir James Goldsmith.

"With our cameramen, he attempted, not unsuccessfully, to develop an all-hardhats-together, deze-and-doze-guys-of-the-world-unite type of bantering relationship."

Following the Cambodia debate, the former President, as he leaves, makes his one visit to the Frost team's monitor room. Left to right: Reston, Birt, the former President, Zelnick.

An impromptu press conference outside the Smiths' residence.

The former President's personal protector, Manolo Sanchez, in his working attire.

The Secret Service was an imposing shield. (The mystery of the question mark on the sign was, however, one it was unable to solve.)

The former President and an Orange County admirer photographed after one of the sessions.

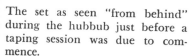
The set as seen by viewers and the camera lens.

Frost leaves the production trailer after a conversation with John Birt.

The set as seen "from behind" during the hubbub just before a taping session was due to commence.

Director Jørn Winther selects a camera angle in the production trailer during one of the tapings.

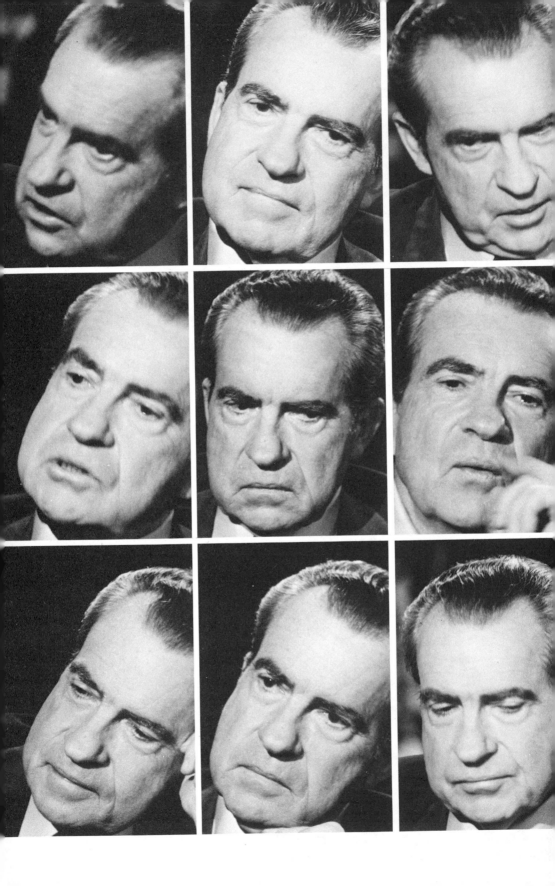

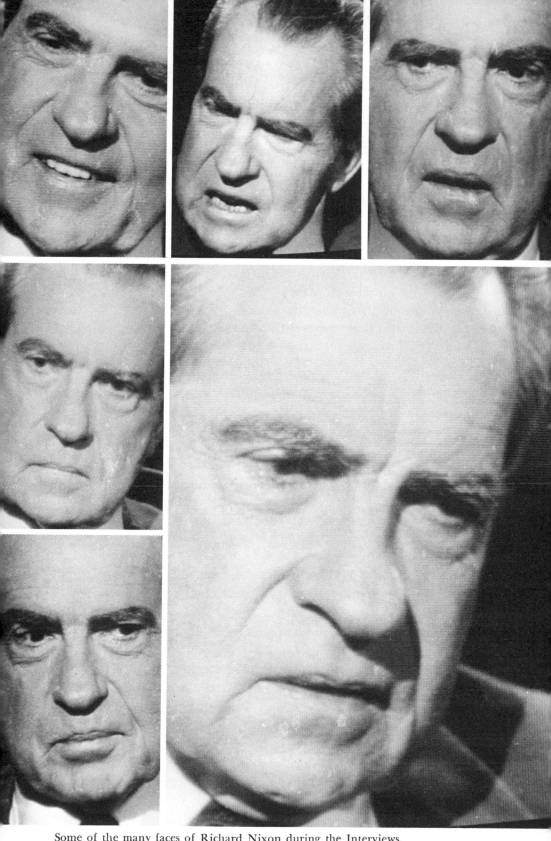

Some of the many faces of Richard Nixon during the Interviews.

money I was making, I became so incensed I almost choked on my caviar."

For the first time during all the months I had dealt with him, Nixon broke into a really hearty and apparently spontaneous laugh. Then he repeated his offer to provide the intelligence data which would support his assessment of the Cambodian operation.

Nixon and Brennan left, but the two staffs lingered. We poured a bottle of Pouilly Fuissé and gossiped a bit in the spacious living room with its majestic view of the ocean and the beach. I had a growing concern I wanted to voice.

"Ken," I said at one point, "the material is so fascinating and the President has so much he wants to share with us, how would you imagine he'd feel about extending the sessions another four or five hours?" John and I had briefly discussed that possibility after the first day's taping. Now it was doubly clear that we were falling considerably behind schedule.

"I think it would be out of the question," Khachigian replied. "The President has a very old-fashioned view about the sanctity of contracts, and ours calls for a flat twenty-four hours. In fact, since you've run about fifteen minutes long on each of the first two days, I don't even see how we can manage twelve sessions." So we were being timed that closely! "But that's just as well. Quite apart from the President's own wishes, I think we'd all like a full week's break during Easter and on the sheet we're still scheduled to tape on Good Friday. So why don't we just drop that date and you can keep running ten or fifteen minutes beyond two hours on the remaining days."

Birt and I exchanged glances. That wouldn't do at all. On the ride back to the Hilton, Zelnick was even more exercised about the problems of time than we were.

"Three or four extra hours, even if you get them, aren't going to do the trick. For God's sake, I covered the Chapin trial, the Plumbers trial and the Watergate trial. And I've seen defendants spend ten or twenty hours in the stand, even with the tightest rules of evidence in effect. We've got a maximum of eight hours after Easter in which to explore every single alleged abuse of power, including Watergate. Unless we establish a different pace and control now, it will be too late."

"I do agree about the time problem," said John. "But I think we'll work that out. And it may be that Vietnam should not be a part of foreign policy, but the major part of the first program." Since we were working on the assumption that Watergate would be the concluding program, and since we could not lead with a "soft" program like Nixon's conduct of Big Power relations, and since the domestic policy and non-Watergate abuse areas were as yet unstructured, the idea made sense.

"Anyway," said John. "We're halfway up the mountain. On Monday, we've got to try to reach that peak. And then all we have to do is stay there for the next three weeks."

The weekend brought a refreshing visitor, Mike Wallace of *60 Minutes*. He and his crew had long been at work on the story. Early in the spring they had sent a team to London to film my comings and goings and I had inadvertently obliged them by diving for a ball in a charity soccer match, getting kicked in the face and emerging with the biggest black eye it had been my misfortune to see—or half see. Harry Moses, Mike's producer, had responded as I would expect a fellow producer to respond. "I'm terribly sorry about the black eye, David," he had said soberly, and then brightened up. "But it was great television!"

The impending story on *60 Minutes* had been a source of some trepidation among the team. Doomsayers had predicted a hatchet job on the project with a kind of "David in the Lion's Den" theme. But the Wallace team had done a careful job. They had soon realized that our preparation had been more thorough than most outsiders would have suspected, and that our approach to the task was indeed serious. So Mike and I were liberated for an amiable joust as he probed for details about my contract with Nixon and asked what I would do if Mr. Nixon didn't cooperate. I suggested the stonewall approach was not necessarily the one that Nixon would take.

FROST: I hope the approach he takes will be the one of a cascade of candor.

WALLACE: A cascade of candor from Richard Nixon? Is this what you expect?
FROST: No, it was just a phrase that I thought would appeal to you.

Mike also wanted to know about the advertising. We were not selling out yet, were we? The advertising had started "slowly," I said somewhat euphemistically, but now it was picking up. That was so: there had been some progress. But of course it was progress not so much from a "slow" start as from a motionless one. There were to be twelve minutes of commercials in each ninety-minute program—six minutes to be sold by the local stations, who retained the resultant revenue from them, and six to be sold by us. As I spoke to Mike we had sold half of our six minutes per show, but only thanks to selling one further minute per show back to the stations. Radio Shack had come in, as had Hilton Hotels, but we were not yet anywhere close to breaking even, despite the fact that the Interviews were already underway.

Indeed, when Mike and his crew left, I spent the next few hours catching up on telephone calls to possible advertisers and overseas networks. I asked Ian Gordon, my managing director in London, to fly to Paris after the weekend, as the French contract was still not officially signed. Back in the States, Universal had acquired the nontheatrical rights for 16-millimeter film, and Ed Little of Mutual Broadcasting would be networking the programs simultaneously on radio, but without at least one major breakthrough—one advertiser taking sixty seconds in all four shows, for example—it was going to be tough to end up in the black. But from balancing the books—my only "relaxation" during this period—it was time to get back to studying them, and underlining them.

"Where will he lay the blame for the collapse of Saigon?" I asked Bob in a quiet moment at Monarch Bay before taping began on Monday morning.

"On the Congress," Zelnick replied.

"Because they passed the War Powers Act and legislated an end to air operations over Indochina, you mean."

"Yes."

"And because of their failure to support the increased aid requested by Ford?"

"I don't think he'll have the balls to say that," replied Zelnick.

A knock on the door, and Brennan entered. "Good morning, David. It's negative on the extra time request," he said, with the sort of firm handshake and big boyish grin that one would normally associate with good tidings. "And you guys are running so far over on each taping session, you were going to lose a day anyway. So it might as well be Good Friday."

"Why don't we get together after the taping this morning. We can talk about that, and go over what subjects we'll be able to cover in the few days remaining to us."

"I'll be glad to bring Ken in and meet with you folks," said Brennan generously, "but what you ask him is really up to you. The time thing is a dead letter, though."

Maybe, I thought. John and I had discussed a couple of ways of bringing it back to life. It was vital, we felt, and reasonable. After all, our shortage of time was not unconnected with the length of some of Mr. Nixon's answers. Well, anyway, we would see after the taping.

The taping that morning was delayed for approximately ten minutes, as one of the cameras was not working properly.

Nixon unhooked his microphone and excused himself.

"I'll wait in the room," he apologized. "You know, when you get yourself ready for one of these things, you lose your edge if you let your concentration wander."

When we got under way, I turned quickly to the question of the Vietnam Peace Accord itself. I wanted to lay the groundwork for our thesis that the Christmas Bombing had been a tragically reckless act, and that the key contributing factor in it had been the conduct of Thieu, rather than that of Hanoi.

FROST: Now the interim agreement Dr. Kissinger took with him to Saigon for Saigon's approval, and, by all accounts, the result was a minor eruption or a minor earthquake. I mean there was violent response to it.

NIXON: Well, I would say that's typical British understatement when you say a minor eruption. It was, basically, a major eruption . . .

Kissinger had returned from Paris jubilant. "Well, the President now has three out of three," he had told Nixon, referring to their three great first-term foreign-policy goals, China, détente and Vietnam. And "based on what the South Vietnamese representatives in Paris had said they would agree to," Kissinger anticipated no great problem from Thieu himself.

Thieu, however, would have none of it. He wanted the North Vietnamese out of his country. He wanted the cease-fire to be immediate, so the North Vietnamese "wouldn't grab up a lot of territory prior to—after it was announced and before it was implemented." Provisions regarding the DMZ and the election machinery had to be spelled out more clearly. And, Thieu "presented it so hard-line that there was no way for Kissinger to break the bottleneck." So instead of flying on to Hanoi, as Kissinger had planned, and the kind of emotional rapprochement that would have symbolized brilliantly the success of the Nixon Vietnam policies, Kissinger had to return instead to Paris for that "one more meeting" that would turn into countless frustrating sessions before breaking off a week before Christmas.

As the days multiplied, Nixon's messages to Thieu "became increasingly tougher and tougher." He was also sending stark warnings to Le Duc Tho in Paris.

But, I insisted, the initial problems had been with Thieu, and the changes we had sought for Thieu.

"That's right." Nixon conceded that point. But, he added, after the election the North Vietnamese "took a totally stonewall position, with regard to even the most minor suggestions for improving the agreement."

It would not strain credulity, I thought, to suppose that the North Vietnamese felt they had been lured into a trap. To get a preelection agreement, they had agreed to let Thieu remain in office. Now the election was history with no accord achieved. And here was Kissinger back in Paris asking for still further "improvements."

But Thieu seemed still to be the principal holdout. So Nixon wrote him one of those now-famous letters, dated November 14, 1972, pledging that "if Hanoi fails to abide by the terms of this agreement, it is my intention to take swift and severe retaliatory action."

"What," I asked, "did you have in mind at that point?"

"Well, that was simply a letter that had as its purpose giving him the self-confidence that he needed to sign the agreement," Nixon replied. Thieu, it seems, "didn't trust Hanoi."

"I therefore wanted him to know that he had my commitment, my personal commitment, to take whatever action I could as President, having in mind, of course, the reservation that he knew that I always had to have in mind . . . I'd have to have congressional support on the appropriations side. But, in any event, I gave him that assurance hoping that would get him to be more reasonable in terms of accepting the terms of an agreement."

Nixon was baldly stating matters we thought we would have to extract from him. And it was imperative that I get him to spell out exactly what he had in mind.

> FROST: But you felt that you could get congressional approval for "swift and severe retaliatory action" with full force?
> NIXON: Ah . . . with regard to "swift and severe retaliatory action," I felt that if the North Vietnamese, which they had so often done in the past, flagrantly and blatantly violated the agreement, that I could go to the country and to the Congress and get the support that was necessary to bring them into line.
> FROST: In other words, you'd have—
> NIXON: I didn't think—I didn't think, in other words, to use the Chinese term that Chou En-lai often used with me, I didn't believe this was an empty cannon. It wasn't an assurance that I didn't feel that I could keep.

Moments later I came back to the subject even more explicitly: "You felt you could go to the Congress and, ah, address the nation and say the war was over. We had peace with honor. We must go back in again and do this?"

Not only that, Nixon replied, but at the time, prior congressional approval wasn't even required. "I could have taken that action, and then the only question is whether or not the Congress would have aborted the action by denying funds for it, which they could have done."

But he did not feel that anyone would tamper with his bombing funds. Congress would be willing to pay "for keeping a peace that we had won."

But the difference, I stressed, was that on all the other occasions when he had taken his case to the people, he had been able to tell them the United States was in Vietnam and what he was doing would help it to get out. Now, having come out, he would have been trying to rally support for going back in, at least with considerable air power. Bombing "for keeping a peace we had won" seemed a contradiction in terms.

But Nixon would have none of it. He would have ordered the air strikes and he would have gotten public support. He was adamant. "I would have broke the case strongly. It would have been swift. It would have been massive. And it would have been effective."

"Un—bloody—believable," said Zelnick. "I can't believe that David got him to say that."

"The rest is a bonus," Birt whispered to no one in particular from his cramped space in the production trailer.

On set, I felt that while Nixon was making some striking admissions, crucial points were still to be made. The period between October 1972 and January 1973 was one of the more intriguing in the recent diplomatic history of the United States. And Nixon —one of the few who knew the record in its totality—would never be more disposed to talk candidly about it than he was at this moment.

> FROST: The massive infusion of military aid to Saigon during this period—was that also one of the Thieu conditions for going along with the October pact?

Nixon didn't answer directly. "Ah, I must say, I think that that helped Thieu's attitude in getting him eventually, while he did so reluctantly, even to the last, to go along with the peace agreement."

FROST: But did he set it as a condition that "I must have more—"
NIXON: Oh, no, no. No, he didn't set it as a condition.
FROST: But, now—
NIXON: He suggested it, but not as a condition. I wouldn't have accepted that.

And the Christmas Bombing, was one of the purposes there "to reassure President Thieu as much as to attack North Vietnam?"

Nixon quibbled with the term "Christmas Bombing." "There was no bombing on Christmas, of course. We had a Christmas truce for forty-eight hours. At the end of that truce, I ordered the biggest strike of the war." (In the monitor room, Zelnick began a rendition of "God Rest Ye Merry, Gentlemen.") "And, within one day after that strike, on the twenty-eighth of December, it worked. The North Vietnamese agreed to come back and negotiate without conditions, and that meant going back to the October 8th proposition, and in fact, we were able to improve upon it . . ."

Regarding the effect on President Thieu, "There isn't any question that it had, I believe, a salutary effect on Thieu, in that it indicated that the United States was going to still take action against the North Vietnamese, if the North Vietnamese backed away from what we considered to be not a formal agreement, but at least a tentative agreement which they had made many, many months before. So it helped his morale."

The bombing, of course, became a mortally divisive issue in the United States. It was regarded as a breach of faith from the White House, which had, two months earlier, assured the nation that "peace is at hand." It was terribly costly in lives, P.O.W.'s captured by the other side and lost equipment. It seemed horribly illogical and it was unexplained. Vacationing in Key Biscayne over the holidays, Nixon confided, he received very few Christmas salutations, even from his Republican allies on Capitol Hill and members of his Cabinet. As a result, "it was the loneliest and saddest Christmas I can ever remember, much sadder and much more lonely than the one in the Pacific during the war."

But what about Kissinger? I wanted to know. Did he support the bombing? Sources very close to him had implied that he did not. Joe Kraft, for one, had said he had been dangled that particular bait himself.

No, Nixon replied, Henry had strongly supported the bombing. Getting Hanoi back to the negotiating table "without conditions" was the key to achieving peace before the first Nixon term expired. "And the only shock treatment that Kissinger could think of, that I could think of, was air strikes."

Their only disagreement had been on "tactics." Kissinger had wanted Nixon to go on television and rally the nation behind his policy. That Nixon declined to do. "The reason I didn't go on television and explain it, was because I wanted results, not the publicity. I felt that if we could get the peace, if we could get them back to the table, that was the big thing. And I knew that while a speech might gain more support and more understanding of the bombing in the first place, that it might, on the other hand, in terms of the enemy, be counterproductive. And so I made the tough decision, if we can get the enemy back to negotiate, that's what we want."

Now for a value judgment, and a tough one from this man. "In retrospect . . . given a choice, wouldn't you say it would have been better if the October agreement, imperfect as it was, could have been signed? Or was it better to have the Christmas Bombing and a slightly different agreement?"

Nixon disputed my term "slightly." He felt it was a "substantially" better agreement. Even so, "when you attempt to weigh, ah, balance the cost of getting it, the need to renew military action as we did in order to get the people back to the conference table, and you weigh that against what we could have gotten if Thieu had gone along with the October agreement and if the North Vietnamese had gone along with it, ah, as well, I would say in retrospect, certainly from our standpoint, my personal standpoint, those of us in positions of leadership within the administration, the American people, that we would have preferred to have taken the October 8th agreement, ah, and taken our chances with those, without those quite significant improvements that were made, having in mind the fact that in the end, ah, two years after the cease-fire, the North

Vietnamese totally broke, and violated the agreement."

Like many answers in which the former President conceded his policies may have been in error, here again he had approached the point circuitously, in grammar so convoluted as to defy comprehension, and with so many qualifiers injected into the response that you almost forgot the question, but the underlying message was clear: the Christmas bombing had been, at best, a waste.

South Vietnam collapsed in April and May 1975, I recalled. "Had you been in the White House in May 1975 . . . do you think you could have done something to save South Vietnam?"

Part of Nixon's answer we had anticipated. No, because of the bombing cutoff legislated by the Congress effective August 15, 1973, and because of the War Powers Act.

But Nixon unabashedly took that next step which Zelnick had thought impossible. Congress had caused the collapse of Saigon "because they cut off Thieu's water, in effect, to speak in the vernacular, by refusing to comply with the peace agreement, ah, our obligation to replace his equipment on a one-on-one basis." When the Communists started their offensive in the Central Highlands, Thieu found himself outgunned; he was fighting a "poor man's war." And why, Nixon asked rhetorically, did this happen? "It happened because the Congress refused to grant President Ford's request to provide the funds for the South Vietnamese to defend themselves. If the South Vietnamese had had the necessary equipment I believe they could have held on."

I had a very clear recollection of the South Vietnamese Army in April 1975 running out of will, rather than guns, but Nixon returned to his theme and warmed to it.

"I do know that the Congress was wrong in having America fall down on its commitments. That the Congress has to be held responsible for that, and that, had the Congress kept its commitments, the commitments we had made to South Vietnam, then we wouldn't even be discussing this esoteric question—"

FROST: But, nevertheless, Congress didn't keep us in Vietnam.
NIXON: As a matter of fact, the Congress lost it. And that's the tragedy and they have to take the responsibility for it.

I moved Nixon on to another controversial subject, his secret pledge of assistance to North Vietnam. "We finally got down to a figure of around, as I recall, three billion dollars," he said. This was not an unconditional promise. For one thing, "there would have to be congressional approval; and, two, there had to be compliance with the peace agreement."

In fact, he claimed to have emphasized this second point to Henry Kissinger, when Kissinger visited Hanoi in February 1973, to review implementation of the agreement. He claimed to have sent Kissinger a message on February 12, 1973, saying, in effect, "You must take the firmest possible line with them on this point. I will under no circumstances ask the Congress of the United States for any funds whatever for North Vietnam if those funds are to be used for the purpose of maintaining forces in Laos or Cambodia or any foreign country."

But did he really think Congress would approve economic assistance for an enemy the United States had been fighting for a decade?

"Yes," the former President replied, "it's rather an American tradition to help our enemies, ah, after a war. In fact, perhaps help them even more than our friends. Who rebuilt Germany? Who rebuilt Japan? And in this case it was North Vietnam . . . "

Excursions aside, the Nixon Peace Accord, then, rested on two political assumptions. First, that he could win majority support for an aid program of some three billion dollars or more for North Vietnam. And second, that if the admittedly "fragile" agreement broke down, he could convince the Congress and the nation to endorse his military reintervention, at least as regards the use of air power. Not the safest assumptions I had ever heard.

"Let's come back to that Domino Theory," I suggested. "If the Vietnam War was worth fighting mainly to prevent countries like Singapore, Malaysia, the Philippines and Indonesia from falling, and now, two years after the fall of Vietnam, those countries remain secure, isn't this proof positive that the initial assumptions were in error?"

Nixon's response was a tentative one. For two years after the accord, "we stuck to our guns" and gave the South Vietnamese a chance to survive. That had a salutary effect on other countries in the area, but as to the effect since the fall of Indochina, it was "too early to judge."

"But we were talking about the same length of time there," I pointed out. He had defined two years as a mightily long time when it was the length of time that the South Vietnamese had held out. It was also just two years since the fall of Indochina. "The two years can't be interpreted in two different ways, if you see what I mean."

We were drawing to a close now. Nixon had an intriguing example of how Vietnam had complicated his dealings with Moscow and Peking, though that I am sure was not the purpose of his telling it. During an early meeting with Chou En-lai, the Premier had told him, "We note some press reports to the effect that you're coming to China for the purpose of getting us to help you on the war in Vietnam. We want to make it very clear that our position is one of support for our comrades in North Vietnam and South Vietnam, the so-called Vietcong. And we believe you should get out."

Nixon recalled his reply: "If the United States doesn't prove to be an ally or a friend one can trust in Vietnam, we aren't an ally or friend that other nations may be able to trust. That's what's on the line there, and therefore, we're going to see this thing through to an honorable conclusion."

And so to a final question. We had wanted something to link Nixon's conduct of the war to the domestic policies he devised to build and maintain support for it. And indeed to discourage dissent from it.

It was Bob who first suggested asking Nixon whether he regarded himself as the "last casualty" of Vietnam. John and I had liked the term but not the question itself. Standing alone, it made Nixon seem more the victim than the perpetrator, more the sinned against than the sinner.

We worked further on the idea. The question had to be structured so as to make it clear that Nixon's fate was not predetermined at the time he took office, that the policy decisions he made, perhaps

reluctantly, were conscious ones and that the consequences to himself grew out of those conscious policy decisions. In that context,
the term "casualty" would not connote the fate of an innocent by-
stander or a mere pawn in someone else's grand design.

As I put it to Nixon, the question went: "If the Vietnam War
had not gone on throughout your presidency, there probably would
have been less—much less—domestic discord, and the unifying policies that you adopted at the beginning might not have led to an
atmosphere of polarization, and many of the so-called abuses of
power might never have occurred, or come to light, or been necessary. In that sense, someone has said—I wonder if you agree—that
in that sense, perhaps, you were the last American casualty of the
Vietnam War?"

Nixon's face suddenly became a mask of pain, as if somewhere
deep inside himself an old wound had been reopened. He paused.
He drew a breath. His lips tightened. And then he spoke.

"A case could be made for that, yes," he began. "Ah, there isn't
any question but that in the conduct of the war I made, ah, enemies
who were, from an ideological standpoint, ah, virtually, ah, well,
paranoiac, I guess. Oh, the major newspaper publisher told Henry
Kissinger one night right after the peace settlement, 'I hate the son
of a bitch's guts.' And, naturally, ah, coming right after the time
that we had been able to have the peace settlement, it's an indication how deep those passions ran. Ah, because that kind of attitude
developed over a period of years. I mean, my political career goes
. . . over many, many years. But the actions, and many of them
I took with great reluctance, but recognizing I had to do what was
right, the actions that I took in Vietnam: one, try to win an honorable peace abroad, and two, to keep the peace at home, because
keeping the peace at home, and keeping support for the war was
essential in order to get the enemy to negotiate. That was, of course,
not easy to do, in view of the dissent and so forth, that we had.
And so, it could be said that I was, ah, if I, that I was one of the
casualties, or maybe the last casualty in Vietnam. If so, I'm glad
I'm the last one . . ."

CHAPTER

7

As we gathered with the Nixon staff in the master bedroom of the Smith home following the conclusion of our Vietnam discussion, John and I had not fully solved the mystery of what it was they most wanted preserved for posterity. Even so, however, we assumed that Nixon himself was probably most concerned about his foreign policy in general, and his two major Big Power initiatives in particular. Those would have to be our trump cards if Brennan and Khachigian continued to resist what we regarded by now as our almost desperate need for extra time.

Very pleasantly, but very firmly, they did precisely that. Equally pleasantly, and equally firmly, John took the initiative in making our point. "Well, the way we're running on, we've got to make some very hard decisions. We are already through three full sessions and we've covered exactly one topic. And remember, we have iron-clad commitments to four foreign networks."

"Oh, yes," Brennan recalled. "Britain, France, Italy and Australia."

"Exactly," said Birt. "Now that's three hours already committed. And with domestic policy and Watergate, that simply doesn't leave much time for anything else. So we've got to cut our losses. Given a choice between treating every area superficially and excluding one or two entirely, I would prefer to exclude one or two and let the President deal with them in his memoirs. Wouldn't you, David?"

"Yes, I am afraid I would," I agreed sadly.

"Well, then, we are looking at détente and normalization, the Soviet Union and China," Birt continued, conscious that he now had everybody's attention. "Those are our two big time-savers. Now you say the President regards the contract as sacrosanct. I respect that, and we will have to abide by it. We would like more time but we'll live without it. China, I am certain, must go."

"China . . . goes . . . ," Brennan repeated like a diplomat who has just negotiated away his beloved colony.

"Exactly," replied Birt with emphasis. "Now on détente, I am pretty sure we can save either SALT or the Middle East, but not both. Why don't you discuss that matter with the President and decide which area he feels would be a more useful topic? Then you can call us this afternoon so we will have time to prepare."

There was a moment's pause. Then Brennan broke the silence. "How much more time do you think you would need?" he asked.

"I think I'd feel comfortable with another four hours," I replied.

"Yes, I think that would probably be adequate," agreed John.

"And what would you do with it?"

"What do you mean?"

"Well, I'm not about to recommend a single extra minute devoted to Watergate."

We had anticipated that. And it was understandable. Any suggestion that any of the extra time would be delayed until after Easter would be regarded suspiciously, we had decided.

"We are not suggesting that either, Jack," I said. "We suggest an extra hour for each of the four taping days before Easter, in order to do justice to foreign policy and domestic."

"All right," said Brennan. "Call us this afternoon."

At 4 P.M., Marv Minoff called Brennan, who requested that we

144

meet at San Clemente the following morning. By then Brennan was able to inform us that the President had indeed agreed to approximately four extra hours of taping. The Good Friday session stayed dropped. The morning tapings could continue to run two hours and fifteen minutes each. Four afternoon sessions, each of one hour, would be added to the schedule. The President would not want to eat any lunch during the break—not even one of his "Hawaiian hamburgers" (as Brennan called them) of cottage cheese and pineapple—so the shorter the crew's lunch break, the better. And there was no suggestion—not even a hint—of any additional payment.

Brennan shook my hand as we left. "You owe me one," he said. As it happens, he has never attempted to use the I.O.U., but at that particular moment I could not disagree. It certainly helped to erase any lingering memories of the nightmare negotiations over the delay. Though, ironically, just because of that delay, John Birt was about to have to leave for London for seven days of "minding the store" at LWT—the only way he had been able to arrange to switch his dates. Before John left, Bob and I decided that we felt sufficiently confident about the content of our Vietnam discussions to proceed with the plan of editing the first rough cut of the first program on the assumption that the war in Indochina was going to be the major topic. Not that we all thought it was perfect. Zelnick, I knew, was concerned that I was still permitting Nixon to make too many demagogic points. My habit of mentally editing out certain topics as we went along, and therefore sometimes allowing Nixon to complete a point at leisure, concerned him. Birt had felt that on some points—where I had made the decision to let Nixon's words speak for themselves—we could have benefited from a more sustained and emphatic restating of the record from us. I was concerned that some of our more complex arguments might end up being either too short for comprehension or too long for the attention span.

Jim Reston had been deeply concerned about the Vietnam debate all along. He felt that the very fact that Nixon could gird himself in the robes of a statesman, at least when he was discussing his dealings with other world leaders, deflected from the moral bankruptcy that we had to demonstrate.

And Marv Minoff took time off from his executive duties to look ahead to the finished product, and said concisely, "It's too PBS. Look, don't get me wrong. I like PBS. But we have to aim for a home run. It's not that people feel that the Vietnam War or the Paris negotiations, or the Christmas Bombing are not important. They just feel that's all behind us. What they want to know about is Nixon the man, his illness, his daughters, all the stuff that you haven't been asking because of your concentration on the hard historical material."

Marv had another objection. "I don't think you're doing as well against Nixon as you guys think you are. I even heard one of the P.V.I. bosses say to him, 'I have never voted for you in my life, but if you ran for office now, you'd get my vote.' And then he asked Nixon to pose with him."

Zelnick made the most hard-line response. "If somebody wants to offer Nixon his vote just in order to get him to pose with him, that says more about Hollywood than it does about the quality of our discussion. If you don't believe me, drop by Disneyland sometime and see how many people are posing with Mickey Mouse. If that little rodent ever ran for governor out here, he'd unseat Jerry Brown."

Deep down, though, Minoff's words troubled us all. If what he reported reflected the views of the other laymen watching the proceedings at Monarch Bay, then we had a problem. For while editing could sharpen the focus of the debate, it could not—and indeed must not—alter the outcome. John, Bob and I just had to hope that the audience would share our view of the proceedings rather than Marv's or Jim's.

While there were already these disagreements among the team—with more to come very soon—everyone was unanimous that the tone of our sessions on the Soviet Union and China need not have the adversary flavor of our earlier discussion on Indochina or our later ones on Watergate. We did not want to search for false confrontations. They would only detract from the real ones. At times

Nixon would be talking about genuine achievements; at other times he would be fleshing out a historical record as only he could.

It soon became clear to me that Nixon cherished his contacts with the Chinese leaders and felt a unique affection for them. Nixon and the patriarchs of the Chinese revolution, it seemed, were almost soul brothers beneath the skin, their diverse ideologies notwithstanding. And each seemed to recognize that. At one point Nixon recalled that Chou had spoken "very glowingly of not what I had done as President, or as Vice-President for that matter, but of the comeback. To him . . . and Mao also mentioned that . . . told me he'd read *Six Crises* and paid it a rather nice compliment, saying 'You know, it wasn't a bad book.' And that, from Mao, is high praise. But in any event, what interested him most about it was not the achievements, not the crisis, but the comeback, the comeback. But when you look at Mao and Chou En-lai and Hua and all the others, Mao and his generation and Chou En-lai being part of the Long March, you can see why a comeback means so much more than inheriting the job or being elected to the job and getting it rather easily, and then doing it. Because it's struggle that appeals to them. It's triumphing over adversity. It's climbing to the summit, and not being on the summit."

Yes, Nixon could relate easily to such men. It was the kind of struggle and self-reliance that an unpopular outsider from Whittier, California, constantly having his nose bloodied by the academics and the media, could understand. And it was easy for him to speak their language. Terms like resisting hegemony came easily into his conversation and easily into his communication. In his own mind, he had been resisting the hegemony of the Eastern liberal establishment all his life.

Nixon seemed to be reliving rather than merely recounting his visits to China. Indeed, constantly throughout our discussion he would speak in the present tense when describing moments with Mao and Chou. It was as if, in his private pantheon, they were very much still alive.

How had the Soviet Union reacted to his early China initiatives? I asked him.

147

Privately, not very well. They had learned early about his use of Yahya and Ceausescu as intermediaries. And late in 1970, in a conversation with Kissinger, Ambassador Anatoly Dobrynin complained, "I just want you to know that what President Nixon is doing in terms of a possible new relationship with China, that is a very neuralgic subject as far as my leaders are concerned."

Kissinger, according to Nixon, replied, "Mr. Ambassador, you should know that your support of our enemy in North Vietnam is a very neuralgic subject as far as President Nixon is concerned."

Nixon received advice at the time from four former U.S. ambassadors to Moscow, including Chip Bohlen, that "any opening to China or any moves toward China would torpedo the opportunity to have a better relationship with the Soviet Union."

"They proved to be wrong," Nixon continued. "Because it had exactly the opposite effect. As we moved closer to China, the Soviet Union didn't want to be left behind . . . they moved closer to us. And the same was true in reverse, as it turned out."

Or, as the former President would later say, "The Chinese game made the Russian game work and the Russian game made the Chinese game work." The language may not be as erudite as political scientists employ when they talk of the "delicate triangular relationship" established by Nixon, but it was a good deal more expressive.

Nixon recounted that during his February 1976 visit with Hua Kuo-feng, "Chairman Hua, after discussing Korea and after discussing Taiwan and these other difficult issues where we disagreed, said, 'But the important thing about our relationship is our stand against hegemony by any major country. And as long as we stand together on this, then these other issues can be brought into better focus.' "

So the Chinese, like Mr. Nixon himself, were masters of realpolitik. Nixon would later recall that they favored a strong NATO because they "don't want, basically, a one-front war with the Soviets." When he told Hua in 1976 that Communist advances in France and Italy could undermine the U.S. commitment to NATO, Hua's enthusiasm for Communist success in these countries quickly paled. For the Chinese, Nixon said, the choice is one between ideology and survival. "And when any nation makes that choice, even a Communist nation, survival comes first."

Nixon too showed himself something of a journalist. Mao, he felt, had suffered a stroke or some other debilitating illness even before that first visit in 1972. But even four years later, although close to death, "Mao was in charge of himself and he was in charge in China. And all of those around him referred to him as being the one in charge."

He was also, in 1976, "shriveled and old . . . But if you watched his hands—the thing that I remembered in both cases, in '72 and '76, his hands never got old. They were very fine, delicate hands." It seemed as good a moment as I would find for one more direct pass at the Nixon psyche: "Did you feel at that moment in almost another world in the sense that you were reliving in '76 the triumphant visit of '72? Back here at home you'd had to resign as President. Did you feel almost in a sense that you'd gone into a time machine and the clock had been rolled back four years?"

Instantly, the spell was broken.

"You know, I know those, those movies, you know with time machines and so forth are very interesting," he said condescendingly. "My daughter Tricia rather likes them and Julie to a less extent. But I never watch them and I don't read much about them . . ."

This was, in a sense, my final formative lesson in the arcane art of trying to persuade Nixon to reveal himself in a personal sense. He knew all about the psychohistorians, and the moment he felt that I was trying to put him on the couch, he ran for the hills. All his defenses went up. All his admiration for "control" came back to the surface. Tricia had been "just as controlled" in the final days as she had been on her wedding day. At another moment, he had paid Pat the same high compliment: "she's a very strong, very controlled person." Even his speech writer Ray Price had got a special mention for being "a very controlled person who seldom shows his emotion." And of course, as Nixon himself had said, "I don't like to show my emotions either."

No, the only way to get Richard Nixon to reveal himself was not directly, but indirectly. At moments in the days ahead there would be openings—moments when the psychological barricades were not being manned, or when Nixon was so caught up in a question or a topic that he would provide me with the chance to press him to go a little further. But I had to wait for the opportunity to present itself, then follow up without using any of those psychiatric "buzz words" that would break the spell.

I asked Nixon for a final judgment on the possibility of a mending of differences between the two great Communist powers. Here he was quite emphatic. He had discussed the matter at considerable length with Hua in 1976 and found the current Chairman still contemptuous of the Soviet "revisionists," still with fresh memories of the 1968 "rape of Czechoslovakia," and still desperately concerned about Soviet notions of geopolitical hegemony.

"He refers, as the Chinese do in all of their public statements, to the Soviet Union as the 'Polar Bear' reaching out its hands, and while he spoke with the threat as being one that the Chinese were not afraid of, it was quite obvious that he recognized that it was a very serious threat."

Chairman Hua told him of the 1965 meeting between Mao and Kosygin. After days of marathon discussions, Mao told his host, "Our differences are going to continue for ten thousand years."

With gusto in his voice, Nixon continued, "And Kosygin said, 'Well, Mr. Chairman, after these long discussions we've had and the reassurance I've given you, don't you think you could reduce that somewhat?' And Mao, with that devilish sense of humor he has, said, 'Well, in view of the very persuasive arguments that the Premier has made, I'll knock off a thousand years. Our disputes will continue for nine thousand years.'

"And then Hua went on to say, 'That's the way we look at it now.' "

Nixon was at his most articulate on the subject of the SALT agreement. He had won the original Senate vote for a limited ABM system by a single vote. "And I've never made more telephone calls to senators, seen more, and I don't twist arms, but I talk very firmly." This was what gave him the leverage with the Soviets when they proposed a mutual ban on ABM's.

But Nixon wanted to halt the momentum on development of offensive systems, and so, rejecting the advice of "an editorial in *The New York Times*" and "many of the soft-heads in the press," he told the Russians there would be no agreement on ABM's alone, and without a comprehensive SALT accord, there would be no corollary agreements on scientific and cultural exchanges, increased trade and environmental cooperation, all of which the Soviets deemed desirable.

Nixon offered a defense of the final SALT agreement in language calculated to gladden the heart of the most liberal member of the arms-control lobby. "If a nation is able to move forward and commit enough resources to the development of a thick nuclear system, ABM system, this would mean that it might gain enough sense of security that it would be tempted to launch a first strike offensively. And, therefore, that would change the balance of power in the world and increase the danger of war. In other words, you would no longer have the balance of terror. So, by limiting defensive weapons, this new breakthrough, limiting them and practically eliminating them now, it means that option is not open to the leader of either of the two major powers, or any power for that matter in the world, which becomes a major power in the future. Because if you cannot defend yourself against a counterstrike, you are not going to launch a first strike."

That explained the mutual ban on ABM's. But what of all those conservatives who argued that the numerical limits enjoyed by the Soviets in terms of offensive launchers—both land- and submarine-based—meant we had struck a bad deal?

"Ah, now, as far as numbers are concerned, there comes a point when they don't make that much difference. Because, unless you can strike . . . knock out your potential opponent's ability to have a counterstrike, that gives you unacceptable damage. That, in other words, it kills 40, 50, 60, 70 million of your own people. Then you do not have an advantage, even though you may have more in numbers."

And, even were a leader insane, he cannot risk losing up to 100 million of his own people in a second strike, said Nixon emphatically. "That's not an option."

As a postscript to the grain deal which followed soon after, Nixon recounted in passing that Andrei Gromyko, the Soviet Foreign Minister, had once tried to soothe his feelings on the deal by recalling, "We were just acting like capitalists in the purchase of this wheat. It was a good deal for us. If you had negotiated differently, your people, maybe you would have gotten a better deal."

All of which led us to the origins of the Yom Kippur War of October 1973 and the Soviet role in the events leading to it. During the next thirty minutes, Nixon set forth the story of the war from his perspective and provided a gripping behind-the-scenes account. My role had changed again. For the next half hour I was Boswell to his Johnson, stepping in with observations to refresh his recollection only when the Nixon narrative lost steam.

Nixon recalled, as he had at our first meeting, the San Clemente session with Brezhnev at Summit II. For three hours in that small second-floor room where Franklin Roosevelt had once played poker, "Brezhnev hammered me on the Mideast. He said, 'You must force the Israelis to withdraw from the occupied territories and you must do it soon.' "

Nixon refused. " 'You can't impose a settlement,' I said. 'It must be worked out between the parties.' " He wanted Israel to negotiate with its neighbors, he thought it would serve their long-run interests. But he also knew that the Israelis "would not and could not simply withdraw to the '67 borders, and that for me to tell Brezhnev and to promise him that I would force the Israelis to do it, and he'd go tell the Egyptians and the Syrians, that would be a promise that I couldn't deliver and I refused to make it."

Nixon tried to impress upon the Russian the need for both powers to restrain their clients. But Brezhnev was adamant. "It is my concern," he warned, "that unless the Israelis do withdraw that the Egyptians and the Syrians are going to attack and they're going to attack soon."

Nixon replied, "If they do attack, we will not let Israel go down the tube."

Nixon's narrative, and I would suspect, his actual conversations with Brezhnev and other world leaders, were often punctuated with such spicy, if not undiplomatic, utterances. In our conversations, countries would go "down the tube" with much the same regularity that their leaders would go "up the wall."

If Brezhnev's alarm affected U.S. policy in any way, it remains a mystery. Rather, as the months wore on, Nixon seemed to discount the probability of an Arab attack, and neither Israeli nor U.S. intelligence could provide much assistance. In fact, on the day before the October 6 Canal crossing, Nixon took off for a long weekend at Key Biscayne.

Nixon was bitter in recalling the C.I.A.'s failure to predict the imminence of an attack. The failure of Israeli intelligence was something else again because it "is probably as good as any in the world, next to perhaps the Russian intelligence." But the fact that on the day before the attack the C.I.A. reported that an attack "is possible, but unlikely," did not, in retrospect, appear strange. "I was not surprised to see our intelligence drop the ball," he said.

Had we dissuaded the Israelis from launching a preemptive strike as persistent accounts of the period had claimed?

No, Nixon replied. To the extent that we did so, it was only because we did not believe the attack would occur. "As far as specific restraint, if they had given us hard intelligence that a strike was coming, we would not have restrained them."

The attack came, and in its initial stages it was highly successful. The Egyptians dug in on the East Bank of the Suez, the Syrians in the Golan Heights north of Galilee. The Egyptian missile defenses were murderous, Israeli aircraft losses fearful. Both sides quickly needed heavy equipment from their superpower friends. The Soviets came rapidly to the aid of the Arabs.

But the American response has been a subject of speculation ever since. For at least eight days after the first urgent Israeli resupply requests were received, the United States did nothing. Some say the responsibility rested with Secretary of State Kissinger, who wanted to increase his bargaining leverage with the Israelis. Others place the blame at the doorstep of Defense Secretary James Schlesinger at the Pentagon, where pro-Israeli sentiment has long been restrained and where a number of military planners were wary of exhausting U.S. inventories of critical weapons.

I wanted Nixon to resolve these contrasting accounts, beginning with the messages he received from Israeli Prime Minister Golda Meir.

Her first calls came early in the war, Nixon said. "She needed equipment. So, there were all sorts of messages that went back and forth. She said that if we didn't get equipment . . . if she didn't get equipment, that they were going to suffer a great defeat. Then came the Russian airlift. And with the Russian airlift, they became, of course, the Israelis, almost terror-stricken."

Nixon asked the Pentagon what we could respond with. He got back "an option paper," which came down on the side of disguising U.S. planes as El Al planes in order to avoid the political fallout from a U.S. resupply effort. But, said Nixon, "I finally cut through all of the red tape and I said, 'Look, I mean, it isn't going to fool anybody.' I said, 'Second, what kind of an airlift is it going to be?' They said, 'Well, we thought we ought to send about three, maybe two, but possibly three C-130's, and we thought that's all the traffic would bear.'

"I said, 'Look, how many C-130's have we got?' And, I think the number came back, eighteen, twenty, twenty-five, irrelevant. I said, 'I want every C-130 that can fly to go in there. If we're going to do this, do it big, do it right, and do it quick.' "

Nixon would later explain that he had, in a sense, overruled both Kissinger and Schlesinger, in part. Schlesinger had wanted to delay. Kissinger had wanted to send fewer planes. He sensed the reaction in the Arab world would be strong. But Nixon had argued that the U.S. would take "just as much heat" for sending three planes as thirty, so his final instruction to Kissinger was to "send everything that flies."

Nixon's account may well be disputed in other memoirs, but he made the point that the Israelis themselves regard him as their friend. Golda Meir has already written, as Nixon accurately recalled, that "I never made a promise to her that I didn't keep."

With the help of U.S. supplies and their own brilliant improvisations, the tide of battle soon turned in the Israelis' favor, and they crossed the Canal. After the first of two U.N. cease-fire resolutions conveniently failed to take hold, the Israelis completed their encirclement of the Egyptians' Third Army. Now the Egyptians were desperate. According to the Nixon narrative, Sadat requested the intervention of a joint U.S.-Soviet force consisting of two divisions provided by each side.

That proposition was totally unacceptable, Nixon related. "Look, I remember one day in the Cabinet Room, very clearly, I said, 'This idea of the Russians having two Russian infantry divisions going to the Mideast and puttin' themselves down in Egypt and Syria, and we send two American marine divisions in order to keep the peace there,' I said, 'This is sheer madness.' " It ran the risk of Big Power confrontation, as well as the loss of domestic support.

With the Sadat proposal rejected and the noose tightening around the neck of Egypt's Third Army, Brezhnev dispatched his famous note to Nixon, the one that triggered the U.S. nuclear alert.

"Was it a threat?" I asked.

"What?"

"Was it a threat?"

"Ah, ah, I prefer my . . . ah, I prefer my words," said Nixon cautiously. "The note had an . . . ominous sound to it because he, in effect, said that the United States and the Soviet Union should move in, as the Egyptians had requested. He knew we had rejected that, and he said, 'If you do not move in and if you cannot restrain the Israelis, as seems to be the case at this point, or is the case at this point'—and I'm paraphrasing and it's my recollection— he said, 'It will be necessary for us to move unilaterally . . . unilaterally into the situation.'

"Unilaterally," was the key code word to Nixon. A Soviet move could tip the balance against the Israelis. It ran the risk of super-power confrontation. And it would have established the precedent of a Soviet presence in the Middle East.

And what was Nixon's reply? I sensed he was writing history again here. Even in their memoirs, Nixon and Kissinger would have to be cautious in their use of classified data or communiqués. "Did you tell him you were going on a nuclear alert?"

"No, no," replied Nixon, "I just said in my reply, and, and, it isn't proper, of course, to divulge the exact words of it, and I can't recall them exactly. All that I can say is that my reply indicated our total opposition to, first, our going in, we would not agree to go in. I indicated, second, we would be glad, of course, to partici-pate in a U.N. group with a small number of advisers, and so forth, to supervise a cease-fire, and third, that third, that we took a very dim view—I used stronger words than that—a very dim view of any unilateral action on their part of moving in."

There remained the question of how Nixon and Kissinger had managed to restrain the Israelis short of their desired goal of eradi-cating the Egyptian Third Army. Israeli zealots in the U.S. had suggested that Kissinger had confronted the Israelis with ultima-tums. No cease-fire, no American aid. Stop now, or we may have to accept the Russian proposal for a joint U.S.-Soviet force in the area.

Nixon denied the reports. It was a question of making the Israelis look beyond the short-term advantage of a crushing vic-tory. Their enlightened self-interest dictated a saving of Arab face. Had the second cease-fire resolution not been obeyed and had Egypt gone down to ignominious defeat, "Somebody would have come into power in Egypt, probably worse than Nasser, oriented toward the radical point of view. Egypt would have become a total Soviet satellite state, and Israel would have won a Pyrrhic victory. They would have planted the seeds for a war of revenge such as you've never seen. And, therefore, we were right in restraining Israel, right from their own self-interest."

Yes, but what form did the pressure take?

"Conversation," Nixon replied. By then, "I had some money in the bank with them. They trusted me." He could cite the airlift and the alert. "So we had some leverage with them," Nixon continued. "But the point was, in exerting this leverage, it was for their own good. Because, in the final analysis, Israel is not going to be able to conquer all their neighbors. Israel is not going to be able to continue to exist, unless it has a better relationship with its neighbors, which they're presently working for."

I wanted even more specificity. "So what was, what was the bottom line, really?" I asked. "That you had the leverage and the bottom line, probably never stated, was: if you don't go along with this cease-fire, the United States will not be able to dot, dot, dot . . . ?"

Again Nixon resisted. There had been no threat, no ultimatum. "What we did was to reason with them, but to reason [with] them in a way, we in effect, if I may paraphrase from *The Godfather*, we gave them an offer that they could not refuse. And the offer was, 'Look, the United States will continue to stand by you. We have demonstrated that we will come to your aid with arms if you come under attack, but on your side, if we will take such risks, including not only the airlift, but an alert in order to save you, you must listen to us, at least in terms of being reasonable in talking to your potential enemies.'"

Throughout the discussion, Nixon's admiration, his genuine affection for the Israeli people, if not all their supporters in this country, was evident. He spoke of their brilliance, their toughness, their commitment, with undisguised esteem. And when he recited accounts of policy disagreements, he left no doubt in my mind that he was indeed as concerned with the best long-run interests of the Israelis as with the geopolitical dilemmas of his own government.

In a sense, Nixon's feelings about Israel were as revealing as his obvious reverence for the Chinese leaders. For if the Chinese patriarchs had exhibited in their personal lives the ability to struggle, to fight, to lose, to come back, to fight again, to triumph over adversity and to continue to struggle even after reaching the top, then Israel's character as a nation was also rich in the sort of symbolism that Richard Nixon appreciated and revered.

157

No Harris poll would show the Israelis unwilling to fight, and Nixon knew that. No bearded unkempt Israeli minions would storm the Knesset urging peace at any price. The Israeli people did not seek haven as exiles when their country was in peril. Rather they struggled to return home, to take up arms and to join the battle as soldier-citizens.

Israeli leaders were not forced to seek fig leaves. They sought victory. Israeli victories were swift and certain, not agonizing and ambiguous. When Israel fought, there was no discussion of dominoes. There was only one domino the Israelis cared about and they knew it would fall the first time they lost a war.

Israel was smart and tough, two qualities which, when combined by Nixon, comprised the ultimate compliment he could bestow upon an individual or a nation. Israel would never be a superpower like the United States. But it would never be a pitiful helpless giant either.

Nixon could add little to the Israeli character. But he could provide a little advice, a few words of wisdom. So he had used our session to urge repeatedly that the Israelis listen to reason, that they adopt a more conciliatory position towards their neighbors, that they show a willingness to compromise on the short-run issues in order that their long-run survival could be assured.

And as we concluded our session and he rose from his chair, he said softly, "Hope the Israelis are listening . . ."

Next on our agenda was Chile, a subject which had outraged world opinion probably even more than it had domestic opinion. The way that the Nixon administration had played havoc with the internal politics of a smaller country had stirred almost universal concern, a concern that we all shared.

Yet, oddly, for the first fifteen minutes the debate obstinately failed to catch fire. In the monitor room my staff were waiting patiently—wrong, impatiently!—for me to go on the offensive: on the set I was waiting for an opening. It took too long, but eventually it came.

It began when I asked Nixon what he "had in mind" when he

told C.I.A. Director Richard Helms that "you wanted the C.I.A. or you wanted America to make the economy scream" in the course of a meeting that took place on September 15 between the date of Allende's 36 percent plurality and the date the Chilean Congress voted him formally into office.

"Well, Chile, of course, is interested in obtaining loans from international organizations where we have a vote, and I indicated that wherever we had a vote where Chile was involved that unless there was strong considerations on the other side that we would vote against them . . ."

I was not quite sure why Nixon would have chosen his C.I.A. chief as the vehicle for such sober economic strategy, but he proceeded to justify the instruction on the basis of all the property that Allende was expropriating.

"He hadn't done that on September 15," I interrupted.

Recognizing that he had been caught in the web of his own obfuscation, Nixon explained that he "knew that was coming" because of Allende's campaign promises. In fact, he recalled Allende saying, " 'With Cuba in the Caribbean and with Chile on the southern cone, we'—he meant Castro and Allende—'will make the revolution in Latin America . . .' "

Nixon then went on to read a short litany of Allende's allegedly repressive acts: running a Marxist program on the government-owned station, cutting back advertising in private papers he didn't like, shutting down the UPI office in Santiago for a short time, closing the newspaper *El Mercurio* for a day.

I would have dearly liked to dwell for a moment on *El Mercurio,* a paper notorious for having been heavily subsidized by the C.I.A., but there was a more important point triggered off by Nixon's answer.

"When you look at the closing of the UPI office, for instance, and things like that . . . all of those things are trivial compared with what followed Allende. I mean, Allende with the . . . all of that list looks like a saint compared with the repression of Pinochet."

Nixon backed off a bit. "That's right . . . I am not here to defend and will not defend repression by any government, be it a friend of the United States or one that is opposed to the United States . . ."

He then made the one argument for his cause of at least colorable validity. "But in terms of national security, in terms of our own self-interest, the right-wing dictatorship, if it is not exporting its revolution, if it is not interfering with its neighbors, if it is not taking action directed against the United States, it is therefore of no security concern to us. It is of a human rights concern. A left-wing dictatorship, on the other hand, we find that they do engage in trying to export their subversion to other countries. And that does involve our security interests."

True enough in the abstract, I thought. But totally absurd when applied to Allende.

"In fact," I responded, "what they have now with Pinochet *is* a right-wing dictatorship. What they had with Allende was a left-wing or Marxist democracy. It was never a dictatorship."

NIXON: Let's understand . . .
FROST: Was it . . . was it though?
NIXON: No, I don't agree with your assertion whatever. I . . . oh . . . I would . . .
FROST: It was not a dictatorship, was it?
NIXON: It was . . . you said it was not a dictatorship, and my point is Allende was a very subtle and a very clever man . . ."

Dictatorship, Nixon added, was Allende's ultimate goal.

FROST: But the C.I.A. reported shortly before his death that he was not a threat to democracy. He wasn't planning to abolish democracy. And he was going to lose in the next election.
NIXON: Based on the C.I.A.'s record of accuracy in their reports, I would take all that with a grain of thalt—salt. They didn't even predict that he was going to win this time. They didn't predict what was going to happen in Cambodia. They didn't even predict that there was going to be a Yom Kippur War . . .

This was tenuous ground for Nixon. He had begun the discussion by making his case for his Chilean actions by hypothesizing a

Cuba-Chile axis. When that didn't seem to work, he had moved on to Allende's antidemocratic actions inside Chile. Then he had moved on to Chile's alleged attempts to export revolution, but that had made little headway. So now he was reduced to grousing about the C.I.A. again, an all-purpose defense to any flawed policy. But the implications there were disastrous to his cause. If a President can't rely on the intelligence provided by his own intelligence agency, does he simply sit at his desk and follow blind intuition?

Not quite. Nixon was ready with a new source of wisdom, this time "an Italian businessman" who came calling on the White House months before Allende's 1970 election. "And he said, if Allende should win the election in Chile and then you have Castro in Cuba, what you will in effect have in Latin America is a red sandwich. And eventually it will all be red. And that's what we confronted."

"A red sandwich"? What an outrageous piece of Cold War hyperbole, I thought.

> FROST: But—but that's madness of him to say that. I mean, how—
> NIXON: It isn't madness at all. It shows somebody saying, cutting through the hypocritical double standard of those who can see all the dangers on the right . . .
> FROST: No . . . no . . . but surely, no . . .
> NIXON: . . . and don't look at the dangers on the left.
> FROST: No, but surely, Mr. President . . . there's two . . . you've got little Cuba and little Chile, and all those enormous countries in between. It's like . . . If it's a red sandwich, it's got two pieces of bread here [I raised my arms as far apart as possible] and an enormous bit of beef in the middle. I mean, are you really saying that Brazil should feel itself surrounded by Cuba and Chile?

Nixon was fighting to hold his temper. Though I didn't know it then, Khachigian had warned Zelnick days earlier that the former President had a short fuse on the subject. Getting rid of little left-wing upstarts—or at least trying to—was something of a minor sport among American Presidents, a bit like falconry to the medieval English princes. Look at Ike and Guatemala, J.F.K. and

Castro, Johnson and the Dominican Republic. And now, just because it was Richard Nixon, people are up in arms. Well, screw 'em.

"All I can say is that as far as Brazil is concerned, as far as Argentina is concerned, the other countries in that part of the hemisphere . . . I have visited most of them—in 1958, for example —and I can testify to the fact that many of their governments are potentially unstable. I can testify to the fact that also they do have a problem of subversion . . ."

No, he was not saying that Argentina or Brazil need fear an invasion, or Venezuela an amphibious assault, but "Castro has caused plenty of problems to his neighbors," and, with Allende in Chile, the threat was doubled.

So his Italian friend had not been a madman. "Well, he's mad like a fox, because what he's doing is taking the historical view, and that is, he knows the nature of Communism . . ."

But Nixon wanted to move on.

"I didn't mean that it was an immediate threat," he concluded, "but I meant that if you let one go, you're going to have some problems with others. So, we'll just let the red sandwich sit right there because, obviously, you've got other subjects to cover."

For the first time, I sensed that he could be debated to the point where he actually wanted to break contact and retreat.

"Well, ah, we'll stick with this one," I suggested.

"Oh," said Nixon with a shrug, as if to suggest he had merely been trying to be helpful, "I can take this one as long as you want . . ."

We had already gotten some clue as to the way that Nixon would deal with the subject of Henry Kissinger during our Vietnam discussions.

"The American people had been told that peace was at hand" on October 26, Nixon had said. While Kissinger's words had been "totally true" at the time, nevertheless Henry, "who is hard on other people in his criticism" and also "hard on himself," had had second thoughts about the wisdom of his statement. "That, he realized, boxed us a bit into a corner. Because by saying 'peace is at hand' it put the North Vietnamese in a position where they realized that, ah, we had to have peace."

"Did the fact that the number of liberal columnists at that time gained the impression from Henry Kissinger that he was opposed to the bombing, madden you? . . . It must have irked you a little," I had asked.

"Well, frankly, I was surprised and I was shocked, and he knew that," Nixon had replied. "And I checked it out. I couldn't really believe that he could have talked to these people and found that he had. I talked to him later about it, and as a matter of fact, I talked to him prior to the time that we had done our broadcast, because I wanted to be sure that his recollections were the same as mine. And he says . . . as far as this particular matter was concerned, that he supported the decision to bomb. Ah, he supported it throughout. And that those that claimed that he didn't support it were not representing his views accurately."

Nixon had then offered what was on its face a supportive view of Kissinger's conduct, but which on closer reading would seem patronizing, even condescending. "He used to be very frustrated with some of his friends. But they were his friends. I mean, he ran in that set. He respected them because of their intelligence. And they respected him. And he thought he could leaven their criticism a bit. Ah, consequently, he often took the position with them that was basically more reasonable than the position, that perhaps I was, ah, appeared to be taking. He did not do it for the purpose of making points for himself, in my view, but because he wanted to keep his leverage with them. He wanted to keep his credibility with them."

And in order to do that, Kissinger approached them in such a way that some "may have gathered the impression, which I think was mistaken, that Kissinger actually recommended against the bombing . . . that later on that, uh, it was a mistake to have done it, some have even gone that far." And then the curiously cautiously worded finale: "In my view, that's not my recollection, and that's not Dr. Kissinger's recollection: and we ought to know, we were there."

Now, several days later, as we dealt with the subject of Henry Kissinger at some length, Nixon's tactics remained the same. Gently, subtly, ever so carefully, he was trying to put Henry down as a brilliant but rather moody, emotionally mercurial, sometimes unreliable fellow who was able to remain effective only because of Nixon's stabilizing influence.

Thus after the Cambodian incursion, which Kissinger "totally supported," then the resulting Kent State tragedy, "Henry came in one day and said, 'You know, I am not sure that we should have gone into this Cambodian thing, and perhaps now has come the time when we should shorten the time and get out a little sooner.' "

Of course, Nixon knew "he wasn't seriously considering it." He just needed a little moral starch. "And I said, Henry, I said, we've done it. I said, remember Lot's wife. Never look back."

And then a sly nudge in the direction of his Jewish colleague. "I don't know whether Henry had read the Old Testament or not. But I had. And he got the point."

That little episode established a pattern in their relationship. Often in the future, Henry would question an initiative after it was undertaken. And "whenever he would come in and say, 'Well, I'm not sure we should have done this or that or the other thing,' I would say, 'Henry, remember Lot's wife.' And that would end the conversation."

Well, since Henry was such an emotional fellow, "how many times, for instance, did he say he might resign?"

"Oh, to me, he would hint it on occasion," Nixon began. The man who retreated each time he suspected a question was probing too deeply into his own psychology now launched into another analysis of Kissinger's. Henry, he said, while "cool and cold and controlled" in his dealings with foreign leaders, "had a tendency to get highly elated by some piece of good news and very depressed by something he considered to be bad news."

True to his own historic pattern of suggesting an obvious conclusion and then withdrawing from making it, Nixon immediately cautioned, "That doesn't mean that he was emotionally unstable . . ."

Of course not, I thought, just your normal, everyday, run-of-the-mill manic-depressive.

It was all, Nixon insisted, a product of Henry's genius: "He can see the heights and also see the depths; and he feels them both."

Nixon contrasted Henry's moodiness with his own Job-like acceptance of adversity, recalling Churchill's admonition that "the brightest moments are those that flash away the fastest."

And he would constantly keep poor Henry on track, reminding him, "Well, Henry, the situation hasn't changed. We shouldn't have been as elated as we were yesterday, and we shouldn't be so discouraged today."

It happened in the SALT negotiations, and in Vietnam, and in the Middle East.

Oh, yes, and getting back to my question, Henry would never really threaten to resign when depressed, just suggest that his usefulness might be through.

"How many times did he come in and say that maybe, maybe he should resign?" I had hoped to get specifics. Instead, I got one of the most revealing insights into Kissinger's dazzling success in seizing the reins of foreign policy in the White House and in holding them against all challengers.

Kissinger had suggested resignation "maybe half a dozen times" directly to him, Nixon said, and to others, like Haig and Haldeman, more often.

"Henry couldn't stand bureaucratic infighting," Nixon continued. He had problems with Secretary of State Bill Rogers, a longtime personal friend of the President.

Rogers, it seemed, had the temerity to want to exert some influence in the making of foreign policy, a not unreasonable desire on the part of a Secretary of State.

This, of course, was out of the question. "There could be only one person to handle some of these major issues, and where secrecy was involved, I mean, secret negotiations, it had to be Henry, ah, in the areas like Vietnam, China, Russia and the Mideast."

Which, of course, left Bill Rogers in sole control of all U.S. initiatives towards Sri Lanka, Finland and Chad.

Not only did Henry elbow Rogers out of the decision-making process, but the unfortunate Secretary, "who had to make public statements all the time and testify and answer questions before the Congress, wasn't informed about things."

"He wanted to be informed," said Nixon. "Well, Henry would come to me—and we had several arguments about it—he would say, 'I will not inform Rogers, because he'll leak.'

"And, I said, 'Henry'—I must have told him this a dozen times—I said . . . 'Henry, the State Department bureaucracy will leak. It always has. It always will.' I said, 'But Bill Rogers will never leak, if we . . . if I tell him it's in confidence.'"

In fact, Henry didn't even want to tell Rogers about the China opening, but here the President put his foot down. "Rogers has gotta know," he said. "You cannot have the Secretary of State not be informed, because he has got to take off the day that announcement is made," informing foreign ambassadors about the move.

The picture of Nixon—who bombed Hanoi and invaded Cambodia, who shook hands with Mao and concluded SALT I with Brezhnev—pleading with Henry to tell Rogers that he would shortly be visiting Peking, struck me as brilliant in its irony.

"Did Henry say that he'd resign if John Connally was appointed Secretary of State?" I asked.

Here again, while trying to take a few subtle pokes at Kissinger, Nixon again revealed his own consummate inability to deal with his foreign-policy adviser.

"Not to me," Nixon said crisply. But, of course, Henry saw in Connally a threat because "everything that Connally touches in the political arena, Connally controls."

And, "Henry, to his credit, was loyal to his former patron, and still his patron, Nelson Rockefeller."

As Secretary of State, Nixon reasoned, Connally would have had a better shot than Rockefeller at the 1976 Republican presidential nomination.

"Were you actually considering John Connally as Secretary of State?"

"Yes," Nixon conceded. "But, in this case, while Henry did not have a veto power—nobody can have a veto power where the President is concerned, any President—but, while he didn't have a veto power, it was indispensable that whoever was Secretary of State be able to work with Henry and Henry be able to work with him."

"In other words," Nixon said with great emphasis, "I had gone through the Rogers-Kissinger feud for four years, and I didn't want to buy another feud with another Secretary of State for the rest of the four years."

The problem, though, was that in trying to find someone Henry could get along with, the putative contender had to be both Henry's intellectual equal and yet someone "Henry would not feel was a competitor who would threaten his position of being the President's major foreign-policy adviser." Having struggled so long and successfully for primacy, "he couldn't therefore tolerate a Secretary of State who would impinge on that position."

There was, of course, only one human being in the world whom Henry would regard as both an intellectual equal and a nonthreat, and that was Henry himself. And with the field thus culled, Henry got the post.

It was all I could do to keep a straight face on the set. For no man prized his prerogatives as President more than Richard Nixon. Few were more diligent students of the uses of power. Few were prouder of their international reputation as an *homme sérieux*. And yet here was Nixon admitting virtual helplessness at the hands of Henry's brilliant palace intrigues.

There was, of course, one question which had to be asked and, I thought, the more informal the approach, the better.

"Dustin Hoffman once made a film called *Who Is Harry Kellerman and Why Is He Saying All Those Terrible Things About Me?* Now as you read accounts, knowing what a successful working relationship you had in many areas, of remarks attributed to Henry Kissinger, whether it's in the *New Republic* or at the Ottawa banquet or whatever, you must sometimes feel, you know who Henry Kissinger is, but don't you sometimes feel, why is he saying all those terrible things about me?"

Nixon nodded his head. The subject, I felt, had not taken him completely by surprise.

"Well, to answer the question quite candidly, it drives my family right up the wall. And it's only because it bothers them that it would bother me at all."

Mentally, I started to total up the points Nixon would score on this one. One: Henry's a louse. He drives poor Pat, Tricia and Julie up the wall. Two: Nixon's too big a man to let it bother him.

"After such accounts appear, I know that I always get a call from Henry on the phone explaining that there's been either a misquotation or misinterpretation. And, I have always said to him, 'Forget it . . .'"

Three: Henry comes crawling back, tail between legs. Four: Nixon forgives.

"And I think what we have to understand too is that Henry likes to say outrageous things. He's kind of like Alice Longworth that way. She, as she puts it, she says, 'You know, I like to be naughty sometimes. I like to say things that are devilish.'"

Five: Henry's a bit frivolous. Six: The Old Man deserves a point for that imitation of Alice Roosevelt Longworth. Lips puckered, face crinkled. Outstanding.

Henry's different from other intellectuals, Nixon continued. They're only interested in a person's brains. "But Henry, on the other hand, was fascinated first by the celebrity set, and second, he liked being one himself."

Seven: Deep down, Henry's shallow. (And have you heard about that ego?)

Nixon related that he used to be invited to Georgetown and Hollywood dinner parties all the time. He stopped going because he realized that he was being invited to entertain the guests with tales of the rich and powerful. But Henry still goes. "Well, anyway, that's Henry. Henry, when he goes to these parties, and he likes parties. I despise them, because I've been to so many. I used to like them, but Henry will learn to despise them too after he's been through a few more."

Eight: Henry has a lot of growing up to do.

In any event, "I can see exactly what happened in Canada. He runs into a lady who has a very low opinion of me and so Henry feels that really he's defending me and that the best way to defend

168

is to concede that, well, he's sort of an odd person, he's an artificial person . . ."

Nine: You're too good, Mr. President. You're just too good. Can't you see through that phony, two-faced ingrate?

"The only problem was that he didn't think to turn the microphone off. On the other hand, I didn't turn it off either in the Oval Office on occasions, so I never held him for that!"

Ten (a knockout): Self-effacing humor—and more forgiveness—from Richard Nixon. Amazing!

Weeks later, just before our foreign policy show was aired, I was speaking on the telephone with Henry Kissinger in Washington.

"I suppose that this week you take off on me," he said. "I expect that I am portrayed as a sort of neurotic genius in need of strong leadership."

"Henry, are you sure you haven't been bugging the sessions?"

"Oh, no," said Henry. "I just know my boy."

CHAPTER

8

I AM RARELY RENDERED SPEECHLESS. BUT RICHARD NIXON ACHIEVED that feat the following Monday morning. Not on the set, I am glad to say, but on our way to the set.

Small talk is not the greatest of Richard Nixon's gifts. It is serious talk that he prefers. Indeed, it has often baffled me how he managed to get through thirty years of political fund raisers and cocktail gossip. He does try, however. With our cameramen, for example, he attempted, not unsuccessfully, to develop an all-hardhats-together, deze-and-doze-guys-of-the-world-unite type of bantering relationship. Now on this particular Monday morning as we moved toward the set he must have felt the moment had come for us to be "one of the boys" together too.

"Well," he said as we crossed the Smiths' kitchen, "did you do any fornicating this weekend?"

For a moment, I could not believe the evidence of my own ears. Richard Nixon didn't say that, did he? He couldn't have. I must have heard it wrong. But no. One look at the startled faces of the people near us convinced me that I had indeed heard it right. In-

171

wardly I had to smile—to warm to the sheer clumsiness of his words. And I knew that really he did not want to know the answer.

So I said, "No comment. I never discuss my private life," as if at a mock press conference, and by then we were on the set.

That Monday morning we were about to tape an hour of special material for Italy and a half hour each for Australia and France, before beginning domestic policy in the afternoon. On the previous Friday afternoon, we had taped an hour of material for Britain.

We had asked the distinguished foreign producers who had flown out for the sessions to prepare the basic questions themselves. They were sophisticated, probing, and quite relevant to the conduct of U.S. foreign policy under Nixon, and often tough. Angelo Campanella and Gul Wines of RAI of Italy, Jacques Chattard of TF1, the first network of France, Mike Ramsden of the National Nine Network of Australia and Peter Pagnamenta of the BBC all focused, of course, on the areas of special interest to their own audiences. But in effect that is what foreign policy is all about anyway: conducting relationships which sustain the vital interest of one's own country while remaining palatable to the natural objects of the country's diplomatic "bounty."

Nixon fielded all the questions with grace and seriousness. He had obviously worked just as hard preparing for these three hours as for the remainder of the sessions, though his motive was somewhat different. For in responding to interrogation intended for a domestic audience, Nixon was addressing a group which regarded him, by and large, as an exile, disgraced among the community of decent citizens. He was fighting to regain as much of his good name as he possibly could and to place even those actions which did not lend themselves to facile justification within the context of his larger domestic and foreign initiatives.

But Nixon had betrayed no mandate from citizens abroad. He had threatened none of their institutions. (No Chilean producers were present.) Many had not understood or had been shocked by his treatment in the United States. Some still regarded him as a consummate world statesman. Most still took him seriously. And even among his harshest foreign critics, there were many who regarded him as a tragic figure in the classic sense: a man of limited character who had striven valiantly to rise above his own limitations, succeeding for a while but destroyed in the end by his own inherent flaws.

So in responding to domestic audiences, Nixon was in a sense fighting to win back something of what he had lost. In responding to foreign audiences, he was fighting to keep whatever he still had. And both objectives called for the utmost skill and preparation.

Most of all during the three hours, the sense came through of how much Nixon had enjoyed dealing with foreign leaders, regardless of their philosophies. As John Birt would later remark, "People who run things get along very well with one another. They may be competitors, but the level of personal communion transcends the divergent interests they represent."

This "level of personal communion" had survived Nixon's Watergate ordeal and his forced resignation. He spoke of such leaders as Rabin, Sadat and others who had telephoned during visits to the United States. The Chinese ambassador had also come to Casa Pacifica, and the People's Republic of China had of course invited him to Peking to commemorate the fourth anniversary of his 1972 visit. Ceausescu's son had stopped by and such longtime colleagues as Italy's Andriotti and Australia's Menzies had sent supportive notes during his darkest hours. And there were many others, Nixon assured us, who might be embarrassed by being named in our broadcast.

These men had all been to "the mountaintop." They knew both the exhilaration and the evanescence of power. They greeted each other with one, or both, out of office as enthusiastically as when meeting Prime Ministers or chiefs of state. Theirs was a lonely, unstable world which created its own moral precepts. Once having accepted the fundamental rightness of their own national interests, it was only a matter of time before notions of expedience and morality merged. Pragmatism in the conduct of international business was not an alternative to morality. It became its ultimate expression.

To many of these men, the abuses of power of which Richard Nixon stood charged seemed petty at best, if not a contradiction in terms. Power was abused only when it was used stupidly, un-pragmatically, recklessly—that is to say, against one's national interest. Richard Nixon had wielded the power of the United States in a way that commanded their respect. He had been undone by do-gooders. In exile he remained an *homme sérieux* still in good standing in the international fraternity of those who had known power.

Domestic policy as such had always posed something of a problem. Zelnick had written months earlier: "There is little question that Richard Nixon knew less about domestic than foreign policy, that he cared less about it and that he accomplished strikingly little in the domestic realm during his presidency.

"Welfare reform, consolidation of the bureaucracy, tax reform, national health insurance and some form of assistance to the nation's declining cities remained programs to be written by Jimmy Carter on a slate left virtually clean by Mr. Nixon. Energy policy remains unsettled. Nixon left a modest revenue-sharing program and a more conservative Supreme Court, but little else." Even his new economic game plan of August 1971 seemed undramatic now, created as it was to combat figures of 5.5 percent unemployment and 4.5 percent inflation, which already appeared almost as an economic paradise. And had not Richard Nixon himself told author Teddy White before his election in 1968 that he felt that domestically the country could just about run itself?

Candidate Nixon had gone on to tell Teddy White that he felt that the President could make his most profound contribution to his country in the area of foreign policy. Indeed, more and more we were beginning to see the Nixon domestic policy as an outgrowth of his foreign-policy decisions. We decided to test the Jonathan Schell thesis. In his book *The Time of Illusion* Schell had argued that Nixon's need to rally a domestic constituency behind his Vietnam War policies had led him to fabricate a number of domestic policies which, while devoid of serious content, created illusions of dealing with those issues likely to be of concern to the constituency that Nixon was putting together. The choice was simplistic, divisive rhetoric rather than real solutions to problems, or rather than admitting that real solutions were difficult if not impossible to come by.

"I know it means darting in and out of a great many different subjects," said Zelnick during our brief lunch break. "But with any luck Nixon won't realize quite what we're getting at."

Bob was certainly right about that. Nixon was alternatively expansive, reserved, candid, defensive, friendly and hostile, as we moved from topic to topic in an attempt to demonstrate a complex theory in all too short a time.

I recalled the $400,000 he had pumped into the 1970 gubernatorial campaign of Jim Brewer, in an effort to get Wallace out of politics.

"Oh, it was certainly in my interest that we did not have a third-party candidate, and that we therefore have a clear majority in 1972," Nixon conceded.

"And, incidentally, it's a very common practice in American politics, and one which I guess you would call Republican revenue sharing," he added magnanimously. "We had a little bit more than we needed and we shared it with them."

I moved on into Nixon's much vaunted anticrime battle, wondering whether no-knock, preventive detention and a stricter Supreme Court had really made much of a dent in the national crime figures. "As it turns out, that was an oversimplification, wasn't it?"

Nixon did not agree. He claimed that between his 1969 inauguration and 1972, crime in Washington diminished by 50 percent, the District of Columbia being of course the only area for which he could legislate directly.

Hours earlier, Reston and Zelnick had at my request checked with F.B.I. and Justice Department sources and obtained information showing the substantial increase in violent crime in the District, particularly rape and murder, during the 1969 to 1974 period, Nixon's entire presidency. There now followed a long and at times acrimonious debate over whose statistics were right. It would never be a serious contender for inclusion in any of our programs, but it was important to me personally as a demonstration of the way in which Nixon could be challenged even on statistics he had

175

asserted with total apparent confidence. (And the extraordinary divergence between his statistics and ours was later explained when it emerged that Nixon had inadvertently overstated his case, and that the *increase* in the rate of crime in Washington had diminished by 50 percent during the period he was discussing.)

I suggested that maybe "you raised false expectations, false hopes that there could be a simple cure for the crime rate."

Nixon disagreed vigorously. Did I realize the situation he had inherited? Had I realized that between 1960 and 1968 crime had increased "ten times as fast as the population increased"?

What on earth did that mean? What if, for example, in a particular period the population was to go down? What would that do to such statistics? The increase in the rate of crime could become "minus four thousand times the increase in the population . . ."

Nixon did not have the absolute figures for the increase in crime between 1960 and 1969, and we moved on to his controversial Supreme Court nominations.

"Was your reason for wanting strict constructionists on the Supreme Court partially to send the message that the era of permissiveness was over to the people?" I asked.

Nixon said "Certainly." I asked him if the nomination of G. Harrold Carswell was a mistake. "Yes, it was," Nixon answered. And then having confessed error, he went on into a recital of the mitigating circumstances. I then quoted the dean of the Yale Law School and Nixon again conceded that Carswell's "legal credentials and intellectual credentials, as I look at them in retrospect, were not equal to those of Burger, of Blackmun, or Rehnquist and Powell." Or indeed those of the rejected Clement Haynsworth, whom he described as "a towering intellectual." No, like Haynsworth, Carswell had been disapproved, at least in part, because he was a Southerner and a strict constructionist.

That didn't add up, I replied, because Powell was confirmed and he was a Southerner and Rehnquist was confirmed and he was among the most conservative strict constructionists of all time.

Nixon had made the admission we had hoped for. But we had not been able to recapture the true feeling of the period with the furious allegations back and forth. Maybe that was impossible, but I had the sense that Nixon had somehow diffused or defused his admission.

In the last few minutes of the day Nixon denied that he had a "Southern strategy," claiming instead to have had a nonexclusionary "national strategy." He defended his civil rights record, and we discussed why it had been "misunderstood." But our time was almost up. We would have to continue on Wednesday.

"Are you going to keep on with this civil rights stuff?" Nixon asked as we rose.

"Yes, I think so."

"Go ahead, if you want to," he said. "I can answer any question you raise. But my advice is to leave it alone. Nobody is interested in this anymore."

John Birt arrived back from London on Tuesday, and immediately sat down to view what had taken place in his absence. He was encouraged by what he saw of foreign policy, but decidedly less enthusiastic about what he saw of our domestic policy opener the day before. He summed it up succinctly. "I think you're quite right that Nixon didn't know what you were getting at," he said. "The trouble is, neither did I! Neither will the audience. We will have to complete the civil rights discussion very quickly, and then move right on. I suspect very little of what I've seen of Monday afternoon will survive editing."

I did not fully appreciate it at the time, but as we headed towards the last of our pre-Easter taping sessions and the period of intense round-the-clock preparations for Watergate itself, the project was experiencing a loss of momentum, a decline in morale, and a cloud of doubt which forty-eight hours later would roll over the group as thickly as any Los Angeles smog. In retrospect, it's easy to see that one of the reasons was quite simply tiredness. Almost everybody had been working round the clock. Bob had scarcely looked up from his papers. Apart from the taping sessions, Jim was devoting himself to preparing for Watergate. John had not only been working flat out in California and while he was back in London, but

mixed in with all of that there was a soupçon of jet lag. Jørn
Winther had been spending days at Monarch Bay and nights at
Don Stern Productions editing the rough cut of what we thought
was going to be our Vietnam show. When he sat in the control
room, he expected to be the man with the last word. So did John
Birt. And on this project it had to be John. Which, added to Jørn's
lack of sleep, did not help anybody's temper in the truck.

Even Libby was tired. And that was a very rare phenomenon.
To her room at the Beverly Hilton were channeled the hundreds
of phone calls each day from colleagues, business associates, journalists and advertisers. (No, not advertisers; I had to telephone
them!) She was also my long-distance link with New York, London
and Sydney. And by night she was the typist, working until the
early hours.

"I feel like the hotel tart, running from room to room from midnight until two each morning," she complained on more than one
occasion. "My liaisons are many and my satisfactions few."

But on Wednesday morning, as we set off for Monarch Bay, those
undercurrents were still not really visible. John and Bob both
had points they wanted to make.

"Nixon knew that by making the decisions he did to continue
fighting the war until he could obtain peace on his terms, the
trauma in America would continue," said Bob. "Then later, in the
October or November period, he realizes that he can either change
his policy and quiet dissent, or take the battle to the dissenters by
mobilizing the so-called Silent Majority. The choice that he opted
for was cold and calculated."

"In effect," Birt interjected, "he chose a policy of divide and
rule and there was nothing casual or accidental about it. Indeed,
it was not even limited to the war issue. You've already been exploring its ramifications in areas like crime and civil rights. It was
as fundamental a characteristic of Nixon's leadership style as anything one can mention."

"But what is the alternative?" I argued. "Surrender to the will
of a dedicated minority?"

"In a democracy, that may very well be the alternative, oddly enough," said Birt. "At its best, democracy is a constant shifting process of accommodation to majority and minority sentiment. The convictions of a minority may often be permitted to prevail if they are held with greater passion than those of the majority. In a free society, intensity of feeling is often as important as the mere numbers that would be reflected through the taking of a plebiscite."

"I see your argument," I said. "But I don't *feel* it. I don't think it's a strong case, or a particularly desirable inevitability."

"The best of our leaders have never been dividers," said Zelnick. "The best of our leaders have been unifiers, conciliators, consensus seekers. They use their power, but they remain awed by it. They seek harmony, not twelve-chord dissonance. Lincoln presided over a country beset by civil war. Yet he never lost sight of the need to bind wounds and unify. Had Nixon delivered Lincoln's second inaugural, he would have said 'With malice for all, and with charity for none . . .' "

A good impassioned rhetorical flourish, I thought. But it doesn't get us very far in terms of a face-to-face interview.

"One other thing," said John. "You spent a lot of time in the United States during the Nixon presidency. If you don't recognize the picture he draws of the America he saw from the White House, don't hesitate to tell him so."

We began with a postscript on civil rights. I read into our record, as it were, the comments of respected civil rights leaders like Father Theodore Hesburgh and Roy Wilkins condemning the actions of the Nixon White House. Nixon said he was not insensitive to black demands. Nor was he desirous of severing his own contact with the black community and its leaders. But it seemed that many of these leaders regarded confrontation with him as more helpful than establishment of a dialogue.

He recalled one instance where, at the urging of his domestic counselor Daniel Patrick Moynihan, he had agreed to meet privately with the Reverend Ralph Abernathy of the Southern Christian Leadership Conference, and others among the "more extreme" group of black leaders. "Not extreme in terms of advocating violence . . . but extreme in terms of saying that anything we did was not enough." At the session itself, Abernathy "couldn't have been more understanding or more conciliatory."

Half an hour or so after Abernathy left, however, into the room came "great big Pat Moynihan waving his arms, livid with rage." After that lovely session, Moynihan told him, Abernathy " 'went out and made a totally vicious unreasonable partisan attack . . . He went out and pissed on the President of the United States. And,' he says, 'that's wrong.' "

It was time to turn to our main theme. There were several of our subthemes that I felt were too literary or too pat, about which I felt very little zest for combat. However, if necessary, we could experiment.

I began by reminding Nixon of the unifying theme struck in his inaugural address and the subsequent unleashing of Spiro Agnew, together with his own "Silent Majority" rhetoric. "Now where, in between those two days did you, would you put the Damascus moment, when you realized that all hope of speaking quietly and bringing everybody together was hopeless, and that in fact you had a war on your hands. When was the moment when in effect you said, 'Okay, no more Mr. Nice Guy'?"

I had phrased the last sentence as unofficially as possible, in the hope of forcing him to forsake an official answer. For a moment it worked. "Well, as far as being no more Mr. Nice Guy, a . . . I would not claim that a . . . I never received that ah, particular ah, description before . . ." But eventually he regained his verbal balance, and the flow of rhetoric began. Neither he nor Agnew had "goaded the demonstrators." They "didn't need any goading." Impervious to his efforts to end the war honorably, they were holding massive Washington demonstrations, some peaceful, others less peaceful.

Apart from the violence, a second, even more important, question was, "Are we going to allow our potential enemies, those that we were negotiating with in Paris, [to] gain the impression that they represent the majority? In other words, are we going to have [a] situation where this war would be lost in Washington as the French lost . . . in 1954 in Paris rather than in Dienbienphu?"

For the next hour or so, scarcely anything went right. The Nixon rhetoric was lengthy and generally banal. My attempts to lead him away into other areas were either resisted or proved to be what Nixon himself would have called "dry holes." I talked about him "rallying his support," and tried to get him to define the support that he was seeking. When we talked about "Spiro Agnew going out as the cutting edge," Nixon insisted that it was the media who "struck the first blow there." Nixon's role in the preparation of the Agnew speeches did not take us very far. The first of the passes I was to make that day at the subject of the Eastern media and the Eastern establishment press yielded only a Dean Acheson anecdote, in which Acheson recalled Lyndon Johnson complaining that the press treated him unfairly. Acheson said he told Johnson, "You want the press to love you. And they won't—because you're not a very lovable man." Nixon went on to apply the same story to himself, but sidestepped the follow-up questions. No, he had never felt an "outsider" in Washington. He was stating his position in relatively hard-line terms, but without any "red sandwiches" to seize on.

"But basically," I insisted, "where you started the year by saying we'll speak quietly and so on and then you found loud voices in opposition to you, you thought, well, we'd better damned well speak louder than them."

"Well, just a minute," Nixon replied. And he recalled the things some of his political opponents and critics were saying about him. George McGovern had compared him to a maddened tyrant and had suggested his Vietnam War policies were of a piece with Hitler's extermination of the Jews. Senator William Saxbe, his future Attorney General, had said he appeared to have taken leave of his senses during the Christmas Bombing of Hanoi. And Sargent Shriver, McGovern's vice-presidential running mate, had suggested he was the greatest bomber since Julius Caesar.

Nixon had fun with that last one, recalling that gunpowder had not even been invented until a millennium after Caesar's death. And he ended with an anecdote that struck me as chilling. It seemed that George Christian, Johnson's former press secretary, who became a "Democrat for Nixon" during the 1972 campaign, was in the Oval Office the morning the newspapers carried the story of the Shriver blast.

"I'll bet you that President Johnson is gonna be real pleased when he finds that now they're calling me the No. 1 bomber," Nixon had told him.

Christian wasn't too sure.

"You know L.B.J. He never likes to be No. 2."

Telling the story, Nixon's face broke ever so slowly into one of those fixed, artificial grins which on the surface may seem to reflect a coldheartedness but which to me came to represent the gesture of one to whom humor is alien but who knows that there are certain times in life when one tries to make merry.

As I turned to Nixon's approval of the Huston Plan, I was aware that things had not gone particularly well in the first hour or so of the discussion. But I had nowhere near the sense of evolving disaster of my staff. For one thing, I had long since trained myself to think in terms of usable material. And for another, while I knew I had taken a number of unproductive excursions that morning, hoping to broaden our perspective on the Nixon presidency with some perspective on the Nixon personality, well, that was what twenty-eight hours were for: to get what we had to get, and to probe for things we thought would be worth getting if they were there to be gotten.

The first few minutes of the Huston Plan were, as it turned out, equally turgid. I asked Nixon, for example, why Hoover had opposed the plan, and then used that as the opportunity for which we had been searching to follow up with two or three questions designed to get Nixon talking about Hoover and what Hoover might have had on him. But the fish was not going to bite on that particular piece of bait. And then finally, at long last, our first real "catch" of the day.

> FROST: Now when you were concerned about street crime and so on you went to Congress and got laws passed and so on. Wouldn't it have been better here, though, to have done what you were going

to do legally, rather than doing something that was illegal, and seizing evidence in that and all of that? In retrospect, wouldn't it have been better to combat that crime legally, rather than adding another crime to the list?

NIXON: But basically the proposition you've just stated in theory is perfect. In practice, it just won't work.

The casual way in which he dismissed the negative aspects of a President adding to the crime statistics was, I thought, damning.

"Now in this case," he continued, "to get the specific legislation to have warrantless entries for the purpose of obtaining information and the rest would not only have raised an outcry, but it would have made it terribly difficult to move in on these organizations because basically they would be put on notice by the very fact that the legislation was on the books, that they'd be potential targets. An action's either going to be covert or not."

That was, of course, total nonsense. The authority to conduct covert operations puts no specific group or individual on notice that a particular operation will be conducted at a particular time, just as the authority to conduct a no-knock raid put no particular suspect on notice that one would be conducted against him. Also, Nixon's aversion to placing a matter before the Congress for fear it would have "raised an outcry" represented a rather startling approach to the execution of a President's constitutional duties. We would come back to it all at some length a few days later. Right now, I was trying to push Nixon to go a little further. And a few minutes later, he did.

FROST: So what in a sense you are saying is that there are certain situations in the Huston Plan, or that part of it was one of them, where the President can decide that it's in the best interest of the nation or something and do something illegal.

NIXON: Well, when the President does it, that means that it is not illegal.

Thank God, I thought, he has finally said what I thought he really believed but which I never figured that he'd admit in so many words. I hoped that my face remained appropriately sober, indeed positively understanding, without betraying any elation, as I sought to persuade him to go further.

"By definition . . . ," I said encouragingly.

"Exactly, exactly," Nixon replied. "If the President, if, for example, the President approves something, approves an action because of the national security or, in this case, because of a threat to internal peace and order of significant magnitude, then the President's decision in that instance is one that enables those who carry it out to carry it out without violating a law. Otherwise they're in an impossible position."

Weeks before, Jim Reston had recalled for me the famous colloquy between the Ervin committee's Senator Herman Talmadge and John Ehrlichman. Ehrlichman had also argued that a President had something of a legal King Midas touch turning to gold the foulest of deeds performed at his authorization or direction. Ehrlichman had not even ruled out murder. Let's see how far Mr. Nixon was ready to go.

"So that the black-bag jobs that were authorized in the Huston Plan—if they'd gone ahead—would have been made legal by your action?"

"Well, I think that we would . . . I think that we're splitting hairs here," Nixon replied.

Burglaries were, of course, illegal, he acknowledged. But when the national-security interests are very high, and when the device will be used "in a very limited and cautious manner, and responsible manner when it is undertaken, then, then that means that what would otherwise be technically illegal does not subject those who engage in such activity to criminal prosecution. That's the way that I would put it. Now that isn't trying to split hairs, but I do not mean to suggest the President is above the law. What I am suggesting, however, what we have to understand is in wartime particularly, war abroad and virtually revolution in certain concentrated areas at home, that a President does have under the Constitution extraordinary powers and must exert them. And we trust the President will always exert them . . . as little as possible . . ."

There were flaws in the Nixon line of legal reasoning and, Zelnick would later urge, an important question to be resolved regarding the checks on a President who sanctioned acts which on their face were unlawful. But I still wanted to see how far Mr. Nixon was willing to push his doctrine, so with a mental bow to Reston, I suggested the possibility of a President authorizing a murder.

Right now, Nixon was doing as I had hoped he would. With encouragement, he had voluntarily driven his case altogether too far, and now was not of a mind to retreat. Like many of his actions as President, the Nixon strategy often seemed to be to get from one moment to the next. If he wound up even further out on a limb than when he started, that simply posed a new problem to be dealt with in a new way. Nixon's game was poker, not chess. So now he tried to move to another limb. He suggested that had President Roosevelt ordered the assassination of Adolf Hitler before World War II, the action would have raised a "tough call" for constitutional authorities.

But, I stressed, we were talking about dissent in this country. "If you're saying that a presidential fiat can in fact mean that someone who does one of these black-bag jobs, these burglaries, is not liable to criminal prosecution, why shouldn't the same presidential power apply to somebody who the President feels in the national interest should murder a dissenter? I'm not saying it's happened. I'm saying what's the dividing line between the burglar being liable to criminal prosecution and the murderer?"

Nixon fell back to flattery.

"Because as you know from many years of studying and covering the world of politics and political science, there are degrees, there are nuances which are difficult to explain but which are there . . ." And again, he repeated his contention that he was President during a period of "wartime abroad and at home and virtual revolution in some parts of the country at home . . ."

So the only real dividing line, I persisted, "is the President's judgment?"

"Yes," Nixon concurred. But just so we don't get the impression that a President can "run amuck" in this country, remember that "a President has to come before the electorate" and has to obtain appropriations for covert C.I.A. and F.B.I. activities from the Congress. Traditionally such activities "have been disclosed on a very limited basis to trusted members of Congress."

"Yes," I said somewhat sardonically, but "I don't think that reading the documentation that it was ever intended, was it, that the Huston Plan and the black-bag robbery should be revealed to the electorate."

"No," said Nixon, "these were not. That's correct. That's correct."

I then asked Nixon whether he could name a single former President who had personally approved black-bag jobs.

Nixon demurred, suggesting that "if they were intelligent people" they must have known of such operations conducted against foreign embassies.

So I restated the question to exclude foreign embassies.

Again, without directly responding, Nixon suggested that his Huston Plan "was basically a better approach. It did formalize it. Ah, I think requiring presidential approval was a good idea."

"Because," I again said, somewhat tongue in cheek, "it may be illegal, but at least it makes it tidier."

We had virtually come to the end of the morning. As we were nearing the luncheon recess, I permitted the discussion to wander, as it often did, following heated clashes. It was the former President's way of unwinding while still on the set, and it was not at all unpleasant for me either. But after listening for a few minutes to tales of traveling through Europe without the White House bed, which the Secret Service had offered to bring along, I decided that we were sufficiently unwound, and suggested that we adjourn for lunch.

But I would have no lunch on this particular day.

I entered the viewing room with my mind still buzzing with the extraordinary statement I had obtained from the ex-President regarding his inherent power to violate the law. To my astonishment, I found Birt and Zelnick standing there, looking gloomy, even angry.

"What on earth is the matter?" I said. "Didn't you just hear that exchange on the Huston Plan?"

"Yes, that was quite something," said Zelnick. "But I don't think you followed it up a bit well. You let Nixon couch his argument in terms of the criminal liability of subordinates acting pursuant to express presidential instructions."

"Oh, rubbish. We were quite clearly talking about a President and his powers to break the law, and how far his deodorizing power could reach."

"A valid point, but a secondary one," John continued, taking his baton from his teammate like runners in relay. "The principal problem this morning was your unwillingness to stand behind the points you were trying to make."

"I am perfectly willing to stand behind the points *I* am trying to make," I said grimly. "I am not necessarily, invariably prepared to stand behind all the points that *you* are both trying to make."

"Fair point," said John. "But take that point we discussed in the car, about not recognizing his vision of what America was like. Twice he talked about America and parts of it being in a state of revolution and you didn't call him on it once."

"That's quite true," I said. "But do you remember when those two moments happened? They both happened in the middle of what I regarded as a far more important priority at the time—defining how far the President could go in terms of lawbreaking. And both of those references if followed up would have interrupted that flow.

"However, I agree with you that it's a point that has to be raised. And I agree that the first hour was a dead loss," I went on. "I agree it was far too directionless. Most of the experiments this morning got nowhere, at least for the first seventy-five minutes. In fact the two things go together. An experimental session where the experiments do not succeed is by definition directionless. And we got a whole set of 'goddamn self-serving statements' from Nixon as a result. And there are other gaps that we have to go back in and fill, I agree about that. But I still say, don't miss the wood for the trees.

"And one other thing, Bob," I added. "You must remember that we are dealing with a television interview here—not a prepared lecture. Or an editorial. We will never make all the points that you have labored day and night to put in a list or something. Even when they may be some of your pet theories. Why? Because when you make your list, you are its sole author. When we have a dialogue on television, then two people are contributing to the proceedings. Maybe only half of the points will ever get covered in the way you would wish, but one interchange that really illuminates an attitude, or a personality, can have ten times the revelatory impact of a whole essay. Or a whole book.

"And believe me, that Huston Plan moment was like that. It was worth everything we endured this morning."

I was sure I was right about that. But John and Bob were certainly right about the gaps, and I began the afternoon session with them.

"Just rounding off, first of all a couple of things . . . we were talking about this morning. On the time when you were considering and so on, and approving the Huston Plan, at that moment in the middle of June, early July 1970. How bad was the situation around the country in terms of disorder?

In reply, Nixon recited his by now familiar litany of the campus closings triggered by the Cambodian "experience," the activities of the Black Panthers and the Weathermen, and the fifty thousand bomb threats and three thousand bombings.

FROST: But when you said that there were parts of the country in a virtual state of revolution, which parts?
NIXON: Primarily in the . . . in the major cities in the Eastern part of the country. And, primarily in those areas against education . . . near to educational institutions, which, ah, ah, might have a more liberal activist element in them.
FROST: But, thinking back to that period, it seems to be a massive

exaggeration. I don't remember that time in America in the East, there being a virtual state of revolution. Revolution implies so much that I thought—

NIXON: Yea, but . . . you, yea, but . . . don't, don't put words in my mouth. You remember what I said earlier; I didn't say revolution throughout the country, I said revolution in certain parts of the country. And I would say that if you were in Detroit, where bombs were planted and discovered just before they went off; or in New York, or in other parts of the country where we had these kinds of attacks, you would have thought it was a revolutionary matter . . .

Could any reasonable viewer accept the picture this man drew of his country? I doubted it. That Nixon himself sincerely accepted it I had fewer doubts. From the Nixon White House, the United States was a strange, alien country. Dark and threatening forces were loose in the land. We must return to those forces and that view later, I told myself.

We talked a bit more about the nature of the dissent of that period. But when I twice asked him whether most of the discord didn't spring from his decision to stay in Vietnam, he refused to concede the point, citing the racial disturbances of the mid-1960's to prove that the unrest had many roots.

He seemed more on the defensive now and, as I again reflected upon the politics of the Nixon White House, he showed flashes of the old savagery of campaigns gone by, rather than the mellowed senior statesman quietly insisting that he not be denied his just place in history.

There were two key political stages, really, I said. The first was when he realized that to continue the war would also continue dissent. And having made the decision to continue the war, "you saw the divisions that had divided America into two groups that we discussed earlier—the Eastern establishment and the minority groups and the media, versus the middle America, the patriotic Southerners and the urban ethnic groups, etc. . . ."

"And a lot of decent people too," Nixon jibed.

"Sure . . ."

"I mean, even though they may not have gone to college."

"Right. And you saw those divisions and you realized that the war would continue with dissent; continue with a divided America, and also, wherever you could in other policies, you tried to build that group that were your support, play to them politically to increase your majority in '72—and the result was an America that was already divided, you divided even more, on a principle that the only way is to divide and rule."

That was the nub of the charge against the pre-Watergate Nixon and I felt better for having stated it at some length. The fact that Nixon would respond to it well disturbed me not at all. What we had sought in this area from the beginning was the best possible statement of opposing views on the Nixon presidency.

"Well, let me just say that . . . that's an interesting thesis," Nixon began. "But why did I go to China then? Why did I go to Russia? Why did I take the positions that I did with regard to biological and chemical warfare? Why did I take the position for family assistance, a very progressive position, which I deeply believe was one of the greatest mistakes the Congress made in not passing it?"

And again, the central Nixon point: "I knew that in order to get the enemy to take us seriously abroad, I had to have enough support at home, that they could not feel that they could win in Washington what they could not win on the battlefield. And I had that support. That's what the election was about. It was a clear-cut issue. McGovern was for buggin' out and I was for seeing it through in an honorable way. And the people voted 61 to 38 my way, whereas, the press, incidentally, voted 3 to 1 for McGovern."

I sensed we had come upon one of those prized moments, impossible to plan for, when Nixon was worked up enough to share some of his real emotions with us. And so, departing totally from our planned line of questioning, I asked him to compare the power he had held as Chief Executive with that wielded by the media, the three networks and the leading national dailies.

The hunch proved correct. With only the most gentle further prodding, he launched into a lengthy verbal treatise on the power and concentration of the media, their ability to spew the same line day in and day out, and the control by single families and corporations of some of the most influential media conglomerates.

His supporters had to be able to "resist the pounding they took night after night from television commentators who were tearing me to pieces, limb from limb . . . " I must have missed the Evening News on those nights, I thought.

> FROST: Well, maybe you should have been president of a network or chairman of the *Washington Post.* Do you feel you'd have had more power?
>
> NIXON: Oh, yes. At the present time . . . let's talk about power. I think it is very significant. The greatest concentration of power in the United States today is not in the White House; it isn't in the Congress and it isn't in the Supreme Court. It's in the media. And it's too much . . . It's too much power and it's power that the Founding Fathers would have been very concerned about. Because the Founding Fathers balanced the power. The presidency balances the Congress, balances the Supreme Court. And when you have balanced power, you have checks, each on the other. There is no check on the networks. There is no check on the newspapers . . .

According to Nixon, the leading Supreme Court libel case, *Sullivan* vs. *The New York Times,* was "really a license for the media to lie." That was why he couldn't sue people about false stories to the effect that he had foreign bank accounts or had sold ambassadorships. A network commentator had put out a story to the effect recently "that I wrote twenty-six love letters to some countess in Spain for three or four months before I resigned. It was proved totally false. I had the Postmaster General investigate it. They were forgeries. It was never retracted. Somebody called me and said, 'Why don't you sue them?' You can't.

"And so my point is," he continued, "let's just not have all this sanctimonious business about the poor repressed press. I went through it all the years I've been in public life and I have . . . they never have been repressed as far as I am concerned. I don't want them repressed, but believe me when they take me on, or when they take any public figure on, Democrat or Republican, liberal or conservative, I think the public figure ought to come back and crack 'em right in the puss."

Nixon recited the words slowly and with great relish, his eyes alive with fire, his voice dwelling on every syllable of every word. And what an interesting opening he had provided. So "to get the record absolutely straight," we went back over the ground he had mentioned. He had never written love letters to a foreign countess. And what about assets abroad?

> NIXON: I not only don't have any assets abroad, I never had a foreign bank account in my life . . . I have no foreign bank accounts, had none, don't have any at the present time, and I hope I have the opportunity sometime to maybe write a check in a foreign land on my bank account in San Clemente.
> FROST: But no foreign assets at all . . .
> NIXON: I have no foreign assets at all. None.
> FROST: And no secret bank accounts in the United States?
> NIXON: No secret bank accounts in the United States . . . There is absolutely nothing to any of these charges. They are totally false, and yet I think most of our audience probably think I am sitting here with a whole bundle of cash someplace that people have paid me through this year . . . And let me tell you, anybody who can find any foreign account, anyplace in the world, in my name, let me say I will contribute it to his favorite charity, which is probably himself. Finders keepers.

During his answer, Mr. Nixon had mentioned that his children didn't want anything left to them. He said that when he and Mrs. Nixon depart this good earth, they plan to leave their money to the Nixon Library.

All of our experiments this afternoon, I thought, have worked as well as they didn't work in the first hour this morning. Perhaps this is the moment when the ex-President would be open enough to talk about Mrs. Nixon. Indeed he was.

His reply began quietly enough with a report on her physical improvement since the stroke: the paralysis gone from her face and her left leg and only a bit remaining in her left arm. The prognosis was for complete recovery.

"But it hasn't been easy, and particularly let me say, I've mentioned the stories that have been written, and some written by, ah, some book authors"—here Nixon feigned an inability to remember the names of that obscure *Washington Post* team of Bob Woodward and Carl Bernstein, looking querulously at the ceiling for guidance— "and so forth, which reflected even on her, on occasion, what her alleged weaknesses were. They haven't helped, and, as far as my attitude towards the press is concerned, I respect some, but [for] those who write history as fiction on third-hand knowledge, I have nothing but utter contempt. And I will never forgive them. Never!"

The words were spoken with utter hatred. A moment or two later he added: "All I say is Mrs. Nixon read it, and her stroke came three days later. I didn't want her to read it, because I knew the kind of trash it was, and the kind of trash they are . . ." And then, having sown the seed, the familiar Nixon disclaimer: "But nevertheless, this doesn't indicate that that caused the stroke, because the doctors don't know what caused the stroke. But it sure didn't help."

Nixon tried to indicate, not altogether convincingly, that criticism was fine as far as he was concerned. "I'm in the arena. I have the ability to fight back. And I mean that I expect it. I may not like it and I may not like them, but I say that when they criticize a member of my family, and unjustly, I don't like that worth a darn. Expletive deleted."

On the narrow issue of his marriage to Mrs. Nixon, and her right to privacy, I could scarcely disagree since we had drawn the line there ourselves. But in general it had been a mind-boggling hour. I hardly knew what to make of it. I sensed the material was perhaps the clearest window on the Nixon personality we might be able to obtain during the entire course of the tapings. But what, I wondered, would the Nixon people think of it? I had complete editorial control, of course, but would we now be subjected to a whole series of requests and pleas not to let his series of outbursts run too long, to keep them as brief as possible?

Jack Brennan greeted me before I reached the door. He grabbed me by the arm.

"This is the greatest material yet," he said, smiling broadly. "If you cut this out of the show, I'll put out a contract on your head."

"Jack," I said sincerely, "I wouldn't dream of it."

As a group, we were dreadfully out of sync on the return ride from Monarch Bay.

My own spirits were high. The afternoon session had provided some memorable exchanges. If a key element in our thesis was that Mr. Nixon's jaundiced view of critics in the press had colored the atmosphere in the White House, providing a context for later excesses, he had given us a rich blend of supporting material—and a remarkable insight into his own personality. We had filled in many of the gaps in the politics of polarization in the opening minutes of the afternoon. And I knew that the former President's dissertation on the prerogatives of the Chief Executive to bend and break the law would demonstrate just how imperial Nixon's visions of the imperial presidency were.

My colleagues, however, shared little of my enthusiasm. Minoff and Reston had circulated among the production crew at the end of the session and heard little but praise for the way Mr. Nixon had "stuck it to the press." Fair enough, it's a free country, I thought, that did not worry me. Zelnick's mind was more concerned with opportunities he thought had been missed rather than with openings seized. And John's mind was focused more on the disappointments of the morning than the extraordinarily high quotient of riveting material in the afternoon.

The team was thus scarcely in an ideal frame of mind to view a rough cut, which can be a fairly harrowing experience at the best of times, even to people who have sat through as many rough cuts as John and I had. In fact, at the viewing of the rough cut of what we still thought was going to be our first show, there were too many people. Rough cuts are for one or two, not for a group. Somehow it then starts to feel like opening night itself. But we wanted Bob and Jim and Marv to judge the program with us, and I particularly wanted Clay Felker, who had arrived in town, to see the program from the point of view of somebody right outside the production team.

When we got back to the Hilton, we got the bad news that the edited tape would not be ready until nine thirty, and that it would be running approximately two and a quarter hours, which was even longer than we had estimated. At that point, we ought really to have postponed the screening, as midnight at the end of a tiring day is not the best moment to achieve a profound overview. However, our schedule was so tight that we had to go ahead.

Jørn Winther arrived from Don Stern Productions with the tape at nine twenty. The opening music and titles were already in, and having a general idea of what I wanted to say, I had simply ad-libbed a few sentences at the beginning to give some sense of time and pace. Jørn and Don had edited the program on the basis of content, working from the "paper edits" that John and I had given them, marked on the transcripts of each day's proceedings. (The transcripts had been typed through the night following each day of taping by two transcribers, Jenifer Shell and Lucinda Smith, who always managed to finish in time for our viewings the next morning.) Where there was a jagged edit, Jørn and Don had rightly left it jagged. Where another shot was required, Jørn and Don had rightly not stopped to find it. Rough cuts are, in short, very rough and very raw.

John and I had edited hundreds of programs for television in the past. And it nonetheless never ceased to amaze us how much time could be chopped out of raw material while preserving the essence of what had been recorded and the atmosphere of the session itself. And how sometimes the smallest of cuts could clarify the meaning and disproportionately multiply the impact. As our lengthy first look at Vietnam began to unroll, it soon became clear that there was a great deal more editing to do. Somehow the details of the tortuous negotiating process between Kissinger and Le Duc Tho, the background to the dramatic May 8, 1972, decision to bomb Hanoi and mine Haiphong Harbor, and the refusal of Thieu to sign the October accord all seemed much longer than they in fact were.

When the viewing ended around midnight, Clay Felker's eyes were closed.

"Wake up, Clay," said Zelnick. "Peace is at hand."

Clay blinked rapidly. "Oh, I wasn't sleeping," he said. "I've been having to do two hours of eye exercises every day for the past week, and they make my eyelids very heavy by nightfall."

"They must be some exercises," Bob said. "They not only make your eyelids heavy, but they make you snore as well."

Clay laughed, paid his respects to the program and left the room. He and I would have a private talk about it next day. The rest of the group lingered. We had spent the better part of three two-hour sessions on the war but clearly the program in its current form did not work.

Marv's reaction to the show was what it had been all along. "It's too PBS."

Jim was even more worried. "This program does the one thing that I warned all along that this series should never do, and that is, make Nixon look presidential. You may win a point or two on the way, or even the debate viewed as a whole. But it will seem like two rational, reasonable men discussing a policy which, in my view, amounted to murder."

"In the abstract," said Bob, "it seems incredibly dramatic for Nixon to admit, first, that the whole question of whether or not to keep fighting the war was a very 'close call,' second, that the Christmas Bombing was a mistake—or even a waste, as you put it, David—and, third, that the whole failure in Vietnam could be laid on the doorstep of the Congress for not providing emergency aid after the rout of the Central Highlands. His positions are untenable. They will be reviewed and regarded as such, and that is an extraordinary achievement for an interview with a former President. But again, all that is overshadowed by the fact that the past two and a quarter hours were boring. And I don't know why. I've never worked on anything like this before, so I don't know what it will look like in final form. But I'm worried."

"David and I will have another stab at this," said John. "Let's not worry any more about it now. We will do what we can with it. And there are other possible options if it still doesn't work."

The next day, Thursday, April 7, was my birthday. I began it with coffee with Clay. He told me that the word back East was that things were going less than well on the project. Joe Kraft had returned from the first day's taping with a feeling that Nixon was in control, a fact which he had confided to Clay. The rumors around Washington in general were that I was in "over my head," a term that would shortly be incorporated into one of Nancy Collins' short-lived "Gossip Columns" in the *Washington Post*.

I said that was nonsense. "We had a rough first day. But we learned a lot from it. However, that's not the point. In the light of all you've been saying, Vietnam is just not strong enough to lead off the series, is it?"

"No," said Clay. "It isn't. I thought it was good in parts, but you have to realize how many people there are out there, lying in wait for these Interviews. If you put a foot wrong, they'll kill you."

Given the differing points of view, our viewing that day of the previous day's taping was likely to have been contentious in any case. It was not improved by being continually interrupted by telephone calls regarding a story in that morning's *New York Times*, which had to be put right. It turned out from the story that Pacific Video's $290,000 had been provided not by the company itself, but by a group of nineteen investors, almost all of them from San Diego. That was fine, and no business of ours. Unfortunately, however, the investors had gone on to state that Mr. Jack Meyer and Mr. Frost "will begin editing the twenty-four hours of raw tape into six hours of broadcast material." Pacific Video Industries of Hollywood was described as "co-producer of the Nixon series in a speculative joint venture with Mr. Frost."

We probably overreacted, but to us the story seemed potentially dangerous. We thought we had clarified for the world that we had sole editorial control. Anything that blurred that fact, that suggested that nineteen San Diegans, members of a relatively conservative community, might have some obscure say in the editing process, seemed to us harmful in the extreme, particularly in the light of what Clay had reported.

Phone calls buzzed back and forth between the Beverly Hilton and the New York Times building in New York. And next day *The New York Times*, with its traditional respect for fairness and accuracy, put the record straight:

> David Frost reasserted last night that he and his company had sole control over the content and editing of the forthcoming interviews with former President Richard M. Nixon.
>
> Richard D. Kirshberg of New York, the attorney for Pacific Video Industries who drew up the agreement with Mr. Frost and his company, Paradine, said that under the "joint venture" Mr. Frost would have "absolute editorial control" over the series.
>
> Mr. Frost said that Mr. Meyer would not be involved in either editorial or technical decisions about the editing . . . and five organizations, including Pacific Video, "will be receiving an 'in association with' credit."

The Pacific Video interruptions ended about four thirty, and the viewing ended at about five. As John rewound the tape and Marv and Jim started to get up, all of Bob's fears for the project, not to mention his intermittent disagreements on tactics with me, or failures to understand my tactical approach, came to the surface at one and the same time. Exacerbated, maybe, by the tension caused by the sheer proximity of Watergate. Whatever it was, it was very real.

" 'Damascus moment' . . . who is this you're interrogating, St. Paul? . . . 'Mr. Nice Guy'—what sort of phrase is that? . . . Look at this answer—ten goddamn minutes of bullshit and you didn't say so once . . . Poor Nixon, the victim of all those nasty dissenters . . . Why didn't you tell him that the Acheson story didn't begin to respond to your point . . . the issue was not whether he was a lovable man, but why he was making a cold and calculated decision to tear the society apart . . . Look at all this time you wasted on Hoover—do this with Watergate and you'll run out of time before March 21st . . . Who cares about whether he brought the White House bed to Europe when he traveled? Cut him off, it's just a distraction . . . Jesus, David, look what you're letting him get away with . . ."

"Bob," I said. "It's pointless for me to reply to every one of your comments. Some of them in particular are absurd. The thing is, though, that this was a devastating day for Nixon. We've already talked about that one sentence in the Huston Plan discussion. But much of the remaining material in the afternoon was also very strong. So I really don't know the basis for your extreme dissatisfaction with what went on."

"David, I'm not saying that he didn't hurt himself on Wednesday," Zelnick replied. "What I am saying is that it was a self-inflicted wound."

"And leading someone to the point where they will willingly do that is one of the jobs of an interviewer," I said. "It's certainly a damn sight more productive than criticizing him for telling the Dean Acheson story."

"Look," said Bob. "We can review this session and every item I have criticized until we are both exhausted. And you'll have a response for everything I say. You can tell me that at one point you were trying to win his confidence, or at another that you wanted him to go on until he tied himself in his own knot. But the plain fact is that you hardly laid a glove on him. You let him carry the day. You may have a good reason for not doing what you set out to do yesterday, but the bottom line is that you never did it."

"But we have confronted him where it really matters. Look at Chile. I certainly did not let him carry the day there."

"Red sandwiches and beef," said Bob. "I thought for a while that you were in a goddamn delicatessen. Don't kid yourself. He's set up perfectly now for kicking your tail from one end of Monarch Bay to the other. He knows he can get away with anything he finds necessary. When he wants to lie, he lies. When he wants to filibuster, he filibusters. When he wants to mistake the law, he does so. When he wants to draw false historical analogies, he draws them. The only thing he has to watch out for is overconfidence. And that's not the position we should be in after more than two weeks on the set."

"That is not an accurate summary of the situation, any more than a goddamn delicatessen is an accurate summary of the Chilean confrontation. You're forgetting the Kissinger material, and the Mideast material. And you're forgetting that when we had to confront him, I did confront him. I confronted him on Chile, on Cambodia, even on those crime statistics in the District of Columbia. Watergate will be like that, only ten times more so."

"Again," said Zelnick, "this is the one area where I would tend to trust my own experience as a print journalist more than yours as a television interviewer. For God's sake, David, I covered the Chapin trial. It lasted a week, most of that time with Chapin himself on the stand. I covered the Watergate trial. It began in October and ended the following January. You've got eight hours left to cover Watergate, and the other abuses of power.

"Don't you know what you're up against? This man is not only one of America's cagiest politicians, he's been a member of the bar for almost forty years. He's tried cases at trial, presided over committee hearings, argued before the Supreme Court of the United States. You've seen how formidable he is on matters he knows something about. Well, let me tell you, by next Wednesday, he will have committed every word on every Watergate tape to memory. He'll know every statute cold. He'll have rehearsed his answers. He'll call you every time you put a comma in the wrong place. He'll respond to your damaging references with dozens that support his interpretation of the facts. He'll put everything in a factual context that will take ten minutes to fabricate. You're in against a master, man, a master. Everything he wanted these interviews to accomplish for him will be on the line beginning next Wednesday. And he's a fighter."

"Yes, you can't back down with Richard Nixon," said John, echoing the sense of foreboding in Bob's words, "because he takes it as a sign of weakness. There's no mercy in the man, not as a warrior and not as an antagonist in this setting. He takes what he gets. You've got to stop him on the spot when he misrepresents the record and say, 'No, Mr. President, I know this better than you do, and I'm not going to let you rewrite the record.' Just look at this transcript and see how long his responses are. You have to declare your points. You have to stand with them.

And you have got to destroy his points. Otherwise we will fail. You will fail."

"And right now," said Bob, "that's where we're heading."

Towards *failure?*

I have rarely felt torn by so many conflicting emotions in my life. This whole atmosphere of critiquing the project and critiquing me was something I had tried to establish from the beginning, and wanted to maintain—indeed, *had* to maintain. It might prove crucial, as we examined and reexamined our strategy, if the first Watergate session did not go according to plan, for example. But this level of pessimism was nonsense—and dangerous nonsense.

There have been several times in my life when I have realized that my main job was to make colleagues I was working with share my faith in a successful outcome, however unlikely that may have seemed in cold rational terms. There have been times when I have denied to colleagues dangers that I have admitted to myself. Times when lifting people's spirits has been an almost physical effort.

From the pure "gloom" standpoint, this was one of those moments. And then again it wasn't. Because pure optimism in this situation, however potentially inspirational, would almost certainly be counterproductive, since one of my colleagues' deepest fears seemed to be that I might be complacent, or unaware of the problems that faced me six days later.

I was, actually, also rather annoyed that they could not be a bit more perceptive. A former colleague of mine, Ned Sherrin, had once written, "David always learns from his mistakes without ever admitting that he's made any." The same was true of unfavorable odds. Just because I had never admitted them publicly did not mean that I did not recognize them privately for what they were. Surely they could see that?

In fact, the more I thought about it, I was not just annoyed; I was angry. What I'd heard was an absurdly lopsided account of the past few days, and indeed of the next few days. It was overkill. And it could be extremely destructive. So I decided to say so.

First I reiterated the point that I thought should have been obvious without my having to mention it. Yes, I was daunted, too.

Intimidated by the sheer scale of the challenge. I realized how far we had to go. And time was indeed a commodity in terrifyingly—and legally limited—short supply. But that was no excuse for this sort of masochistic orgy.

Why just take all of the gloomy portents of the past few days, for God's sake? Sure, the Vietnam viewing had been depressing—but that was a problem to be solved, not an excuse for cardiac arrest. That was the whole point of the project. If we made mistakes, then, if we had the intelligence, we had the time to correct them.

Granted, the first hour of domestic policy the day before had been Toilet City, but get the Huston Plan into perspective. "If anything in this project is, then that is our 'smoking pistol,' " I said.

Not only did I not believe their low estimate of our chances. I did not believe that deep down they did either.

"However, if there is anyone who really thinks that we are going to fail, it is better they leave this project now. It would just make the next few days too depressing . . ."

Silence. The moment had passed. The taboo word had been uttered, faced and rejected.

"Now," I added, "in case you've forgotten, you're all invited to my birthday party—by Caroline, I hasten to add. Why on earth she thinks I want to spend my birthday with such a miserable bunch of manic depressives I cannot imagine, but there it is . . ."

The meeting broke up in good humor. In retrospect, I suppose it was probably a marginal plus. It could have been a disaster, of course. The original air of gloom, despair and despondency, if not dispelled, could have destroyed everybody's powers of concentration, including mine, for the next few days. But that did not happen. And where we were always going to work fifteen hours a day up to Watergate, maybe we managed sixteen. And where we were going to order two courses from room service maybe we saved time and only ordered one.

With the air cleared, Caroline's party could not have been better timed. And later that evening, reflecting on the events of the day with a little more detachment, I thanked God for a team that was clearly as emotionally involved in this project as I was.

We had already divided the next five days into two: three days for separate effort, then two days for conferring together as required. On Friday, Saturday and Sunday. I would hardly lay eyes on any member of the team, phoning John, Bob or Jim only to request additional reference material or, perhaps, to check a point of law or a stray fact. I referred to few of the books about the Watergate period. They had been fine early on, when I sought an overview of the subject. Now it was the original source material that I wanted to stick with, the White House transcripts released by Nixon himself or obtained by Leon Jaworski or the House Judiciary Committee, the material unearthed by Reston more than six months ago and, miraculously, I thought, still undiscovered by the press, excerpts of the Watergate trial testimony meticulously compiled by Reston during his research work, and the stunning summary of the case by trial counsel James Neal as he made his closing argument to the Watergate jury.

I read them, reread them and read them again. I made notes to myself on the backs of folders and in yellow legal pads. Receiving two sets of first-draft lists of suggested questions, one prepared by Zelnick and one by Reston, on Sunday afternoon, I began making marginal notes, while at the same time writing my own.

I was not yet at the point where I felt it necessary to develop a complete theory of the case against Nixon. That could await our discussions beginning Monday morning. But I did begin to think in terms of what it was that I could specifically prove against the former President. I made little lists, checked them against the portions of the transcript I had underlined, added to them, subtracted from them, changed the wording, put them aside, and began compiling new lists from scratch.

I was satisfied that I could prove that Nixon had ordered Haldeman on June 23, 1972, to order the C.I.A. to request the F.B.I. to curtail its probe of the break-in.

I could prove that on January 8, 1973, Nixon had given Colson favorable signals with respect to clemency for Howard Hunt.

I could prove that on February 13 and 14, again in discussions with Colson, he had staked his entire second term on the continued silence of the seven convicted defendants. The only problem would be "if one of the seven begins to talk."

I could prove that on March 13 he had ignored clear statements from Dean regarding the criminal involvement of current members of his administration, including Strachan and Magruder.

I could prove that beginning March 20 he had leaned on Dean to write a phony document absolving White House personnel of culpability in the break-in and cover-up.

I could prove that during the March 21–22 marathon Watergate discussions he was told of blackmail payments in process and, later, that they had been paid, and had—at the very least—done nothing to turn them off.

I could prove that on March 21, he had coached Haldeman on how to commit what any reasonable person would call perjury without getting convicted.

I could prove that after Dean fell out of his good graces, he had turned Watergate matters over to Ehrlichman, who was himself deeply implicated in the cover-up conspiracy.

I could prove that between March 27 and April 14, he had attempted to get Magruder and Mitchell to come forward and take the rap, hoping the investigation would stop with them.

I could prove that through Haldeman and Ehrlichman, he had offered suggestions of clemency to Mitchell, Magruder and Dean in order to coax them into not implicating those even closer to him.

I could prove that he had shamelessly betrayed Henry Petersen's confidences by relaying his accounts of the investigation to Haldeman and Ehrlichman.

I could prove that between April 14 and 17 he had worked on "lines," "scenarios" and "drafts" with his two colleagues in order to explain their involvement in the earlier hush money payments.

I could prove that he recommended no immunity for those suspected of criminal wrongdoing after Ehrlichman told him on April 17 that such action might be the best way to remove Dean's incentive to talk.

I could prove that on April 20 he recalled authorizing the blackmail payment to Hunt.

And I could prove that he had repeatedly and egregiously lied to the American people regarding his own state of knowledge at various times and his efforts to unravel the truth within his own White House.

And what could I not prove? That list was almost as important as the first, though, I must confess, it was a good deal shorter.

I could not prove that he had prior knowledge of the Watergate break-in.

I could not establish a motive for the original crime.

I could not establish a motive for his initial involvement in the cover-up.

I could not prove that he was aware of Kalmbach's and Hunt's activities during the summer and fall of 1972.

I could not prove that he knew of the blackmail payments before March 21, 1973.

I could not prove his personal involvement in the erasure of eighteen and a half minutes of his June 20, 1972, Watergate-related conversation with Haldeman.

I could not prove that he had personal knowledge of who erased the tape, or, indeed, how the erasure occurred.

I reviewed my list of "could not proves." With respect to some items the circumstantial evidence was strong. Would, for example, Ehrlichman and Haldeman have dared to enlist the President's personal attorney for the raising and transmittal of blackmail money without clearing it with Mr. Nixon himself? Would Haldeman have released $350,000 from his White House safe without Nixon's knowledge and consent? The gap in the tape had been created through at least five manual erasures. Stephen Bull and Rose Mary Woods were the only ones with the possible motive to cause that erasure, except for the President himself. Would either of them have acted alone?

Still, it seemed the better part of wisdom to ignore these episodes, or relegate them to a secondary line of questioning. Some would have to be covered just for the record. Others might simply be listed as additional questions concerning Nixon's conduct throughout the period. But I was convinced our approach all along was sound. Stay with what we know we can prove. Keep within the essential cover-up period—June 1972 to April 1973.

It also struck me that I might find myself in mild disagreement with Bob's approach to the case. He had always stressed the trend of events—the fact that Nixon's chief lieutenants quickly organized the cover-up and stayed with it until it came apart. These were men personally selected by Nixon and trusted by him as faithful interpreters of his will. It thus strained credulity to suppose that they had acted without his approval.

True enough, I thought, but it gives Nixon an out. Straining credulity was never a task he felt himself unable or unwilling to tackle. What we couldn't prove, he would deny baldly. (We had found that out earlier when we had tried to discuss the Anna Chennault incident with him, without having a primary source for our questions.)

The best proof was his own words, right out of the transcripts. No one reading or listening to that material could fairly deny his involvement in the cover-up, perhaps not even Nixon himself. And while one phrase or sentence, or two, or five, or eight, could be passed off as ambiguous, or taken out of context, the mere repetition of incriminating statements, the hundreds that veritably littered the transcripts, had a cumulative impact quite beyond the significance of the individual items alone. At some point, I concluded, it might be worthwhile to simply list a dozen or so of the most incriminating items and let Mr. Nixon attempt to interpret them all at once. I was convinced the exercise would be damning. And I made sure that I had dozens of such statements ready on my clipboard.

Khachigian had already made one tactical mistake. Shortly after their first meeting in San Clemente, he had given Zelnick the galley proofs to Victor Lasky's revisionist book, *It Didn't Start with Watergate.*

"Lasky's principal biases seem to be against original research, good writing and persuasive argument," Zelnick had reported at the time. "And most of his false trails we have already discussed."

But now the Lasky book started Zelnick thinking again. Perhaps he had dismissed its implications for our project too cavalierly. After all, Lasky had been almost an official historian for Nixon in his time. His little red herrings would likely be used by Nixon. Plus, Nixon was inventive enough to devise a few of his own.

So Zelnick began work on a short but brutally effective paper, "Likely Nixon Detours," in which he set forth the possible excursions Nixon might lead us on in an effort to get us off the trail of his own criminal culpability. And he outlined the kinds of responses we would need to abort each such frolic and get us back in hot pursuit of the game.

Were Nixon, for example, to suggest an innocent motive for his abuse of the C.I.A., we would come back to the fact that a man is legally responsible for the consequences of his own actions. Thus, even had Nixon sought to divert the F.B.I. for political reasons, the fact that curtailing its investigation would have permitted guilty men to go unapprehended rendered the President's conduct criminal.

There were other "likely detours" listed—eleven in all—ranging from Haldeman's interpretation of the March 21, 1973, Nixon-Dean conversation (Nixon was just "probing," advancing possible theories, in order to find out what was really going on) to the basic defense put forth by James St. Clair to the House Judiciary Committee. (However circuitously Nixon went about unraveling the cover-up after March 21, the fact is that he took the actions necessary to unravel it.) In each case, a list, sometimes voluminous, of Nixon's words and actions rebutting the more benign interpretation was included.

Meanwhile I was reexperiencing one of the private pleasures of reading the White House transcripts: seeing cover stories with which the culprits would later "go public" concocted before our very eyes. Both in Hawaii and again now during this period, having run across one of Nixon's public alibis, I would then search back through the transcripts until I was able to locate it in the scheming stage.

Some of the more blatant examples:

In a March 1, 1973, conversation with Dean, the cover story regarding Dean's access to the early F.B.I. Watergate data was devised. From then on, the public White House line was that the access was needed to support the investigation Dean was conducting for the President.

On March 13, Nixon decided to prevent the Ervin committee from getting too close to the case by asserting executive privilege with respect to "present and former" members of his White House staff. He christened the occasion by putting Colson back on staff as a part-time counselor. The ploy was abandoned shortly thereafter in the face of political pressure.

The idea of devising a "Dean Report" whitewash on which the President could later be said to have relied was developed in stages, most notably on March 17, 20, and 22.

The "national-security" rationale for the Ellsberg break-in was hatched on March 21, in a presidential meeting with Dean and Haldeman.

The line—"not a lie, but a line"—that money was paid to the defendants to keep them from talking to the press, or, in Hunt's case, possibly writing a book, was advanced by the President himself on April 14, in a meeting with Haldeman and Ehrlichman.

I asked Bob to see if he could find some more. He managed to list fourteen in all. He entitled his list, "Nixon Cover Stories Conceived in the Transcripts and Later Used." As a novelist, Jim found that rather unimaginative and, with a bow to our old friend Dean Acheson, recommended instead "Present at the Creation."

By the time Monday morning arrived, I felt positively buoyant. I knew the transcripts inside out, better in fact than any of my colleagues. I had Zelnick's questions, Reston's and mine: I had Bob's latest road maps, intended not as a text but as a guide, embracing as much supporting documentation as feasible for purposes of following up. They were already complemented by my own copious notes, as well as numerous excerpts from the exclusive Reston research material. What I had before me represented a true team effort.

"All right," I said to the assembled group. "Our first question will ask him for a characterization of his role in the cover-up. So what we are looking for is an opening statement from defense counsel. A clue to his line of defense."

"Yes," said Bob. "If he lays out a theory of his case, then you know what targets you have to shoot at. If, as is more likely, he rejects the opportunity, you can be pretty certain that you're going to have to take him transaction by transaction and prove his guilt at each step."

"Let's go through what it is that I would have to prove were this a criminal conspiracy trial." Today I wanted Zelnick the lawyer.

"You have to show the existence of a corrupt conspiracy, plus at least one overt act taken to further it," Zelnick explained. "For example, if the four of us discuss plans to rob a bank here in town, we are not yet guilty of a crime. But if I then go out and purchase a gun, or if Jim drives downtown to case the premises, either of those would constitute an overt act in furtherance of the conspiracy and all of us who participated in the plan would be guilty of conspiracy to rob the bank."

"Then the overt act does not itself have to be illegal."

"Absolutely right," said Zelnick. "So long as the design itself is illegal, any step taken toward its implementation takes on an illegal coloration."

"And I would be just as guilty as you or Jim, even though I sat here in the hotel."

"Right. Once the existence of a conspiracy has been established, any of the individual conspirators become legally responsible for the acts of their co-conspirators. In fact, that is one of the reasons few civil libertarians much cared for the conspiracy laws until Richard Nixon got tangled up in them."

"Then everything that Ehrlichman, Haldeman, Dean, Magruder, Kalmbach, Ulasewicz, Hunt and the others did during the summer of 1972, and, indeed, prior to March 21, 1973—when Nixon will claim he first learned of the cover-up—implicates him, even if he had no specific knowledge of it?"

"Yes, that's right. Provided you can establish, as I think you can, that in ordering the C.I.A. to halt the F.B.I. investigations on June 23, 1972, Nixon willingly joined the criminal conspiracy to obstruct justice."

"And this is where we'll get into our first real dispute," I predicted, "because he'll claim that his motives on June 23 were innocent, that his only concern was political embarrassment."

"Yes," said Zelnick. "And this is the essential point you have to win without any question. Remember, the June 20th Nixon-Colson conversation that Jim discovered, together with the June 23rd conversation itself, shows conclusively that at the time he directed Haldeman to approach the C.I.A., he knew at the very least that Hunt was involved, that Liddy was involved and that Mitchell was involved. Now had his instructions been carried out with the intended consequences, these individuals would not have been apprehended. Now right there you have Nixon implicated in a conspiracy to obstruct justice, because there followed a number of overt acts in furtherance of the scheme—the most immediate being Haldeman's approach to Helms and Walters."

"And motive is no defense," I repeated.

"None at all."

"Then why do prosecutors always seek to establish motive?" I asked.

"Motive can be an important aid in the investigation of a crime. Unless they are insane, people who commit crimes usually have a reason for doing so. Find a motive and you've found a potential suspect. It can also be helpful in establishing intent, which *is* a necessary ingredient for conviction. For example, if I run over Jim in my car, the act itself is not a crime. To convict me of murder, a prosecutor would have to show that I intended to hit him with the vehicle. Now if, in searching around, they discover that I had recently taken out a million-dollar life insurance policy on him, suddenly they know I had a motive for wiping him out and from there they can seek to establish the intent necessary to convict me of a felony. On the other hand, if in searching my room they discovered a taped conversation in which I told you, 'Tomorrow I am going to run Jim over with my car,' and then I proceeded to do it, they would have pretty clear proof of my intent, even if they did not succeed in establishing a motive."

"So the absence of intent is a defense to a crime," I replied. "But the absence of a motive, or the existence of an innocent motive, is not."

"Exactly," said Zelnick. "Getting back to our bank analogy, if you walk into First National and point a gun at the teller's face and demand money, it is no defense to the crime of robbery that you did not intend to keep so much as a cent of it, that you wanted to give it to a sick sister, or donate it to charity. Your motive may have been pure as the driven snow, but so long as you intended to walk into that bank with a weapon and force the teller to hand over the contents of that till, you're guilty."

"Is it legally possible for one to withdraw from a criminal conspiracy while the conspiracy itself continues?" I asked.

"I suspect that would be a darn close case," Zelnick replied. "At the very least, it would have to be a clear, unambiguous withdrawal—in this case, a good deal more than telling Gray to do a good job after learning that the C.I.A. would not carry the White House's water and that Gray was already going ahead anyway. I suppose, as involved as Nixon was in the early stages of the conspiracy, he would certainly have had to make some early effort to ascertain the facts and to instruct those whom he knew to be involved to turn themselves in, or at least to do absolutely nothing to obstruct or impede the investigation."

"Yes," I said. "And both the circumstantial and the direct evidence point to Nixon's nonwithdrawal from the conspiracy between the period July 6, 1972, and March 21, 1973. During 1972 it's mainly circumstantial. We have the activities of Kalmbach and Ulasewicz, plus the perjury of Magruder, Strachan, Mitchell and Porter. In November, there is that meeting at Camp David where Dean plays the Hunt-Colson tape for Haldeman and Ehrlichman and then flies to New York City to play it for Mitchell and Stans. In December we have Haldeman's transfer of $350,000 from the White House to CREEP. In January it starts to be more direct. There is that Colson-Nixon conversation about clemency for Hunt. In February, we have those two fantastic conversations with Colson that Jim discovered. And even before March 21, we have discussion about keeping aides from testifying before the Ervin committee and the beginnings of that 'self-serving goddamn statement' he wanted Dean to begin writing."

"That's exactly what I would hit, David," said Birt. "I'd take him through to March 21 on the first day."

"Including that evening talk with Colson about the hush money," I suggested. "Another Reston exclusive."

We gathered again briefly Monday afternoon and then for several hours on Tuesday. A good part of the time was spent discussing the conspiracy, the activities of others in the cover-up conspiracy. We searched the theories of the law with which we were unfamiliar, the revisionists' arguments that we had not already rebutted among ourselves, and ambiguities in the transcripts that we had not yet resolved. We could find gratifyingly few. From the despair of the previous Thursday, the team now seemed brimming with confidence. Ian Gordon, who had flown in from London, was wandering round the hotel, asking people why there had been such gloom when he arrived.

Then it was Tuesday night, and some of the butterflies came back. Birt realized again that the fate of the project would be decided the next day. He stopped by Zelnick's room. "Are you nervous?" he asked.

"No," Zelnick replied. "I'm a fatalist, like Nixon. We've all done our best. We've worked hard and honestly. And I can accept whatever happens."

John went back to his room. It was after 1 A.M. that I responded to a faint knock on the door. It was Libby.

"Sorry to disturb you, David, but John asked me to deliver this to your room." She handed me an envelope, wished me good luck tomorrow, and left.

Inside the envelope was a handwritten note John had penned on the hotel's stationery. It was, at one and the same time, the most inspiring and the most constructive letter I can remember receiving. The expressions of confidence in me, coming from a man who could not, indeed would not on principle, exhibit an ounce of false schmaltz to save his life, moved me more than I can say.

And his recital, which followed, of the basic components of our mutually agreed strategy could not have been more economical or to the point.

> Today you should review only the evidence that would have been brought up in a court of law: and you should not depart from that evidence:
>
> It is not a conventional interview: you are exchanging interpretations of the known facts; you should talk almost as much as he does:
>
> Most importantly, don't be tempted to put brief and "pointed" questions that elicit long and vague answers: when he paints a picture that you know to be false, respond by painting, at the same length he does, the alternative picture as you understand it:
>
> Always keep firmly in mind that Watergate is a difficult subject for a mass audience to follow and at each stage consider that it is your responsibility to point out clearly to that audience the implication of any question, fact, event, statement or admission that you consider relevant:
>
> Stay cool and firm, but be polite: only raise your voice if and when you are pushed to:

I stopped reading for a moment. John was right to bring that up. It sounded very simple, even obvious, but I had been thinking a lot about it myself. It was one thing to talk about Nixon the archconspirator and for Bob or anyone to talk about that "son of a bitch" and so on in his absence. But it was quite another thing to say something like that to his face. It was not just the fact that here was a man who had faced and outfaced the most powerful men in the world, who had successfully "psyched" some of them. Though that was part of it. It was also that here was a polite, sometimes almost cordial, man with whom a conversation was about to take place in which the dictates of simple courtesy or good manners and the dictates of nailing the truth might be totally at odds.

John's note went on: "And finally, keep up the pressure at all times: You will win only if you can, so to speak, sprint the mile."

As so often, John had hit the nail on the head. I could not afford to relax *at all*. And that was in some ways unique. It's not that you "relax" fully in any interview, but in almost every other interview there were the odd moments in which it was possible to freewheel mentally—to gather one's thoughts, albeit only for a few moments. An anecdote by the interview's subject might be in progress in which the interests of both parties would coincide; both would want the story to be as witty and interesting as possible, for example.

But as far as tomorrow was concerned, that simply did not hold. At no point, even for a moment, were our interests going to coincide. My aim was to nail the basic truths about his involvement in the Watergate cover-up during an all too finite period of time. His aim was to filibuster, perhaps, or rather, to use his own words in our first interview, "to demolish." In a situation like that, anything I was going to get I was going to have to win.

It was a long, remarkably quiet ride to Monarch Bay. I remember John saying something to the effect of "You know something, you also have to stay *physically* in charge, as well. There is something that you do sometimes . . . you did it on Cambodia, and although I wasn't there at the time, it seemed to me as though you did it with Chile . . . and you did it with Ian Smith in Rhodesia . . . " Most of the time, however, I was reading silently, transcribing additional notes, and I had but few occasions to request additional information.

But as we neared the guardhouse at the Smiths' subdivision, I had one further request.

"We've talked a lot about the conspiracy to obstruct justice. Has anyone here read the actual statute?"

"Just a minute," said Jim. "I think there's a copy of it here in the Judiciary Committee volumes."

He quickly found the place and handed me the book. I began to read aloud: " 'Whoever corruptly endeavors to prevent, obstruct or impede the administration of justice . . .' Bob, that sounds pretty wide."

"I recall John Dean telling the Ervin committee that the definition of the crime was coextensive with the capacity of man to devise ways to prevent, obstruct or impede the administration of justice. In a sense, then, it means everything because it means nothing."

"A corrupt endeavor to prevent, obstruct or impede," I repeated. "Thank you, Jim. It may come in handy."

CHAPTER

WE ARRIVED EARLY. I WANTED TO ADDRESS BRIEFLY ALL OF THOSE WHO
had shared the experiences of the past weeks with us and who
would shortly be privy to the climactic moments of our encounter.

Even in the most casual of contacts with our crew, one quickly
became aware that for none of them was this just another job. The
term heard most often was "history." They knew that the interrogation of any former President was an event of some consequence.
And in the case of Richard Nixon, no part of the confrontation
would escape future examination. Scholars would scrutinize his
words. His demeanor would be studied by lawyers and laymen alike.
His voice would be tested by oral polygraph machines manned by
both amateur and professional sleuths for indications of falsehood
or veracity. The quality of his performance would be analyzed
by drama coaches. Even the quality of his makeup would be looked
at by those who recalled his damaging first debate with John F.
Kennedy.

So in a very real sense, the cameramen and assistants, the audio
men and technical directors, the electricians and our makeup man,

Ken Wensevic, were all sharing a historic moment and contributing to it. And I wanted to thank them and alert them to the pressures we would all be under in the days ahead.

"Gentlemen, you've all been superb," I said as the group gathered in the small front courtyard. "You have done your jobs magnificently and I simply wanted to say thank you. Today, we begin the most dramatic subject of all: Watergate.

"Many of you have already been contacted by the press on more than one occasion. You have resisted brilliantly the temptation to share your thoughts and observations with them. During three intense weeks, we have not had a single leak of any consequence, a single breach of confidence on anybody's part.

"Well, I can assure you that the pressures will not only continue, they will mount. Every reporter in the country wants to know what the former President has to say about Watergate. I must ask you not to tell them. Don't even tell your wives, or the woman you love. In fact, please don't tell either of them. Thank you again."

There was a sprinkling of applause. Several of the men shook my hand, or patted me on the back, or simply said, "Good luck, David," as I entered the house to change.

Birt asked Zelnick to join him in the production trailer. If something went wrong this morning, he would want the comfort of an instant second opinion.

Nixon arrived at his customary time, ten ten. As usual there was a small group of local residents gathered by the curb to greet him. He waved and smiled and shook a few hands. He looked good. He exuded confidence. He would be tough.

A tall, slender, gray-haired man stepped out of the Nixon car.

"Who is that?" Birt asked.

"It's Dick Moore," said Reston.

"He was one of Nixon's public-relations men at the White House," Birt recalled.

"And a fellow unindicted co-conspirator," Zelnick added. "He lives in New York now."

A second car pulled to the curb. Out of it climbed Diane Sawyer and Frank Gannon, two familiar faces from the negotiation period, neither of whom had attended the previous sessions.

They joined Moore on the sidewalk in front of the house, along with Ray Price, Khachigian and Brennan, who had, as usual, arrived early.

"They're all here," said Birt.

"Yes," said Reston. "All the President's Men."

On the set, we shook hands. The countdown began.

"Stop," said Don Clark. The outside doors were not properly closed. He started again.

"Ten, nine, eight . . ." Clark counted down.

This is it, I thought.

"Seven, six, five, four . . ."

The first question . . . The overview . . . The opening statement . . .

"Three, two, one."

"Mr. President, to try and review your account of Watergate in one program is a daunting task. But we'll press first of all through the sort of factual record and the sequence of events as concisely as we can to begin with. But just one brief preliminary question. Reviewing now your conduct over the whole of the Watergate period, with additional perspective now, three years out of office and so on, do you feel that you ever obstructed justice or were part of a conspiracy to obstruct justice?"

Nixon was about to admit nothing. The best thing, he said, would be to do exactly what I had said we would do and "go through the whole record in which I will say what I did, what my motives were, and then, we . . . I will give you my evaluation as to whether those actions or anything I said for that matter amounted to what you have called obstruction of justice."

That was fine with me, I said. I began with the June 17 break-in itself—the break-in and the various debriefings conducted by Dean and reported to Ehrlichman and Haldeman in the days that followed. By June 20 Haldeman knew enough to order Gordon Strachan to see that his White House files were "clean." And Ehrlichman knew enough to order Howard Hunt out of the country, only to rescind the order a short time later.

"Now that was just some of the background to what had been going on as you met with Haldeman on the morning of June the 20th, for that conversation with the memorable eighteen-and-a-half-minute gap in it. Now what in fact did Haldeman tell you that morning about Watergate?"

Nixon was disappointed. He had apparently expected me to take a pass at establishing pre-break-in knowledge on his part. The fact that I had not done so would not in the least dissuade him from answering the question I had not asked.

He had no prior knowledge of or involvement in the break-in, he said. In fact, as it occurred on a weekend, he hadn't even discussed the matter with Haldeman until their Monday-evening return flight from Key Biscayne. "I expressed, first, astonishment that such action could occur, because I thought it was stupid . . . crazy. Second, I expressed great concern with regard to whether anybody in the White House might be . . . have been involved."

Haldeman, according to Nixon, said there was no White House involvement, "but that a lower-level person at the committee had been involved."

"So we come back to, yes . . . what did Haldeman tell you during the eighteen-and-a-half-minute gap?"

"Haldeman's notes are the only recollection I have of what he told me," Nixon began.

If his refusal to indicate in answer to my first question whether or not he believed he had committed a crime suggested that he was going to pursue a highly legalistic defense, this sentence was conclusive proof of that intention. For Nixon had already testified from memory to hundreds of conversations, many remote in time and of little consequence. Now, unwilling to give a false account of his conversation with Haldeman, he was taking a route familiar to defendants in the dock and limiting his "recollection" to that which the documentary evidence could establish.

Ah, yes, I thought, perjury is a tough rap to prove.

Haldeman's notes of the conversation reflected, of course, only Nixon's postbriefing instructions to himself. "PR offensive," "Check the EOB for bugs." And so on.

Surprisingly, Nixon sought to use so sparse a record to "knock down one of the most outrageous stories that have ever been published"—that he or his agents erased eighteen-and-a-half minutes of the conversation because it was incriminating.

I took an instant decision. Nixon was clearly eager to deal with the eighteen-and-a-half-minute gap. And from the outset we had known that the question of intentional tape erasure was not one of those which could be proved but was one which had to be asked. I now felt that it might be useful to test Nixon out on an issue important enough to require us both to bear down, but not of central importance in terms of establishing his role in the cover-up conspiracy. The next few minutes on the subject of the eighteen-and-a-half-minute gap and the selection of Senator John Stennis as the man to authenticate the tapes were thus extremely valuable to me in terms of defining the ways in which I could be firm and where necessary interrupt, without sounding rude. They yielded no particular gems for posterity, but I was testing both Richard Nixon and myself, learning that I could press him as closely or as pointedly as I needed to, and learning that I could challenge him on a point of credibility quite directly: "When you put that fact, that body of evidence, together with the fact that the eighteen and a half minutes that happened to be erased was the first recorded conversation between the two of you about Watergate—you're asking us to take an awful lot on trust, aren't you?" Some important bridges had, in short, been crossed. The outcome, however, would depend on what happened when we engaged our main units. I decided that moment had come and said, "Let's come back to the timetable . . ."

I summarized for Nixon the highlights of his June 20 discussion with Colson, one of the conversations which—thanks to Jim's research—Nixon did not know we had. I recalled for him the talk of "pulling it all together," and doing "the right things to date," of all the arrested men being "pretty hard-line guys" and of leaving it "with the Cubans," or "stonewalling it" and Nixon's incautious remark, "If we didn't know better we would have thought the whole thing was deliberately botched."

Nixon's face became taut. It was a crucial moment. Suddenly I was showing material he didn't know was in our arsenal.

221

Still, he dismissed the new evidence as unimportant. He would not challenge the fact that between June 20 and 23, he learned of the possible involvement of Hunt and Liddy, in addition to the five arrested burglars.

But the important thing was not what he knew, but what his motive was. "My motive was, in everything I was saying or certainly thinking at the time, ah . . . ah, was not to try to cover up criminal action . . . but to be sure that as far as any slip-over—or, should I say, slop-over—I think would be a better word, any slop-over in a way that would damage innocent people or blow it into political proportions, it was that that I certainly wanted to avoid."

Nixon went on to list a few items of potential political concern to himself—the D.N.C. civil suit against CREEP growing out of the break-in, some of the allegations starting to surface against Rebozo—but, as far as I was concerned, he was on the threshold of a critical legal admission. Unless our assessment of the law was 100 percent erroneous, whatever motives may have lurked within his heart were utterly irrelevant. If, three days later, he took action to shield a man he knew to be guilty, he then became a willing member of a criminal conspiracy to obstruct justice.

NIXON: In other words, we were trying to politically contain it . . .
FROST: And you knew about Liddy on the twenty-first or twenty-second?
NIXON: I learned about Liddy, yes, on the twenty-first or twenty-second.
FROST: Is that why you raised his name in the conversation on the twenty-third? You had obviously heard about Liddy?
NIXON: Right. Right.

Nixon denied, however, that he had learned enough to believe that Mitchell was criminally involved. He had talked to Mitchell on the twentieth. Mitchell had apologized for "not policing the people in my organization as well as I should have."

Nixon said he took that as an indication that the burglary had been perpetrated without Mitchell's authorization or approval. He did not think Mitchell was criminally implicated. "I didn't believe it. I didn't believe that Mitchell could possibly—I thought he was too smart to appr—to have approved such a stupid thing."

A debatable point, but an irrelevant one, I thought. His knowledge of the involvement of Hunt and Liddy was sufficient.

Nixon, meanwhile, was rambling off on a new subject, this time trying to explain why he had "forgotten" for so many months about the substance of his June 23 conversation with Haldeman, recalling how busy he had been during the period. But this was no time for digressions.

"So you invented the C.I.A. thing that day as a cover?"

Nixon recoiled at the words.

"No. Now, let's use the word 'cover-up' in the sense that it has —should be used. If a cover-up is for the purpose of covering up criminal activities it is illegal. If, however, a 'cover-up,' as you have called it, is for a motive that is not criminal, that is something else again. And my motive was not criminal. I didn't believe that we were covering any criminal activities. I didn't believe that John Mitchell was involved. I didn't believe ah . . . ah . . . that for that matter anybody else was. I did believe, however, that with the F.B.I. investigations moving out all through the government with leaks coming out of the F.B.I., that this could be blown out of pro—out of proportion politically. And under the circumstances, I felt that if possible, if the C.I.A. could reach the conclusion that it was not in its interest, as well as our political interests not to have this investigation move over into the area which would uncover a C.I.A. agent with a long history of distinguished service, including his service in the Bay of Pigs, Howard Hunt—that then . . . that that would be the best way to contain the investigation . . ."

That was one of the historic Nixon tendencies. When he dissembled, he dissembled in all areas at once, partially and totally. The words were attached to each other at random. Inconsistencies didn't bother him at all, not even inconsistencies in the same or consecutive sentences.

Thus in the response to a single question he had denied the existence of a cover-up, admitted involvement in a cover-up, defined the term cover-up in a way that no lawyer would ever define it, indicated that he didn't believe anyone else was involved criminally, and then recalled his efforts to save Hunt, whom he had previously admitted to have been criminally involved.

The time, I thought, had come for one of those long declarative statements in the guise of a question which had become a part of my life in the past two or three weeks.

So as Nixon again denied his involvement in any criminal cover-up activity, I objected.

"But surely, in all you've just said, you have proved exactly that that was the case. That there was a cover-up of criminal activity because you've already said, and the record shows, that you knew that Hunt and Liddy were involved. You'd been told that Hunt and Liddy were involved at the moment when you told the C.I.A. to 'tell the F.B.I. to stop—period,' as you put it. At that point, only five people had been arrested. Liddy was not even under suspicion. And so you knew, in terms of intent, and you knew, in terms of foreseeable consequences, that the result would be that in fact criminals would be protected. Hunt and Liddy, who were criminally liable, would be protected . . . So that's obstruction of justice—"

NIXON: Now just a moment—
FROST: —period.

Nixon quibbled with my assessment, but, after a short tangle, we came back to the same point. He knew that Hunt and Liddy were involved. He asked the C.I.A. to take steps to call the F.B.I. to heel before its investigation reached them. Therefore, he was involved in an obstruction of justice, or at least an attempt to obstruct justice.

Nixon tried another exit from his predicament.

The points to remember, he suggested, were, first, that General Walters had refused to implement the plan and, second, that when Pat Gray called him on July 6 to warn him that aides were trying to "mortally wound you," "I said, Pat, go right ahead with your investigation."

"Yeah, but the point is, that obstruction of justice is obstruc-

224

tion of justice if it's for a minute or five minutes, much less for the period of June 23 to July 5th, when, I think, when he talked to Walters and decided to go ahead—the day before he spoke to you on July the 6th. It's obstruction of justice for however long a period, isn't it? And also, it's no defense to say that the plan failed, that the C.I.A. didn't go along with it. Refused to go along with it. Said it was transparent. I mean, if I try to rob a bank and fail, that's no defense. I still tried to rob that bank. I would say you still tried to obstruct justice, and succeeded for that period. He's testified—they did not interview Ogarrio."

Nixon tried again to back off. The questions seemed to have struck him like blows to the solar plexus. They were not only telling legal blows, but facts buried deep in the records of the various Watergate proceedings. So he decided to play lawyer and put me at a tactical disadvantage.

"Now just a moment," he began. "You're again making the case, which of course is your responsibility as the attorney for the prosecution. Let me make the case as it should be made—even were I not the one who was involved—for the defense. The case for the defense here is this: You use the term obstruction of justice. You perhaps have not read the statute with regard to respect . . . ah . . . ah . . . obstruction of justice."

"Well, I have," I interjected, sorely tempted to tell him that I had inspected it only minutes before coming on the set. But even my more modest claim knocked him off stride to the point where he had trouble articulating his words.

"Obstructed—well, oh, I'm sorry, of course you probably have read it, but possibly you might have missed it because when I read it, many years ago in, ah . . . perhaps when I was studying law . . . if, although the statute didn't even exist then, because it's a relatively new statute, as you know." (At this moment, the laughter in the production trailer could have registered on the Richter scale.)

"Ah, but in any event," Nixon continued, "when I read it, even in recent time, I was not familiar with all of the implications of it. The statute doesn't require just an act . . . The statute has the specific provision . . . one must corruptly impede a judicial . . .

"Well," I interrupted, "a corrupt endeavor is enough."

"Conduct . . . all right . . . we'll . . . a conduct endeavor . . . corrupt intent, and that gets to the point of motive. One must have a corrupt motive. Now, I did not have a corrupt motive."

I reminded Nixon of the conspiracy law—like the obstruction statute itself, another of the tough anticrime measures passed during the early days of his administration. Conspiracy required only an agreement to break the law, an agreement which, in fact, existed among himself and his two aides, Haldeman and Ehrlichman. "And, followed by that, there is an overt act, to follow it. So I would say it's both obstruction of justice and conspiracy to obstruct justice."

Again, Nixon retreated to his first argument. All right, using the C.I.A. was a mistake. In retrospect, he shouldn't have done it. But, "My motive was pure political containment. And political containment is not a corrupt motive. If so, for example, we, President Truman would have been impeached."

I was not going to nibble at that one, though twice Nixon would come back to Truman's instructions to the executive agencies to neither cooperate nor testify in Nixon's subcommittee investigation of Alger Hiss.

To avoid unfairness, however, we would research the point between our two Watergate sessions. Truman did not, to be sure, cooperate with the Nixon subcommittee. But unless he knew that Hiss had committed a crime—and no one has suggested that he did—his actions would in no way be comparable to Nixon's in trying to get the F.B.I. off the trails of Hunt and Liddy, both of whom he knew to be guilty of felonies.

Again, though, it was time to drive home to Nixon our point of law. "The point is that . . . motive can be helpful when intent is not clear. Your intent is absolutely clear. It's stated again. 'Stop this investigation here, period.' The foreseeable, inevitable consequence, if you'd been successful, would have been that Hunt and Liddy would not have been brought to justice."

Nixon appeared to have been shocked by our preparedness to meet his legal arguments head on. He had taken the calculated risk of conducting a highly legalistic defense, plainly similar to a defendant at a criminal trial trying to squeeze through a loophole in the law. While we had always viewed this portion of the interview as an opportunity to put Nixon the "defendant" on the stand, we figured that Nixon would steadfastly resist any such strategy, would want to distance himself from what had happened in court to Mitchell, Haldeman, and Ehrlichman. But he seemed to be the prisoner of some perverse sense of pride, an unwillingness to concede the fact that the Ford pardon had been the only thing to separate him from their demeaning fate. No, Nixon seemed intent on using all his considerable skills to prove that he could have gone through their ordeal and beaten the rap.

If he had succeeded, our project would have been dead. But instead he was now badly bruised. Through a combination of guile and grit he had tried to construct a legal shelter out of straw. We had blown it away. That contingency had not been in his battle plan.

It was important briefly to cover the period of July 6, 1972, to January 8, 1973, when some of the most incriminating of the Nixon conversations would resume. A great deal happened between those two dates, I reminded Nixon. "You would say, I think, that you were not aware of it. I, I think, was arguing that you were a part of it as a result of the June 23rd conversations."

The preceding minutes had heightened the sense of confidence I began to feel during our opening detour. I could assert the gravest charges against the former President in a matter-of-fact conversational tone of voice, but without hedging my words in the slightest.

"You're gonna say that I was a part of it as a result of the June 23rd conversation?" Nixon asked in an incredulous way.

"Yes."

"After July 6th, when I talked to Gray?"

"I would have to say that you joined a conspiracy which you therefore never left."

"No. no. Then we totally disagree on that."

"But I mean, those are the two positions," I repeated in the cause of clarity.

Next I wanted Nixon to stake out his basic position regarding his knowledge of the cover-up. I had a number of questions designed to undermine it once he did.

"Now, you in fact, however, would say that you first learned of the cover-up on March the 21st. Is that right?

"On March 21st was the date when I was first informed of the fact, the important fact to me in that conversation was of the blackmail threat that was being made by Howard Hunt, who was one of Watergate's participants. But not about Watergate. But about activities other than Watergate, which were matters involving highly sensitive foreign-policy matters."

This was, of course, totally inconsistent with the record of that March 21st conversation with Dean, not to mention dozens of Nixon's own former statements about when he learned fully of the Watergate cover-up. But to go after that now would interrupt my line of questioning. I promised only to come back to the point later, and again reminded Nixon of the fact that much had gone on after the Gray conversation.

"No," he said, "I don't know what you're referring to."

"Well, for instance, your personal lawyer, Herbert Kalmbach, coming to Washington to start the raising of $219,000 of hush money approved by Haldeman and Ehrlichman. They went ahead, though, without clearing it with you?"

Nixon said he had checked the record with his two former colleagues and would stick by his statement that he had not been informed. Of course, though, "If I had been informed the money was being raised for humanitarian purposes to help these people with their defense, I would certainly have approved it."

"Right," I said, "and if you'd been told that they were saying that it was for humanitarian reasons but it was being delivered on the tops of phone booths with aliases and at airports, and with people with gloves on . . . would you have believed that it was humanitarian reasons? . . . That's not normally the way that lawyers' fees are delivered, is it?"

Nixon conceded that "of course, I would have had a suspicion about it." Then, perhaps more revealingly, he added, "As a matter of fact, I think that was the great mistake of those involved in contributing the . . . and also in ah . . . delivering the money and providing the money in that period . . . didn't do it openly." He thought the Cuban Committee he had "read about" would have been "perfectly all right."

As an aside, recalling to myself the list of cover stories concocted before our eyes in the transcripts, I mentioned to Nixon that that story of his having "read" about a Cuban Committee was invented at an April 25 meeting to explain his knowledge of it in his March 21 meeting with Dean. Nixon said he really had read it in January.

We moved on to the January 8 conversation with Colson. But as I began the question, Nixon wanted to stress that he was not informed of any transfer of funds from the White House until a March 20 conversation with Haldeman. "But he thought it was for humanitarian purposes," Nixon emphasized.

Yes, but Ehrlichman later said the money had been paid to prevent the defendants from going "off the reservation." And "Haldeman actually admitted that it was because the defendants were 'gonna blow.' Which only has one meaning, doesn't it?"

"Yeah," said Nixon. "Well it has one meaning, but let's understand what the word 'blowing' means too."

Was he really going to suggest that "blowing" meant something other than blowing the whistle on the whole Watergate scheme?

He was indeed. "And as far as blowing is concerned, what they were referring to . . . was blowing in terms of ah . . . as Dean said on March 21st, that they could have sold out to the Democrats for a million dollars in this period before the election . . . ah . . . of . . . or millions of dollars. Ah . . . Ehrlichman said, my concern was not about their talking to the grand jury, ah . . . speaking of the defendants and so forth. My concern was not any criminal activities they might talk about. My concern was about their talking to the press."

Aha! I thought. Another nifty little theory crafted before our very eyes in the Watergate transcripts. "But when he said that, you said, 'Come on, we've got to think of a better story than that.' And you still haven't."

Nixon had no direct answer to that, but kept insisting that he had believed his colleagues. Why, in April, he had specifically instructed them to "get a line, not a lie" on the hush-money payments. That caliber of defense ought to be left to twist slowly in the wind, I thought. It would have been a pity to disturb it. So I again returned to the January 8 conversation with Colson.

I was refreshing Nixon's recollection of the conversation. When the clemency subject had come up, he had said that Hunt was a "simple case," but that he would have difficulty with some of the others. Colson then said that "the vulnerabilities are different." The otherrs, he said, "don't know any direct information." Nixon had then said, "Well, I think I agree," to which Colson had replied, "See, I don't care if they spend five years in jail."

"He forgot the compassionate bit for a moment there," I told Nixon. "And then he went on, 'I can't . . .' "

NIXON: What did I say then?
FROST: Ah, he continued first of all—
NIXON: No, no, what did I say? Go on.
FROST: I don't have your quote here.

I knew the conversation practically by heart. But I had no idea what Nixon was driving at. I could not believe I had left out anything material.

NIXON: I said, "Oh, no."
FROST: "Oh, no," you said, I remember you saying that.
NIXON: Well, why isn't it there?
FROST: Because I was quoting Colson and continuing with Colson.
NIXON: You understand? Are there any quotes from me on the page?
FROST: Ah . . .
NIXON: Why do you leave—
FROST: Yes—
NIXON: —out the—
FROST: Yes, yes, there are.
NIXON: Why do you leave out the one? Why do you leave out the one? Why did your—I don't understand. I, I can't believe you would distort the record that way. I really can't.

230

I had taken no chances on anything like this destroying the integrity of the interrogation. As a precaution, I had taken the complete set of Watergate transcripts onto the set with me. And as Nixon pressed his point, I leafed through the binder until I located the conversation of January 8. And there was the troublesome quote in full context.

> FROST: All right. Let's get the full transcript of this thing.
> NIXON: No, no, no. Go ahead.

And leave that point open? Not likely.

> FROST: Because there's another thing that you said which was: "Perjury, that's a damned hard rap to prove." That's one quote.
> NIXON: That's correct.
> FROST: And, "They haven't got that kind of evidence on Mitchell or anybody else, have they?" Which is important, obviously, for indicating that you're still concerned about Mitchell. But the key quote that I wanted to quote to you was: "See, I don't care if they spend five years in jail." And he continues, doesn't say that you'd agreed or disagreed, and I think, "Oh, no," could be agreement or disagreement. And doesn't affect the record.
> NIXON: Oh . . .
> FROST: "They can't hurt us. Hunt and Liddy: direct meetings; discussions very incriminating to us." Now, all of that linked in with the reference to clemency, doesn't that suggest that clemency and silence were being linked?
> NIXON: Well.
> FROST: In the minds of the two people having that conversation?
> NIXON: They, it, it, may have been . . .

I had beaten back his challenge, a challenge which once again showed both the utter desperation of his position and his complete mastery of the transcripts. The two omitted words had meant absolutely nothing. But again, he had worked like a demon to get ready. He had worked like a lawyer preparing for his once-in-a-lifetime trial. His main problem as a lawyer was the case he had chosen to represent.

He was on the defensive now, recalling the close personal relationship between Colson and Hunt, the compassion Colson must genuinely have felt for his friend, particularly in the circumstances of Mrs. Hunt's recent fatal airplane crash.

But the two of you had also discussed parole, I recalled.

"That, that a parole might be arranged, which I, of course, could not do, but a parole board on its own could. Ah, that could be considered," Nixon allowed.

FROST: And someone said you controlled—
NIXON: On a humanitarian basis—
FROST: —the parole board. (John Dean, as I recalled, had been the speaker in the transcripts.)
NIXON: Now, what Colson's motive was, ah, that could be one thing. What my motive was, is something else again . . .

As would recur later, with respect to Haldeman and Ehrlichman themselves, Nixon had carried his friend's baggage just as long as he could. But now it had become too heavy. And, in a single sentence, he had unceremoniously dumped the load. Colson may have been covering up, but not Nixon.

Colson thus dispatched, Nixon continued with a discussion of his own motives, which he again insisted were purely humanitarian.

"And so March 21st was the first time you really knew about the cover-up?" I asked.

"March the 21st was the date in which the full import, the full impact of the cover-up came to me . . ."

Totally inconsistent, as I had figured it would be, with his statements of a few moments earlier regarding the delicate national-security things he had learned about on March 21, but that was fine. He was now perfectly set up. I let him run on a few moments about some familiar March 13 and March 17 conversations which added little or nothing, one way or the other. March 21 remained key, the cornerstone of his defense.

"But in that case, if that was the first occasion, why did you say in such strong terms to Colson on February the 14th—which is more than a month before—you said to him, 'The cover-up is the main ingredient. That's where we gotta cut our losses; my losses are to be cut. The President's losses gotta be cut on the cover-up deal?' "

Nixon was stung. Again he had been hit with a transcript he had not known was in our collection. He needed a moment's reflection.

"Why did I say that?"

"February the 14th?"

Here Nixon gave another of those waves of the arm and forlorn sideways glances that reminded me of no one so much as the late Jack Benny. "Because I read the American papers . . . and in January, the stories that came out . . . not, not, not just from the *Washington Post,* the famous series by some unnamed correspondents, who have written a best-selling book since then (another Bennyesque gesture), but *The New York Times,* the networks and so forth, were talking about hush money. They were talking about clemency. They . . . ah, ah, ah, for cover-up and all the rest. It was that that I was referring to at that point. I was referring to the fact that there was a lot of talk about cover-up and that this must be avoided at all cost."

A tinge of admiration mingled with my sense of overwhelming skepticism. Not too bad for an ad lib. Hardly a soul in all of Christendom would believe it, but still, not a bad ad lib.

He had a tougher job with the February 13 conversation.

"There's one very self-contained quote, and I read the whole of this conversation of February the 13th, which I don't think's ever been published . . . and there was one very clear quote in it that I thought was—"

NIXON: It hasn't been published, you say?
FROST: No, I think it's available to anybody who consults the records, but, but people don't consult all the records—
NIXON: Oh, just wondered if we'd seen it.

The statement I quoted was from Nixon to Colson, and in its own warped way, it was one of almost elegant simplicity: "When I'm speaking about Watergate, though, that's the whole point of the election. This tremendous investigation rests, unless one of the seven begins to talk. That's the problem."

I lingered over every word. They were all so devastating. All those bragged-about F.B.I. interviews, the grand jury appearances, the "investigation" conducted by Counsel Dean for his Chief Executive. Nixon had dismissed all the McGovern charges about Watergate with a few, brief imperious references to the majesty of the inquiry which had been conducted. The greatest since the assassination of J.F.K., Attorney General Kleindienst had assured the nation, in support of his patron at the White House. In a sense the election did rest on "this tremendous investigation." Not that McGovern was likely to have won anyway. Had Nixon himself been among the captured bandits, that probably would not have elected poor McGovern. But the integrity of the second Nixon term did rest on those presidential assurances. The mandate Nixon sought and achieved rested on them. The reorganization of government, the pursuit of détente, the new conservatism—it was all there before him, "unless one of the seven begins to talk."

"Now in that remark," I said, "it seems to me that someone running that cover-up couldn't have expressed it more clearly than that. Could they?"

"What, what do we mean by 'one of the seven beginning to talk'?" Nixon replied. "I . . . how many times do I have to tell you that as far as these seven were concerned, the concern that we had—certainly that I had—was that men who worked in this kind of covert activity; men who, of course, realize it's dangerous activity to work in, particularly since it involves illegal entry—that once they're apprehended, they are likely to say anything . . . "

Nixon again referred here to the sensitive national-security matters that he was afraid would be revealed by the seven.

The answer was utterly preposterous. Rather than saying "anything" once they are apprehended, trained operatives in the covert intelligence field—certainly at the level of a Hunt or Liddy—are likely to reveal little of their mission. That's not the way the professional spy business works.

However, for the moment, I thought a simple statement indicating that I had not been the least persuaded by the former President's tortured discourse would do.

"I just think, though, that one has to go contrary to the normal usage of language of almost ten thousand gangster movies to interpret 'This tremendous investigation rests unless one of the seven begins to talk. That's the problem' as anything other than some sort of conspiracy to stop him from talking about something damaging to the person making the speech."

"Well," said Nixon, in a tone of voice reflecting something close to fatigue with the effort he had expended for so few returns, "you could, you could state your conclusion and I've stated my views."

"That's correct."

"So now we go on with the rest of it."

The "rest of it" was, of course, Nixon's March 21 conversation with Dean. For days I had wrestled with the best possible strategy for interrogating Nixon about it. The more often I had read the transcript, the more damning it seemed, not because of the total absence of ambiguity and not because one could conclude from it that the $75,000 payment to Hunt later that day was the direct result of a presidential command.

The conversation proved to me beyond a reasonable doubt that it was Richard Nixon, not Dean, not even Haldeman, who urged that the cover-up continue. It was Dean who warned the President in the starkest possible terms that Watergate had become a "cancer on the presidency" which, unless cut out, could destroy the presidency; Dean who warned that several—including himself—would likely go to jail; and Dean who alerted the President to the pending blackmail demanded by Hunt and who suggested that meeting it would not resolve the problem with finality.

Whatever his underlying motives, however "blind" his ambition had been in the past, Dean here was performing as a loyal staffer should, presenting his boss with the complete set of facts on which a decision must necessarily be based. The Nixon White House and legal staff would later go over the Dean briefing with a fine-tooth comb. Here and there it would find a stray fact unreported, a conclusion regarding guilt or innocence not supported entirely by all the available evidence. But the stoutest Nixon defender could not say what missing ingredient could possibly have altered the picture Dean painted for his superior, what the President needed to know that Dean hadn't told him in order to act in accordance with his constitutional responsibilities, why on the basis of what he was told that day he didn't act in a way totally contrary to the way he did.

No, it was Nixon who, throughout the conversation, repeatedly returned to the subject of Hunt's financial demand, to the desirability of meeting it, to the time it would buy, the options it would keep open, to the possibilities of raising more money to meet later demands. And if Nixon could find here and there a saving reference to the difficulty of early clemency, he would find the record barren of any suggestion that he had so much as lifted a finger to bring the course of continuing criminality to a halt. And, if that was not fatal to his position as a man accused of crime, it was most certainly fatal to his position as a President accused of malfeasance.

But I needed a way of driving all of this home. And I had settled upon a simple list of sixteen incriminating items on the tape. I had mentioned nothing of this plan to my colleagues. The right opportunity might never present itself. We would see.

I began cautiously, allowing Nixon the fact that the payment to Hunt was probably set in motion prior to his meeting with Dean and completed later that evening. Nevertheless, had he, during that fateful conversation, endorsed or ratified what was going on with regard to that payment?

No, said Nixon. He hadn't ratified it. He did consider the payment. Not, of course, because of any concern about Watergate, but rather because of some of those things Hunt had done for Ehrlichman, things like the "Ellsberg problem."

Once again, as he had with the June 23, 1972, conversation, Nixon had begun his defense by conceding all the elements of a crime. Even were his statement true—and the March 21 conversation shows no neat cleavage between Hunt's Watergate activities and his other "seamy" business—the payment to Hunt would have been just as illegal had it been conveyed to procure his silence only with respect to the Ellsberg matter. For that too had involved criminal conduct by Ehrlichman, Hunt, Liddy and their associates. Indeed, Mr. Nixon, while still President, had referred to the Ellsberg break-in as "illegal, unauthorized by me and completely deplorable."

"That's the illegal break-in," I reminded Nixon.

NIXON: Which I'd learned about on the seventeenth.

FROST: You'd learned four days—

NIXON: I knew that certainly that it, to have that, ah, come out, ah, while it should have had, as it eventually did when it did come out, the effect of poisoning the case, might poison it, and future events proved that I was right . . .

Still another crime, I thought. Not only was he admitting that he let the Hunt payment proceed to prevent officials from learning of the Ellsberg break-in, but he was doing so because he didn't want to poison the ongoing Ellsberg prosecution—a further breach of Ellsberg's civil rights and an incredible admission for the nation's chief law-enforcement officer.

Nixon padded his answer with reference to the other work done by Hunt, principally uncovering of the famous "Radford leak" regarding his administration's "tilt toward the Paks" in December 1970. I thought the list needed a little fleshing out. "Surely the things we know about now, the things you would have been likely to be more concerned about: the hideously embarrassing, illegal Ellsberg break-in: interviewing DeMott for dirt on Kennedy; ah, the Watergate break-in and details on that: spiriting Dita Beard out of town. I mean, those are the rather seamy, squalid things we know he did. And surely those would have been the ones that would have been embarrassing, because as a 'patriot' he probably wouldn't have revealed the others anyway."

Nixon conceded that he didn't know what Hunt knew or what he would do. "I was very concerned about his emotional stability." Still he had only considered the payment of blackmail; he had not authorized it. From the transcript he recalled saying, "Well, you could raise the money, but doesn't it finally get down to a question of clemency?" And when Dean replied that it did, Nixon recalled saying, "Well, you can't provide clemency and that would be wrong for sure."

"Now," he continued, "if clemency's the bottom line, then providing the money isn't going to make any sense."

The statement, "It's wrong, John, that's for sure," is of course one of the most famous in the Watergate transcripts, and had become one of our catchphrases. In context, having read it dozens of times, it was clear to me that Nixon had been expressing a tactical conclusion with respect to clemency, at least until the Christmas following the 1974 congressional elections.

But as he had done while still in office, Nixon here tried to broaden the phrase to embrace both a moral and a tactical judgment, with respect to both clemency and the payment of blackmail.

NIXON: It would have been wrong in this case to give it to Hunt, when he was . . . when it was given for the purpose of blackmail. In other words, hush money. That would have been wrong.
FROST: Yes.
NIXON: And that's what I meant.

It was time for the list, I thought.

FROST: But when you were talking about the money, the $120,000 demanded, that, in fact, he got $75,000 of, that evening. Ah, bearing in mind what you were saying earlier about reading that in the overall context of the conversation, the . . . is there any doubt, when one read . . . reading the whole conversation:
1. "You could get a million dollars and you could get it in cash. I know where it could be gotten."
2. "Your major guy to keep under control is Hunt."
3. "Don't you have to handle Hunt's financial situation?"
4. "Let me put it frankly: I wonder if that doesn't have to be continued?"
5. "Get the million bucks, it would seem to me that would be worthwhile."
6. "Don't you agree that you'd better get the Hunt thing?"
7. "That's worth it, and that's buying time."
8. "We should buy time on that, as I pointed out to John."

9. "Hunt has at least got to know this before he's sentenced."

10. "First, you've got the Hunt problem. That ought to be handled."

11. "The money can be provided. Mitchell could provide the way to deliver it. That could be done. See what I mean?"

12. "But let's come back to the money. ["They were off on something else there," I said. "Desperate to get away from the money; bored to death with the continual references to the money."] A million dollars and so forth and so on. Let me say that I think you could get that in cash."

13. "That's why your immediate thing, you've got no choice with Hunt but the hundred and twenty or whatever it is. Right?"

14. "Would you agree that this is a buy-time thing? You'd better damn well get that done, but fast."

15. "Now, who's gonna talk to him? Colson?"

16. "We have no choice."

·And so on. Now reading, as you've requested—

NIXON: All right. Fine.

FROST: —within the whole context, that is—

I had gathered momentum as I went along. Nixon remained guarded, his countenance placid through the first several items. Then his lips quivered. His eyes fluttered like the wings of a moth shot through with electric current. His head lurched backward with each new item. He was a man in pain, a man under the lash, but not yet a man ready to concede defeat. Slowly the pain turned to determination. He was collecting himself, putting body and mind back together, rallying his mental and physical resources as a field commander, whose ranks have been broken, rallies his troops in the hope of a counterattack.

"Let me stop you right there. Right there. You're doing something here which I am not doing and I will not do throughout these broadcasts. You have every right to, ah, you were reading there, out of context, out of order, because I have read this and I know—"

FROST: Oh, I know.

NIXON: —it really better than you do.

FROST: I'm sure you do.

Nixon: I should know it better, because I was there. It's no reflection on you. You know it better than anybody else I know, incidentally, and, ah, you're doing it very well . . .

His defense rested on the inconclusive nature of the last several minutes of the March 21 conversation. One of his last remarks, he said, was, "But ya never have a choice with Hunt. Do you ever have one?"

"Rhetorically," Nixon went on, "ya never have a choice with Hunt. Because, when you finally come down to it, it gets down to clemency. Now, why after all of that horror story—and it was—I mean, even considering that, I mean, must horrify people. Why would you consider paying money to somebody who's blackmailing the White House? I've tried to give you my reasons. I was concerned about what he would do. But my point is: after that, why not? Why not you do what was not done by Mr. Jaworski in his book? What was not done by Mr. Doar before the House Judiciary Committee? Read the last sentence. The last sentence which says, after that, 'You never have any choice with Hunt, because it finally come down to clemency.' And I said, six times in that conversation, you didn't read that in your ten things, six times I said, 'You can't provide clemency.' "

I wanted to be fair. But I could never make the link Nixon and his supporters had urged us to make between clemency and the immediate blackmail demand by Hunt. Clemency was a tough, long-term proposition. A better solution would have to be found. The $120,000, though, was simply a "buy-time thing." There was nothing mutually exclusive, or indeed even mildly inconsistent, about ratifying the blackmail payment and declining to go ahead with clemency. And it seemed to me that Nixon's own contemporaneous recollection was that he had approved the blackmail payment. He knew it was in the works on March 21. He learned it had been paid on March 22.

And I had one more tape to call on.

"Let me quote to you then, I've been through the record. I want to be totally fair. . . . But the last thing in the transcripts I can find about this subject was you talking on April 20. And you were recollecting this meeting and you said that you said to Dean and Haldeman, 'Christ, turn over any cash we got.' That's your recollection of the meeting on April the 20th when you didn't know you were on television."

"On April 20th," Nixon admitted, "it could well have been my recollection. But my point is: The question we have is whether or not the payment was made as a result of a direction given by the President for that purpose? And the point is, it was not."

The highly technical, legalistic defense, was doing Nixon no good. But his convoluted statements of fact could be confusing to those in the audience not listening with the rapt attention of jurors at a trial. We had spent so much time debating what Nixon had done on March 21. Now, with the session about to end, perhaps it was time to consider what he had *not* done.

"Well, there's two concerns to be said to that. One is: I think that the time—my reading of the tapes tells me, trying to read in an open-minded way—that the writing, not just between the lines, but on so many of the lines that I quoted, is very, very clear that you were in fact endorsing at least the short-term solution of paying this sum of money to buy time. But the—the other point to be said is: Here's Dean, talking about this hush money for Hunt; talking about blackmail and all of that: I would say that you endorsed, or ratified it. But let's leave that to one side—"

NIXON: I didn't endorse or ratify it.
FROST: —Why didn't you stop it?

Again the question seemed to jolt Nixon. And when jolted, he dissembled until he collected himself. "Because at the point, I had nothing to—no knowledge of the fact that it was going to be paid," he began.

It wasn't a very promising line of defense, though, and he opted for a more reasonable one. "The point I make is this: It's possible . . . it's a mistake that I didn't stop it. The point that I make is that I did consider it. I've told you I considered it. I considered it for reasons that I thought were very good ones. Ah, I would not

241

consider it for the other reasons which would have been, in my view, bad ones."

We had reached the end of our session. Birt and Zelnick had been sitting as if in a trance during much of the past hour. I had scored more heavily than either of them had dared hope. Zelnick patted his colleague on the back and bolted through the trailer door, down the steps and toward the house.

He met me at the door of my room.

"David, it was super. First-rate. Sensational."

We embraced, then looked around for John. He was standing closeted with the Nixon staff outside their monitor room, where Brennan and Khachigian had stopped him as he followed Bob.

"What a mistake," said Brennan. "What a mistake."

"The President of the United States made himself look like a criminal defendant with David as prosecutor," Khachigian agreed.

"We didn't want him to go that route," said Brennan.

"But this was one subject that we simply could not discuss with him. It was just too personal," said Khachigian.

"That's right," said Diane Sawyer, joining in the conversation. "He hasn't written the Watergate part of his book yet. So none of us knew what he was going to say . . . "

CHAPTER

10

THE FOG HAD LIFTED. THE CLOUD OF GLOOM WAS ONLY A MEMORY. It had evaporated once and for all in two and one half hours of brilliant morning sunshine. Marv's face took on the look of a man ten years younger. Jim, a calm presence even during moments of intense dispute, seemed now like a man who had achieved nirvana, his countenance a portrait of total enlightenment and peace. Bob, who gave ground grudgingly when he thought things were not going well, now with equal passion defied one and all to suggest so much as a single imperfection in the morning's proceedings. There were instant replays of every pivotal exchange.

In such moments, John would feel the need to keep us on an even keel. Euphoria, even as well founded as today's, was also a danger. If premature, it could lead to mental relaxation and a corresponding inability to maximize our advantage. Success and failure were not absolute points on a spectrum. It was all a question of degrees, percentiles. Before this morning's session, we were heading for a finish which would place us in the 50 to 60 percent range in terms of achieving what it was possible to achieve. Now we were in the 75 to 80 percent range. If we pressed ahead, with hard work and luck we could score 90 to 95 percent. And then we must strive for more.

Viewing the tapes and reading the transcripts the next morning changed none of our views. The change in Nixon's demeanor as the interrogation progressed was palpable. And the sixteen points I had listed from his March 21 conversation with Dean had an even more devastating quality in the replay than we had recalled. It was so devastating, in fact, that we were posed with an ethical dilemma. One of the conventions agreed upon with the Nixon people at the outset of the tapings permitted Nixon to make minor cosmetic adjustments while the cameras rolled, without fear of embarrassment when the programs were broadcast. Throughout the twenty-eight hours he kept within reach a white handkerchief saturated with ammonium chloride to combat perspiration, applying it sparingly from time to time. But as I had recited the sixteen incriminating utterances from March 21, the camera isolated on Nixon had zoomed in for its close-up. His facial expressions and reactions were telling, and relevant to any judgment. His lower lip had also broken out with moisture. He had reached for his handkerchief and applied the ammonium chloride more than once. The visual impact was enormous and, we thought, a journalistically valid statement of what he was going through. But could we, consistent with both our agreement and our desire to be fair, show the sequence to millions of viewers? We debated the point as seriously as we had debated anything. And in the end, with everybody's agreement, I instructed Jørn to eliminate all shots of the former President not only when he was dabbing his face with his handkerchief, but immediately before and after. Any reaction shots of Nixon during the exchange would have to come from whatever was left. But the picture of the former President during those two minutes would remain with us all. Better than anything else it demonstrated the physical element of our month-long confrontation, the fact that to both of us the contest had been much like an international chess championship match where the players shed weight and become gaunt in the struggle to bear up physically under the burden of mental competition.

But now it was time to look ahead. John had a particular concern. "I don't know what Nixon will come up with on Friday. Jack and Ken seemed so genuinely disappointed when I talked to them yesterday that I feel sure that they will do everything in their power to reach Mr. Nixon and persuade him to take a different line. I don't know what it will be, but I think we will have to be ready for it."

Bob expected no strategic adjustment. "Contrition in any meaningful sense is alien to Nixon's personality. He is psychologically incapable of it. We are going to face the same stonewall tomorrow we faced on Wednesday."

Over the next few hours, our "seminar" went back and forth on the events of March 21 to April 30, the second of our two evidentiary periods. What if the former President had come up with something favorable to "clarify" his position on March 21? Here John suggested the simple response "Let us not go over your every word again. The only question worth asking is, 'Why didn't you call the cops?' "

At the end of our session, I asked the team, "Assuming what Bob said earlier about the stonewall is right, and taking John's point, do you think that at the end we ought to invite him expressly to retract the hard-line approach and go the other route? Do you think the occasion calls for it?"

"Absolutely," said John. "Whether or not you agree with it—and I don't, by and large—I feel he's presented a coherent view of himself and his administration except in these abuse areas. But as long as he remains rigid there, the rest of his record will never be taken and debated seriously." Birt smiled. "It's ironic, isn't it? That's precisely the line we have taken with the Nixon people all along. And we did it mainly for our tactical reasons. And now we're urging him to do it mainly in his own interest."

The discussion continued, and we finally decided that, towards the end of the session, we would indeed present Nixon with one final opportunity to purge himself of this albatross called Watergate which he wore so willingly about his neck.

"Bob," I said. "You've been so adept at anticipating Nixon's responses all along, how do you think he'll reply to an emotive challenge like this?"

"His face will contort," said Bob. "His eyes will glisten. His voice will break. His head will nod gently and sadly. With the weight of history on his every word, he will say . . . 'Screw you.' "

When ten ten the next morning came and passed, we began to get uneasy. Never before had the ex-President been so much as a minute late. Birt and Zelnick took their places in the production trailer, the rest of our group gathered in the monitor room. Don fidgeted uneasily about the set. Jørn said his technical crew was ready. But still no Nixon.

He finally arrived, seventeen minutes late. I was stunned by the sight of him. He seemed to have aged five years in the past few days. His voice was husky with fatigue, his eyes strained and bloodshot. His countenance bore marks of that strange, vaguely terrified look of his last months in office. There on the set, while Jørn made his continuity tests, conversation was desperately difficult. Somehow or other, the name of Henry Kissinger cropped up. I seized on it gratefully.

> FROST: Is ah . . . is Kissinger enjoying his new role as it were, hmmm?
> DON CLARK: We're rolling, gentlemen, ten seconds . . .
> NIXON: Trying to but ah . . . any man that's had his power . . .
> DON CLARK: Four, three, two, one . . .

Like two lawyers returning from a brief recess, our conversation began slowly. The former President had a point that he wished to add to our discussion of the Stennis Compromise. While Senator Stennis may indeed have had a hearing problem—which in fact he is not sensitive about—any bewilderment I might have felt about his selection as the man to listen to the tapes should be tempered by a point that Nixon had not mentioned, namely that Senator

Stennis was chairman of the Senate ethics committee. I nodded and then, for some reason, thought that a moment of humor might break the ice before the day's proceedings really began. I was wrong.

"What you're really saying," I said, "is there's no truth to the rumor that when you picked up the phone and telephoned him and said 'Senator Stennis, I'd like you to listen to these tapes,' he replied 'WHAT?' "

Nixon's face froze in horror. How had I gotten hold of such information? Had another of his cherished tapes leaked to the opposition?

"Hmmm," Nixon mused.

Matters were getting out of hand. I had better try to explain!

"But that's not true. That's a joke . . . That's a joke that someone told after the program yesterday. You are saying his hearing was good . . . Right?"

But Nixon's mind was already on the defense.

"What did 'What?' mean . . . Ah . . . I don't recall the conversation . . ."

A few minutes later, when a light bulb exploded and there was a brief pause while it was replaced, Nixon's mind was still on the exchange. He shook his head disbelievingly. "Senator Stennis would never have said 'What?' He'd have said 'Pardon.' "

The bulb was replaced and we resumed.

"Well, now, let's at that point . . . come back to where we . . . where we left off yesterday. One of the other things that people find very difficult to take in the Oval Office on March 21st is the coaching that you gave them—Dean and Haldeman—on how to deal with the grand jury without getting caught, and saying that perjury is a tough rap to prove. And you said earlier, 'Just be damn sure you say, I don't remember . . . I can't recall . . .' Is that the sort of conversation that ought to have been going on in the Oval Office, do you think?"

Instead of bristling at the new allegation, Nixon seemed genuinely grateful for the opportunity to respond to this new and serious charge.

247

"I think that kind of advice is proper advice for one who, as I was at that time, ah . . . beginning to put myself in the position of an attorney for the defense—something which I wish I hadn't had the responsibility, ah, felt I had the responsibility to do. Ah, but I would like the opportunity when the question arises to tell you why I felt as deeply as I did at that point . . ."

"Give him the opportunity, David," Zelnick implored in the production trailer.

"Patience. Patience," said Birt. "Let David lay out the record."

As always when he made an admission, Nixon quickly appended several mitigating circumstances. He had not specifically told Dean and Haldeman to lie, to say they forgot if in fact they remembered. Like an attorney preparing witnesses for grand jury testimony, he simply wanted to be sure they testified only to facts about which they were absolutely certain. Were there any doubt at all, they should simply say they failed to recollect.

Where to turn next? I wondered. Clearly Nixon had things he wanted to say, statements—perhaps even admissions—he wanted to make. This was virgin territory in the story of the Nixon presidency. I wanted to be certain we did justice to the occasion. History would be ill served by a prepared Nixon speech at this moment. What he wished to say must be drawn from him, refined by my own questions and critique, in order to come nearer the truth. So I decided against immediately pursuing his reasons for playing defense counsel to his two aides.

Instead, I challenged his conclusion that he had not advised perjury in the guise of a faint recollection. And I recalled his own February 13 conversation with Colson where the subject of Mitchell's memory had come up. There Colson had said, "John has got one of those marvelous memories that, 'I don't know, I don't remember what was said.' " And Nixon had ad-libbed, "I was busy at the time."

"I mean, that's getting very close," I suggested. "Wasn't there an admission in that conversation that John's marvelous memory was self-serving?"

Mitchell, Nixon replied, is a "very careful lawyer." He wouldn't testify to anything "that he wasn't totally sure of. I don't think I was indicating that as far as Mitchell was concerned, ah . . . that he was lying and deliberately forgetting things, and deliberately misstating."

Nixon wanted to talk about Mitchell, but not about his role in the cover-up. Rather he thought he could explain how so sensible a man had permitted Watergate to occur in the first instance. I agreed to come back to that point too, later on. There was a lot that Nixon wanted to get off his chest, but I didn't want a single statement of generalities to cover over a multiplicity of specific wrongful acts.

Also, the very process of interrogation was having its effect. Nixon was resisting it point by point, but he was losing ground with each. And as he lost ground, he also seemed to be losing confidence even that his legalistic defense would get by. Thus, when he finally issued whatever apologia he had in mind, it would be less a prepared act of benevolence and more an impromptu introspection by someone who had trespassed on both law and duty. The quality of his ultimate explanation, I felt, would be enriched by the process of recounting the events that led to it.

I turned, then, to the Dean Report. I recalled that in an August 15, 1973, statement, he had explained its origins to the American people by saying, "If anyone at the White House or high up in my campaign had been involved in wrongdoing of any kind, I wanted the White House to take the lead in making that known. On March the 21st, I instructed Dean to write a complete report of all that he knew on the entire Watergate matter."

"Now," I said, "when one looks through the record of what had gone on just before and after March the 21st: On March the 17th, the written statement from Dean, you asked for a 'self-serving goddamn statement' denying culpability of principal figures. When he told you that the original Liddy Plan had involved bugging, you told him to omit that fact in his document and state it was for . . . the plan was for 'totally legal' intelligence operations.

March the 20th, as I'm sure you know, you said, you want 'a complete statement, but make it very incomplete.' On March the 21st, after his revelations to you, you said, 'Understand, I don't want to get all that goddamn specific.' And Ehrlichman and you, and you're talking on the twenty-second, and he's talking of the Dean Report, he says, 'And the Report says, nobody was involved.' There's several other quotes to that effect. Was that the Dean Report that you described? It wasn't the same as you described on August the 15th, was it?"

There was, as Birt suspected, still some fight left in the man. And it took its usual form—a lashing out on all fronts. Sure he wanted the truth, he argued. That's why he had pressed for a full accounting on Donald Segretti's dirty-tricks operation (which, needless to say, had previously been reported and incriminated few of those close to the President).

And, in speaking of the Dean Report on March 22, he had said, "If it opens doors, it opens doors." (Doors, one might add, to the initial break-in, not the cover-up.)

He moved from there to his one and only real attack on Dean, a repetition of the discrediting attacks about the March 21 briefing that had become familiar during the period of desperate White House efforts to save the Nixon presidency. "I should have recognized that what he did not tell me on March 21—the fact that Magruder had confessed to him, which he has written in his book. I should have recognized that he had suborned perjury for Magruder. I should have recognized that he had handled payments for the defendants. I should have recognized that he himself had made unauthorized—they were unauthorized by me—offers of clemency. I didn't know these things. He didn't tell me those things . . ."

I reminded Nixon of just how much information was in fact conveyed by Dean on March 21. The central figures, Magruder, Kalmbach, Haldeman, Ehrlichman, Mitchell, even Dean himself, were all named, their transgressions listed. "And therefore when you say, 'Say this person isn't involved and that person isn't involved,' you knew they were involved."

Nixon repeated his single exculpatory remark, that of opening doors.

> Nixon: I would think you would have found that statement . . . Let's get an impression of the whole story. Let the bad come out . . . there's plenty of bad. I'm not proud of this period. Ah . . . I didn't handle it well. I messed it up.

Here he recalled Mayor Fiorello LaGuardia's famous remark, "When I make a mistake, it's a beaut."

"Well," he continued, "I must say, mine wasn't a beaut—it was a disaster. Ah . . . and I recognize that it was a mistake. I made plenty of them. Ah, but . . . ah . . . I also insist that as far as my mistakes were concerned, ah . . they were mistakes frankly of the head and they weren't mistakes of the heart. They were not mistakes that had what I call an improper, illegal motive, ah . . . in terms of obstructing justice. Ah . . . that's all I'm trying to say."

This, I suspect, was the statement Nixon had come prepared to make. A simple declaration that he had made disastrous errors of the mind but not the heart, but that reading the totality of his words in context, one could see that he had been involved in no criminal conspiracy to obstruct justice. He had made the statement as he was being pushed, and while there was genuine emotion in his voice and a trace of sincerity on his countenance, I felt far less than fully satisfied by what I had heard. I wanted him to come to grips far more specifically with his conduct.

Biding my time, therefore, I returned to the March 22 conversation with Ehrlichman, Haldeman, Mitchell and Dean at which the desired Dean Report had been discussed at some length.

I recalled Ehrlichman's treasured phrase, that the report was to be "a modified limited hangout," reminding Nixon that "You can't have a modified limited version of the truth—I mean, it's obviously not going to be the whole of the truth."

Ehrlichman, I recalled, had gone on to say, "I'm looking at the future, assuming some corner of this thing comes unstuck at some time, you"—"That's you," I said, pointing to Nixon—"are in a position to say, 'Look, that document I've published, is a document I relied on; that is the report I relied on.' "

Nixon had replied to Ehrlichman, "That's right."

"Now you've decided that the document's going to be modified. It's going to be limited. And then you're going to rely on that document and so you're going to be able to blame it on Dean. And it seems to me that that is consistent with all the quotes that I have quoted and not the one 'door' quote that you have quoted."

Nixon disputed the point, but without much apparent conviction, again referring to his "open doors" remark which, in my view, was ambiguous standing alone, and totally meaningless in the context of his many instructions regarding the Dean Report.

Nor was he much more convincing in explaining how, on April 16, he could have described the Dean Report to Henry Petersen by complaining, "The report was not, frankly, accurate; well, it was accurate, but it was not full," when in fact no such report had been written.

Referring to several handwritten pages of Dean's draft that later came to light, Nixon said that was the report he had in mind, although he had not seen it at the time he spoke to Petersen.

He therefore tried to deflect the conversation back towards Dean himself, saying that on March 21, "The mistake was mine in not, as I say, smelling the rat that he was then . . ."

Nixon's responses to the evidence we had marshaled were becoming so unconvincing—even, I felt now, to himself—that the moment might be close.

Minutes earlier he had given me some hints that he was prepared to accept culpability in one form or another. I thought that perhaps—just perhaps—this man, who did indeed seem to be incapable of recognizing any specific act as contravening his legal and constitutional obligation, might respond more fully to a question that brought together and characterized the shortcomings of his conduct in general. And that the best way to do this was to use John's thought about calling the cops. So I again recited for him the things he had learned from Dean on March 21—things about

the original Liddy Plan and the involvement of men like Haldeman, Ehrlichman, Magruder, Strachan and Dean himself in the
cover-up.

"I still don't know why you didn't pick up the phone and tell
the cops," I said. "I still don't know, when you found about the
things that Haldeman and Ehrlichman had done, that there is no
evidence anywhere of a rebuke, but only of scenarios and excuses, etc. Nowhere do you say, 'We must get this information
direct to whoever it is—the head of the Justice Department criminal investigation or whatever.' And nowhere do you say to Haldeman and Ehrlichman, 'This is disgraceful conduct'—and Haldeman
admits a lot of it the next day, so you're not relying on Dean—
'you're fired.' "

Nixon took a deep breath and peered off into space. For a brief
moment his body seemed to go limp. In that instant I knew that
my instinct had been correct—that we were moving to a new phase
of our exploration of the Nixon presidency. The sharp exchanges,
the terse confrontations, the haggling over points of law and
nuances of fact were drawing towards a close. In stages he would
now try to address the totality of his conduct. Up to this point the
confrontation had been Nixon versus Frost. Now the question
became, How much of Nixon could Richard Nixon himself dare
to confront? And my role became one of helping his better angels.

"Well . . . could I take my time now to address that question?"
he began. "I think it will be very useful to you to know what I
felt I was going through. Ah . . . it wasn't a very easy time. Ah
. . . ah . . . I think my daughter Tricia once said that there
really wasn't a happy time in the White House—except in the
personal sense—after April 30th, when Haldeman and Ehrlichman
left. And the Watergate problem obsessed the country . . ."

It was a promising start, but it proved to be only the start of a
tortuous trail that did not yet lead very far. Nixon insisted that
before March 21, he had no detailed knowledge of the Watergate events. That's why he was willing to take the risk of nomi-
nating Pat Gray as permanent director of the F.B.I. He knew
Gray would face extensive examination over his handling of the

Watergate affair and had been assured by Gray that he was prepared to defend that part of his record.

"All right, now, March 21st . . . You really get slapped in the
face with recognition of—or at least you're being made aware of—
the fact that I'd been worrying about the wrong problem. I'd been
worrying about whether anybody in the White House had been
involved in the break-in, but Dean says the problem was—the
cover-up was the problem . . . was what we should be concerned
about."

So unfamiliar was he with the legal terrain, he recalled, that
when Dean first referred to the possible crime of obstruction of
justice, Nixon repeated the law, only he called it, "destruction of
justice." He quickly learned the proper title of the law and the
litany of his aides who had violated it.

"But in any event, we came to this point. We had—as I indicated—contained the matter during the campaign. We contained
it and I tried to contain it for political purposes. Ah . . . because
I didn't feel at that time that any erosion of the strength of the
President in the country—of his support in the country—and also,
I didn't feel that his defeat in an election . . . ah . . . would be
in the best interest of the country."

Had it not been for the obvious anguish that Nixon was experiencing, I would have been sorely tempted at this moment to return
to the harder line. Just like all the other participants in the
cover-up, Nixon now seemed to be explaining his actions in terms
of the "greater good," speaking of himself in the third person, confusing his personal political welfare with the nation's well-being.

It was almost as if he read my thoughts.

"Obviously that's a self-serving statement . . . and intended to
be. I knew that the North Vietnamese in their talks with Kissinger
at that time were finally beginning to buckle. I knew that they
would seize on any indication that my political support was going
away, that they then might decide, well, we'll wait, and we
wouldn't get the peace as soon as we got it."

I was determined now to interrupt, but he returned to the

"human factors"—his personal feelings for Haldeman, Ehrlichman and Mitchell. They were all "decent men."

"I knew their families. In the case of Haldeman and Ehrlichman, I'd known them since they were just kids . . . We weren't close personal friends, but boy they had worked their butts . . . for good causes. And I appreciated that. They told me, after this conversation, 'Look, we didn't intend to obstruct justice.' I mean, they explained the money thing as we've already talked . . . that they were doing it for humanitarian purposes. They didn't consider it was hush money and so forth and so on."

We were slipping back towards the old "lines." I was willing to believe that Nixon's intentions were, at this point, entirely honorable. There was contrition in his mind and in his heart. Whether it was a product of the debacle he had suffered during the first day's interrogation, the conversations with his staff between the sessions, or our continued grappling earlier this morning, I could not be sure. But somewhere, Richard Nixon had concluded that he owed the country and himself more than the sort of technical defense he had previously offered. And now we were fighting, and he was fighting within himself, over the ground his apologia would embrace.

This was a difficult, delicate, painful task for one who had erected so many barriers obstructing his own view of the truth. And it was for the purpose of assisting him in removing these barriers, rather than to cross-examine him further, that I now rejoined the fray. I was not so much impeaching his credibility, as attempting to help him reach towards credibility by discarding more of the discredited 'scenarios.'

"But when it came to March 21st," I reminded him, "and the revelation . . . ah . . . Haldeman and Ehrlichman soon made it very clear to you that these payments, for instance, were not—were not in fact innocent payments for humanitarian reasons—not just the gloves and phone booths and so on—but, I mean, Haldeman said the defendants 'might blow.' Ehrlichman said they were there to keep him (Hunt) 'on the reservation.' "

Nixon was still not ready to concede the point. He talked again of keeping the defendants from talking to the press, from selling out to the Democrats before the election.

"But Haldeman had told you that he transferred the $350,000 in December, so there can't have been any electoral reason for that whatever."

"No electoral reasons, but at that point there could—there could be reasons of embarrassment beyond that . . ."

That would simply not do. I reminded Nixon again of all he had learned from Dean and thereafter, and of all his actions that were utterly inconsistent with an attempt to get at the truth.

"And then you say in your statement, your later August statement, you say that 'On March the 30th, I instructed Mr. Ehrlichman to conduct an independent inquiry and bring all the facts to me.' Now, you already knew he was a prime suspect. That's like asking Al Capone for an independent investigation of organized crime in Chicago. I mean, how can you ask the prime, one of the prime suspects . . . how could he, even if he was the Pope, conduct an independent inquiry, because you knew he was one of the prime suspects?"

The exchange seemed to bring Nixon to a new plateau. Yes, the record of Haldeman and Ehrlichman may reflect things that "indicate otherwise." But he had believed them. "I mean, you believe the people that are close to you. Ah, sometimes you shouldn't. Ah, sometimes when you come in and have any doubts about them, you should just can them. Ah, I didn't do that. Ah, but if I could just take a moment to conclude why I didn't do it, because maybe our viewers would like to know. You see, I had been through a very difficult period when President Eisenhower had the Adams problems, and I'll never forget the agony he went through . . ."

I was not entirely unprepared for the reference to Sherman Adams, the straitlaced former New Hampshire governor who had been Ike's closest aide until a vicuña coat and other gratuities received from Bernard Goldfine brought him to grief. Months earlier, Ray Price had discussed the incident with my colleagues and its impression upon the former Vice-President.

"Here was Adams," Nixon continued, "a man that had gone through the heart attack with him. A man that had gone through the stroke with him. A man that had gone through the ileitis with him. A man that had been totally selfless, but he was caught up in a web. Ah, guilty? I don't know. Ah, I considered Adams then to be an honest man in his heart. He did have some misjudgment, but in any event, finally Eisenhower decided, after months of indecision on it, and he stood up for him in press conferences over and over again, and Hagerty did. He decided that he had to go. You know who did it? I did it. Eisenhower called me in and asked me to talk to Sherm."

Nixon was near tears now as he recounted the Adams episode. And I will maintain to my last day on this planet that he was recounting the truth as he recalled it. Later there would be stories that his mission had been shared with the former Republican National Chairman, Meade Alcorn, and that the actual hatchet had been wielded by the party pro and not the Vice-President.

Did that in fact make any difference? Was Nixon less aware of Ike's feeling? Was he less aware of the blow to the proud and proper New Englander? Was he less observant of the play of human emotions and the agony of two close friends? I doubt it. As would occur repeatedly in this session, subjective truth could be every bit as revealing—perhaps even more so—than objective truth. Who dispatched Sherman Adams was far less important to me, and certainly to Richard Nixon, than the fact that the incident had occurred and he had observed it. Maybe in his own mind he was the one to perform the execution. Maybe he felt guilty for it. Maybe he was transferring the guilt he could not make himself accept for the fate of his own close associates. Whatever the explanation, the emotion was real. Nixon was telling the truth as he had the capacity to see it.

"And so here was the situation I was faced with," he continued. "Who's going to talk to these men? What can we do about it? Well, first, let me say that I didn't have anybody that could talk to them but me. I couldn't have Agnew talk to them because they didn't get along well with him. Bill Rogers wasn't happy with them either, and so, not having a Vice-President or anybody else, and Haldeman—my chief of staff—himself being one involved, the only man that could talk to them was me."

He knew the end was near for his two aides on April 15 when he had the first of his many discussions with Henry Petersen. But even then he resisted the inevitable. "I didn't fully reach that conclusion because I still wanted to give them a chance to survive. I didn't want to have them sacked as Eisenhower sacked Adams, and then have . . . and Adams goes off to New Hampshire and runs a ski lodge and is never prosecuted for anything; sacked because of misjudgment . . . yes; mistakes . . . yes; but an illegal act with an immoral, illegal motive? No. That's what I feel about Adams and that's the way I felt about these men at that time."

As he expressed reservations to Petersen that day, during one of those unrecorded conversations, unrecorded because the tape had run out while he was conferring earlier with Kleindienst, Petersen had reported on the evidence against his two aides and had recommended their immediate dismissal. And Nixon had replied, "But Henry, I can't fire them simply on the basis of charges. They gotta have their day in court. They gotta have a chance to prove their innocence. I've gotta see more than this, because they claim they're not guilty."

Petersen, according to Nixon, had responded, "You know, Mr. President, what you've just said—that you can't fire a man simply on the basis of charges that have been made and the fact that they—their continued service will be embarrassing to you—you've gotta have proof before you do that—that speaks very well for you as a man. It doesn't speak well for you as a President."

"And," said Nixon, "in retrospect, I guess he was right. So, it took me two weeks to work it out, tortuous long sessions. You've got hours and hours of talks with them, which they resisted. We don't need to go through all that agony." As Nixon spoke, I was fighting to make sure that I kept some sense of distance. These were deeply emotional moments for him. He was trying to give an accurate account of things—trying desperately, I believed—but he was still a prisoner within his own walls. And I knew that much of what he was saying would not stand up in cold print.

What in fact had he learned from Henry Petersen on April 15? Nothing, really. Nothing that Dean hadn't told him on March 21 and nothing Ehrlichman and Haldeman had not confirmed for him dozens of times since that date. In telling Nixon of the cover-up that day, Petersen was really telling him only that he, Petersen, knew of the cover-up. That was all that was new. Nothing else could possibly have come as a surprise.

And when Nixon pleaded with Petersen for more time so that Haldeman and Ehrlichman could have their "day in court," it was not that he wanted anything other than for them to beat the rap. Not for a moment did a single one of the cover-up transactions affront his sense of morality or propriety. The laws that governed this elite stratum of society were not those that applied to other mortals. These men—himself included—were problem solvers. Winning the election big was a problem. Using dirty political tricks, up to and including the modified Liddy Plan, was one of several ways that his aides sought to solve that problem. That was a mistake, a misjudgment. The risks far outweighed the benefits. It didn't work. Once the burglars were apprehended, that situation too became the problem and the cover-up was the only apparent solution. It too proved a mistake, a misjudgment, because it wasn't carefully handled. It didn't work. And when it began to unravel, that was the consuming problem to be addressed, and limitation of damage became the solution.

So what Nixon weighed in his heart and in his mind between April 14 and April 30 was not the guilt or innocence of Haldeman and Ehrlichman, but whether the damage to his administration could better be contained by their staying or their leaving. If they stayed, he would have a three-man front in place against Dean, but he would have difficulty keeping the Watergate infection from spreading to himself once the two of them came down with the disease. If they left, he would lack their savvy help, but assuming the organs had been severed in time, he could at least keep the contagion from reaching himself.

Here Nixon committed a critical "mistake" and "misjudgment":

he moved in both directions at once, but neither of them swiftly and surely enough.

First he conspired with Haldeman and Ehrlichman, hoping to isolate Dean, while the three of them devised a cover story that might stick. Then he let his aides go. He was now in the worst of all possible worlds. He had lost the solidarity of a unified front with his two friends and colleagues. And he had moved too late to prevent the Dean allegations from reaching himself. Indeed, his very dismissal of Haldeman and Ehrlichman served only to enhance Dean's credibility. If his later handling of the Butterfield testimony sealed his fate, his handling of matters in the period March 21 to April 30 set him up for disaster.

Yet I could see now how Nixon might sincerely believe that his actions during this period had been motivated more by compassion than by self-preservation. After all, had he been driven by nothing more than a commitment to self-preservation, had there been no desire to protect as many of his own people as could be saved, he could certainly have done things differently. He could have granted pardons to the original Watergate defendants before their trials. This would have invited some harsh political rebukes, but it would have come at a moment when he was at the apex of his political power and at a time when a majority of Americans still regarded Watergate as little more than a prank. Or he could have asserted privilege with respect to his conversations with Dean, and possibly with respect to all of Dean's White House dealings. Dean was in fact the official White House lawyer. His conversations were certainly privileged under the historic attorney-client rule and, arguably, under the less well-defined doctrine of executive privilege.

Only after Dean's later testimony and the published tape transcripts suggested the criminality of the discussions in question did either of these doctrines fall into disrepute. Given the known facts in March and April 1973, Dean could almost certainly have been shielded, had Nixon opted for that strategy.

He didn't because, in my view, he was too proud. He wanted to have it both ways, appearing publicly as a law-and-order President devoted to the unraveling of the cover-up, yet privately conspiring to make the cover-up work. Like his later moves with the dismissal of Haldeman and Ehrlichman and his releasing part of the tape transcripts while asserting executive privilege with respect to other portions, this indecisiveness doubled his problems. Given a choice between one form of damage and another, the President—on three pivotal occasions—chose both.

So now he was trying to explain it all, and despite the benevolent construction he put on his actions during the period, his face was contorted by the pain of it and his voice had broken to a near-whisper. He remembered the weekend at Aspen, the presidential cabin at Camp David where he had retreated with his two aides, the brilliant fields of spring, the blooming tulips bursting with color, the aged Catoctin Mountain rolling against a clean horizon.

Haldeman came in first. He got the news. "I disagree with your decision totally," he had told his boss. "I think you're going to live to regret it." But he agreed to resign.

Then Ehrlichman. "I knew that Ehrlichman was bitter because he felt very strongly he shouldn't resign. Oh, he'd even indicated that Haldeman should and maybe he should stay."

He took Ehrlichman on the porch. "I said, 'You know, John, when I went to bed last night . . . I hoped, I almost prayed, I wouldn't wake up this morning.' Well, it was an emotional moment. I think there were tears in our eyes, both of us. He said, 'Don't say that.' We went back in. They agreed to leave. And so it was late, but I did it. I cut off one arm and then cut off the other arm. Now I can be faulted. I recognize it. Maybe I defended them too long. Maybe I tried to help them too much. But I was concerned about them. I was concerned about their families. I felt that they in their hearts felt they were not guilty. I felt they ought to have a chance at least to prove that they were not guilty. And I didn't want to be in the position of just sawing them off in that way.

"And I suppose you could sum it all up the way one of your British Prime Ministers summed it up, Gladstone, when he said that the first requirement for a Prime Minister is to be a good butcher. Well, I think the great story as far as a summary of Watergate is concerned, and I, ah, did some of the big things rather well, I screwed up terribly in what was a little thing and became a big thing. But I will have to admit I was not a good butcher."

At this moment I was conscious of two things. The first was the overwhelming, almost unbearable emotion of the moment. A former President of the United States, consumed with melancholy recollections of a tragic period in his and his nation's life sat red- and puffy-eyed before me, and I had been drawn into his personal ordeal in an almost metaphysical kind of way. Still, a part of me resisted the temptation to succumb completely. I had followed his words. I knew that once the poignance of the moment had passed, they would be examined closely.

And what had he said, really? That he felt compassion for Ehrlichman and Haldeman. That they had maintained their innocence and he had believed them. That they were entitled to their rights until proven guilty. That he had, in effect, exalted the rule of law over the rule of political expediency. That he had done the right thing, only a few weeks late. That he was too decent to be "a good butcher."

It wouldn't wash. Nixon had still not been able to confront his own conduct, his own words and deeds, his own role in the conspiracy to obstruct justice. I must still play the interrogator if only to move him further.

I in fact asked Nixon to "go a little further." He had spoken in terms of loyalty to his friends and his perceived need to serve as defense counsel for them. But he had also told the nation that his sole concern during the period March 21–April 30 was to get the truth out. "But now, you're telling us your innermost feelings at that time, and I've indicated some of my doubts, and I've got others about the speed with which the truth came out."

Nixon reverted to form. Never before had the metaphor about bleeding the truth from a witness struck me as more apt. With Richard Nixon, the heart would pump, there would be a gush of subjective truth at least, and then the ventricle would close and the flow would cease. Nixon would retreat, seemingly dismayed at how much of himself he had previously revealed.

Now he retreated. The truth came out slowly, he said. He should have called an independent man to do the investigation since "Kleindienst was too close to Mitchell." Or upon hearing Dean's allegations on March 21, he should have called Kleindienst and said, "Look, here are these two people. Dean has made these charges. I want you to haul them down to the dock, fingerprint 'em and throw 'em into the can and put 'em before the grand jury or do whatever. But I'm just not made that way. And I'll admit that. I'm a pretty tough guy. I'm a pretty tough guy. In fact perhaps I'm criticized a bit more for being tough than for being soft. But when it comes to people, you know, I feel for 'em. And when you let your feelings, your heart get in the way of your head, that's when you make mistakes. And that's what I did."

"And that word, I think, is a trigger word with people," I replied. "Would you now . . . would you now say, to clear the air, that for whatever motives, and you've expressed some of them, your feelings about Haldeman and Ehrlichman and whatever we said about the earlier periods, and so on . . . that between the period March the 21st and April the 30th, you were, indeed . . . misled, maybe waylaid by emotion, or whatever you were waylaid by . . . that actually, in that period, you were a part of the cover-up?"

No. Nixon wouldn't buy that. He simply trusted the innocence of his aides. He believed them. And he wanted to give them a chance to defend themselves. I tried again.

"But don't you think that in protecting them you were protecting yourself?"

"No, on the contrary, as far as protecting myself was concerned, the best thing I could have done was not to waive the attorney-client privilege for Dean. I knew that Dean, by April 17th, had totally turned on Haldeman, Ehrlichman, possibly the President. I wasn't sure, but I knew certainly he was a loose can on the deck. I didn't have to waive the attorney-client privilege, even as President I didn't have to, but I did."

The moment was slipping. We had been close, so close to the sort of purging statement that both history and justice required, and then Nixon had backed off.

A break might help, I thought. We had made some progress, progress that we had scarcely dared to believe was possible. But now—how to encourage this reluctant witness to complete his task? I needed time to think. And to talk to my colleagues. Yes, and to talk to Jack Brennan too. A few minutes earlier he had entered the room for the only time in the whole twenty-eight hours and tiptoed over behind the camera, where I could see him holding up a piece of paper. It was difficult to read, but I thought it said "Let us talk." Then he had tiptoed out again. Nixon and I had been in the middle of an exchange, and I had ignored the message at the time, but now perhaps Brennan would have something to add.

I told Nixon that we needed time to "change tapes," asking the crew at the same time to agree to a late lunch break. Although we planned to resume in a few minutes, I had no idea when we would finish.

Nixon rose slowly and returned to his room, where Khachigian dashed to join him. I started for our own monitor room. But Brennan was waiting in the hall. His face was flushed.

He began to talk in a jumble of words. I heard only isolated phrases. "Critical moment in his life . . ." "Can't cross-examine him . . ." "Know he'll go further . . ." "What do you want?"

On the floor lay his piece of paper. It did not say "Let us talk." It said "Let him talk."

Khachigian came rushing out of Nixon's room, whispered something to Brennan and rushed back in. Then Birt arrived from the production trailer.

"What is it you're trying to say, Jack?"

"David has gotta quit playing the prosecutor," Jack said. "This is an important moment in the President's life. He'll go further than mistakes and misjudgments. He wants to make a full accounting. But you've gotta let him do it in his own way."

"What do you mean by a full accounting?" asked Birt. "That he was guilty of a crime?"

"I don't know if he'll say that."

"That he committed impeachable offenses?"

"I don't know if he'll say that either."

"Then David's cross-examination will resume."

"Just a minute. Let me talk to him."

Birt turned to me. "That was exceptional, David. But we can't relent now."

"No, we can't. On the one hand, Jack's right when he says that Nixon won't go much further under adversary pressure. On the other hand, I have to dispute or at least disclaim any categorization of his conduct which doesn't reflect ours."

"Don't change a thing," said John.

Amidst all the emotional turmoil, Brennan returned from the Nixon room.

"He knows he has to go further," he said. "I don't know what he'll say, and I'm not sure he does. But ask him. Just ask him. He's got more to volunteer."

"Look, Jack, we can't plea-bargain with you," said John.

"If he's got something to say," I said, "we'll give him every opportunity to say it on his own. But if he falls short, we'll have to come back at him."

"The interrogation will have to restart. That's all we can tell you now," said John.

"I'll go and tell him," said Brennan. "And if it doesn't happen now, we can always try again on Monday."

John put out his hand and stopped Brennan for a moment. "No, Jack," he said with intense earnestness. "Don't let him feel that, even for a second. Believe me, if he doesn't do it now, having come this far, he'll never do it on Monday."

I have often read of "electricity" in the air. Of a "highly charged atmosphere." But I never expect to experience it again quite as I did as Nixon and I walked back onto the set. Everybody felt it. All over the house. John felt it on his way back to the trailer. He stopped, turned and came back again. He walked across the set to the side of my chair, leaned over, and whispered in my ear. "It is terribly easy for all of us to get caught up in the emotions of the moment. But what happens now and what he says now and what you say now will be pored over by historians. That's the perspective to try and keep."

John made a nod towards the ex-President, and strode out to return to the trailer. "Stand by," said Don Clark. The red light on the cameras went on. I tried to recapture the mood of our conversation earlier.

"To come back to where we were just now, Mr. President . . . because this is a difficult program for you and a difficult program for me. We were talking about the period . . . March the 21st and April the 30th. And you were talking about your emotions as you had to bid farewell to Haldeman and Ehrlichman. And talking about the mistakes that you made and so on in doing that . . . you've talked about the mistakes . . . we're at an extraordinary moment in a way. Would you do what the American people yearn to hear? Not because they yearn to hear it, but just to tell all, to level and so on. Would you go further than the 'mistakes'? You've explained how you got caught up in this thing. You've explained your motives. I don't want to quibble about any of that. But just coming to the sheer substance—would you go further than 'mistakes'? The word that seems not enough for people to understand."

"Well, what word would you express?"

It was the most surprising response I had ever had in my life. I had spent hours cross-examining Richard Nixon. Now he wanted me to testify for him as well. Yet, unless I was able to frame with precision what it was we wanted to hear from him, the moment would be lost, never to be recaptured. As a symbolic gesture, I picked up my clipboard from my lap, and tossed it onto the floor beside my chair.

"Let me say that my concern is now not to—which is why I chucked the clipboard away—not to be legalistic or anything, about obstructions of justice and so on, and things we've discussed so far and so on . . . I think there are three things—since you asked me that heart-stopping question—I would like to hear you say, and the American people would like to hear you say. One is, there was probably more than mistakes . . . there was wrongdoing. Whether it was a crime or not—yes, it may have been a crime too. Secondly, I did—and I'm saying this without questioning the motives, right—I did abuse the power I had as President, or not fulfill the totality, the oath of office. That's the second thing. And thirdly—I put the American people through two years of agony and I apologize for that.

"And I say that—you've explained your motives—I think those are the categories. And I know how difficult it is for anyone, and most of all you, but I think that the people need to hear, and I think unless you say it, you're going to be haunted for the rest of your life."

My recital seemed momentarily to drive all the air from Nixon's lungs. Then he began slowly, circuitously. No, it had not been a good time for the country. He had made mistakes—"horrendous ones . . . ones that were not worthy of a President . . . ones that did not meet the standards of excellence that I had always dreamed of as a young boy."

He had considered resignation on the night before April 30, 1973, when he was to address the American people, following the resignation of Haldeman, Ehrlichman and the others. But Ray Price "didn't put it in" the final draft of his speech, as Nixon had said that he could if Price felt Nixon "oughta."

Yet he "owed it to history" to note some of the positive accomplishments of his office during the last sixteen months—the second and third summits, resolution of the crisis in the Mideast, the continuing process of détente and normalization with the two Communist powers.

Then he started coming back towards the point. He didn't just make mistakes in this period. Some, that he regretted most deeply, involved "the statements that I made afterwards," about his claimed efforts to unravel the cover-up.

"I would say that the statements that I made afterwards were, on the big issues, true: that I was not involved in the matters that I had spoken to . . . not involved in the break-in, that I did not engage in and participate in or approve the payment or the authorization of clemency, which, of course, were the essential elements of the cover-up."

But he had been in a "five-front war" with a partisan media, a partisan Ervin committee, a partisan Special Prosecutor's staff and a partisan Judiciary Committee staff. "Now under all these circumstances, my reactions in some of the statements and press conferences and so forth after that, I want to say right here and now, I said things that were not true. Most of them were fundamentally true on the big issues, but without going as far as I should have gone and saying, perhaps, that I had considered other things but not done them."

> FROST: Well, you mean—
> NIXON: And for all those things, I have a very deep regret.
> FROST: You got caught up in—
> NIXON: Yeah.
> FROST: —and then it snowballed.

"It snowballed," said Nixon. But he quickly repeated his claim that "on the essential issues, I leveled with the American people, and told the truth."

Yet in the face of continuing attacks, his credibility began to go down at home, and it went down abroad. "By the time I resigned, I was crippled. I was crippled even before that . . ."

He would take the blame for that. He was not blaming anyone else, certainly not Mitchell, Ehrlichman and Haldeman and the rest. They have all suffered enough.

"I'm simply saying to you that as far as I'm concerned, I not only regret it, I indicated my own beliefs in this matter when I resigned. People didn't think it was enough to admit mistakes. Fine. If they want me to get down and grovel on the floor, no. Never. Because I don't believe I should."

Those words were spoken with conviction, even defiance. But he quickly came back to his more wistful, conciliatory tone. He was, again, not blaming anyone else, not the C.I.A. and not his Democratic and Republican foes, the so-called impeachment lobby. He would reject the claims of those who called him a victim of a coup or a conspiracy.

"I brought myself down. I gave them a sword. And they stuck it in. And they twisted it with relish. And, I guess, if I'd been in their position, I'd have done the same thing."

I was taking inventory of his answers. He had said some important things. He had lied to the American people. He had been his own worst enemy. He had "brought himself down." He had not gone the C.I.A. route, as we had suspected he might. He had not followed the Lasky line in holding himself out as a man who was singled out for ruin by an unconscionable coalition of enemies.

But he had still not been able to address the crucial March 21–April 30 period. And softly, as gently as I possibly could, I had to call that to his attention. In addition to these untrue statements, could he say with conviction "that you did do some covering up? We're not talking legalistically, now. I just want . . . the facts"—I paused fractionally and dropped my voice slightly in the middle of the phrase as it struck me that otherwise the sentence might sound momentarily like *Dragnet*—"I mean that you did do some covering up. That there were a series of times when, maybe overwhelmed by your loyalties or whatever else, but as you look back at the record, you behaved partially protecting your friends—or maybe yourself—and that in fact you were, to put it at its most simple, a part of a cover-up at times?"

Now we were defining with clarity the grounds for whatever confession the former President wished to make. And whatever the facts, he was making it clear, he would stick to his own conclusions about their legal ramifications.

"I did not, in the first place, commit a—the crime of obstruction of justice. Because I did not have the motive required for the commission of that crime."

Even at this moment, I thought, I have to reiterate.

FROST: We've had our discussion on that, and we disagree on that, but that's—

NIXON: The lawyers can argue that. I did not commit, in my view, an impeachable offense. Ah, now, the House has ruled overwhelmingly that I did. Of course, that was only an indictment and would have to be tried in the Senate. I might have won; I might have lost. But, even if I'd won in the Senate by a vote or two, I would have been crippled and the . . . in any event, for six months the country couldn't afford having the President in the dock in the United States Senate. And there can never be an impeachment in the future of this country without a President voluntarily impeaching himself. I have impeached myself. That speaks for itself.

FROST: How do you mean, "I have impeached myself?"

NIXON: By resigning. That was a voluntary impeachment.

The former President declined again to read legal conclusions, even into his voluntary act of self-impeachment. Nor was he ready to admit greater personal knowledge of the cover-up events between the time of the break-in and his March 21 briefings from Dean. But then his monologue took a dramatic turn.

"Now when you come to the period—and this is the critical period—of March 21st on, when Dean gave his legal opinion that certain things, actions taken by Haldeman, Ehrlichman, Mitchell, etc.—and even by himself—amounted to a legal cover-up and so forth, then I was in a very different position. And during that period, I will admit that I started acting as a lawyer for their defense.

"I will admit that acting as a lawyer for their defense, I was not prosecuting the case.

"I will admit that during that period, rather than acting primarily in my role as the chief law-enforcement officer in the United States of America, or at least with responsibility for law enforcement—because the Attorney General is the chief law-enforcement officer—but as the one with the chief responsibility for seeing that the laws of the United States are enforced, that I did not meet that responsibility.

"And, to the extent that I did not meet that responsibility, to the extent that within the law, and in some cases going right to the edge of the law in trying to advise Ehrlichman and Haldeman and all the rest as to how best to present their cases, because I thought they were legally innocent, that I came to the edge.

"And under the circumstances, I would have to say that a reasonable person could call that a cover-up."

He had ticked off the misdeeds and indiscretions like counts in an indictment. And when he said—this time with a surprising lack of emotion—"I would have to say that a reasonable person could call that a cover-up," he seemed like a man who as both defendant and jury foreman was returning a verdict against himself.

It came as no surprise when this stunning series of admissions was followed by the more traditional Nixon retreat, when he went on to repeat that he himself did not regard his actions as a cover-up and that, had he wanted to cover up, he could simply have granted clemency after the election, easing the political shock by granting amnesty to the Vietnam war resisters and deserters as well.

That was old-hat. I had long since thought through the reasons for his acting as he did: the pride, the stubbornness, the ability to view himself as different people when the circumstances demanded that he play different roles. They were part of the psychology of Richard Nixon, and I thought that by this time I understood them as such.

The retreats were also part of this psychology. So were the digressions. He could reside only so long on the peak of his emotional roller coaster. He went from grueling climbs to terrifying slides to flat periods of intellectual and emotional respite. His statement was a symphony of many movements. It had to be listened to and appreciated as such. At any given point, a variation could be mistaken for the main theme.

"But now we come down to the key point—and let me answer it in my own way—about 'How do I feel about the American people?' "

We were ready for the finale now.

He told of his farewell dinner at the White House with his closest congressional supporters on the evening of August 8, 1974, moments before he would appear on television to deliver his resignation speech. He peered around the table. His friends were crying. And then the President began to cry. And as he rose from the gathering to face an uncertain personal destiny, he said, "I'm sorry, I just hope I haven't let you down."

"Well, when I said, 'I just hope I haven't let you down,' that said it all.

"I had.

"I let down my friends.

"I let down the country.

"I let down our system of government and the dreams of all those young people that ought to get into government, but think it's all too corrupt and the rest.

"Most of all, what I fear the greatest—not that I don't hope and pray that President Carter will be able to make progress in his peace initiatives—I let down an opportunity that I would have had for two and a half more years to proceed on great projects and programs for building a lasting peace, which has been my dream, as you know from our first interview in 1968, before I had any thought I might even win that year. (I didn't tell you I didn't think I might win, but I wasn't sure.)

"Yep, I . . . I, I let the American people down. And I have to carry that burden with me for the rest of my life.

"My political life is over.

"I will never yet, and never again, have an opportunity to serve in any official position. Maybe I can give a little advice from time to time.

"I can only say that in answer to your questions, that while technically, I did not commit a crime, an impeachable offense . . . these are legalisms.

"As far as the handling of this matter is concerned, it was so botched up.

"I made so many bad judgments, the worst ones, mistakes of the heart rather than the head, as I pointed out.

"But, let me say, a man in that top judge . . . top job, he's gotta have a heart.

"But his head must always rule his heart."

CHAPTER

11

THE MAN WHOSE PRIDE WOULD NOT PERMIT HIM TO SAY, "I BROKE
the law; I violated my constitutional duty," had come as close to
admitting both as it was in his pathology to do. I was moved—
awed—by the experience we had just shared.

"You're saying, if I understand it right, Mr. President, you said,
it's a burden you've got to carry with you for the rest of your life.
I think, I think it may be a little lighter after what you've
said . . ."

"I doubt it," Nixon said sadly. He recalled a conversation with
Edward Cox, Tricia's husband, the night before he resigned.
"Well, at least this cuts it off, Ed," he had said. "We'll go out to
California and they'll leave us alone."

"Oh, no, they won't," Cox, a Princeton and Harvard Law
School graduate and former associate of Ralph Nader, had replied.
"You don't know these people. I know them. Let me tell you
something about them. I worked in the U.S. Attorney's Office in
New York. And I went to school with some of these people. They're
tough. They're smart. But, most of all, they hate you with a passion.

Most because of the war, and some because of other reasons. And they and others like them, and the press, they're going to hound you. They're going to harass you for the rest of your life."

"And," said Nixon, "as we conclude this, I can say they have, and they will, and I will take it, I hope, like a man."

We talked on for a few more minutes. When I asked Nixon a question he did not quite hear, he asked me to repeat it and then, harking back to a conversation that now seemed light-years ago, cupped his hand to his ear and said, "I'm like John Stennis— 'What?' " He said ruefully of Watergate, "I fouled up in the area where I'm supposed to be a master; the area of 'just politics.' " But he had survived Watergate, I said. "Have I?" asked Nixon, "Oh, I'm physically surviving it. Mentally, ah, I would say I'm surviving. It hasn't been easy."

The allotted time had long since passed. We had wound ourselves down gradually, almost like divers going through decompression before stepping back into the lighter atmosphere.

There were still two more sessions to go, other subjects to cover. They would have to wait. I promised to return to many things at our next meeting.

"But, as, before we finish, Mr. President, this, ah, this has been more . . ."

"Been tough for you?" Nixon asked good-naturedly.

"Well, no," I replied, "but I was going to say that, I feel we've—"

"Covered a lot of ground."

"—been through a life, almost, rather than an interview, and we thank you."

"Fine. Have a good lunch," said Nixon. "Well, let's get out of here."

And he was up and heading for the kitchen, ready for a sip of water and his usual release of some light post-Interview banter, preferably unrelated to whatever he had just been discussing.

But this time the two staffs would have none of it. As deeply moved as myself, they surged into the living room, surrounding us, congratulating the former President and his interviewer for one of the most extraordinary moments any among us could ever hope to be privy to.

Zelnick shook the former President's hand warmly, the first such salutation since their introduction after the interrogation on Cambodia.

Birt was not far behind.

Khachigian, Brennan and Price took turns shaking my hand and complimenting me on the way I had handled the changing situation. Diane Sawyer kissed my cheek.

"Do you think they'll accept what he said as satisfactory?" Khachigian asked after Nixon had left.

"I would certainly hope so," said Zelnick. "The President was as honest today as God has given him the capacity to be honest."

"It's funny," Diane mused sadly. "You people are journalists, and good ones. And you've probably learned more about Richard Nixon than any other outsiders in the world. Sometimes I think you know him better than we do. But I think we know more about your colleagues than you do. Just watch. They're going to see your show. And they're going to tear him to shreds."

"Wanna bet?" said Zelnick, extending his hand.

"Why not?" Diane replied, clasping it. "We've got nothing to lose."

In retrospect, neither Diane Sawyer nor Bob Zelnick would prove totally correct. There would be those in the media who would feel that Nixon had gone as far in terms of contrition as anyone had the right to ask, let alone expect. Others would feel that his performance was little more than vintage Nixon guile—a string of deceptions coupled with a self-serving claim of compassion for his aides and an effort to transfer his misfeasance to them. Some of them remained unremitting in their demand for a total *mea culpa* on Nixon's part—a self-assessment that mirrored the most hostile views of his critics. But that, I fear, is asking more of human nature than those who earn their livelihoods studying human nature would ever demand. In the weeks after our Watergate program was broadcast, many a prosecutor would privately echo what Henry Petersen would explain to one interviewer: that an acknowledgment of moral culpability is the last thing that can be expected of one accused of crime. Even—to use Petersen's example—a bank robber caught red-handed fleeing with the loot will find reasons to justify what he did. He may plead guilty to the act, but he will never accept its underlying moral depravity.

In any event, there was no division whatsoever among the members of our team. We had all been there. We had shared the emotions of the moment. We had felt with Nixon the catharsis of his self-confrontation. To a man we believed that he had risen above himself, or, more accurately, reached into himself, to find, however briefly, that elusive nobility which those closest to him could from time to time discern, but which even they acknowledged was often buried under his darker qualities. I was aware, though, that even were we able to recapture totally the drama and emotion of those moments, still Nixon's words would appear in cold print in newspapers and magazines across the country. And those analyzing them would compare them to his previous Watergate statements to determine how much further he had gone than ever before.

So when I returned to my suite at the Beverly Hilton, the first document I reached for was his statement of September 8, 1974, accepting President Ford's full and absolute pardon. It was that statement which Ford would later interpret as "tantamount to a confession of guilt," and against which others would rightly judge his words that morning.

Reading the familiar phrases about "mistakes and misjudgments," the Nixon statement accepting the pardon seemed ambiguous and general when compared to the far more precise accounting he had just provided.

The pardon statement mentioned no period during which lies were told to the public.

It included no reference to the coaching of Haldeman, Ehrlichman and the others, one of his activities which Nixon had admitted went "right to the edge of the law."

It referred to no neglect of duty as the chief law-enforcement officer in the nation, or the one with the chief responsibility for seeing that the laws of the United States are enforced.

And—perhaps most important—it included no reference to having let down friends, the country and the very system of government which, according to many constitutional scholars, is the nub of an impeachable offense.

Indeed, Nixon had in a sense conceded that point when he defined his own resignation as "voluntary impeachment."

If Nixon's statement accepting the pardon, then, could be viewed as a concession that he had not been railroaded out of office, his conversation with us was more like a bill of particulars conceding the principal elements in the charges against him.

In fairness, it must be said that Nixon did not confess to each and every one of the allegations included in the nine-count Article One, or "obstruction of justice" impeachment article, prepared by the House Judiciary Committee against him. We had not questioned him specifically about charges that he lied to investigators or withheld vital information, and we had not pressed the question of his breach of Henry Petersen's confidences.

He had specifically denied authorizing overtures of clemency to the Watergate defendants; we had not gotten to his involvement in similar overtures to Mitchell, Magruder and Dean.

He had denied commanding the payment of hush money to Hunt, but admitted considering it, or at least not stopping it. And indeed had also admitted that his recollection a month afterwards was that he had encouraged it. So a fair-minded observer could regard that as an admission of "approving, condoning and acquiescing" in the hush-money payment—the precise language of the Judiciary Committee resolution.

Nixon had admitted counseling witnesses to give misleading testimony to investigators. He had admitted attempting to interfere in the early Justice Department probe and misusing the C.I.A. in the process. And he had conceded "making or causing to be made false or misleading public statements for the purpose of deceiving the people of the United States into believing that a thorough and complete investigation" had been conducted.

So of the six counts in Article One that had been specifically presented to the former President, one had been unequivocally denied, one had been partially denied and partially admitted, and four had been conceded outright. All of this did not, of course, mean that the final Watergate chapter had been written. Haldeman, Ehrlichman, Mitchell and perhaps others were still to be heard from. The vast body of unsubpoenaed White House material would one day bring additional revelations into the public domain, I was convinced.

But the conspiracy of silence among the main Watergate actors had now been broken, once and for all. The man at the center of the conspiracy had spoken. Others would now come forward. We had, in effect, given the apple tree a mighty shake. Over time the fruit would fall one piece at a time.

We were convinced that we would be facing a different Richard Nixon on Monday. In what respect we could not be sure. He might be sullen and uncooperative. Or his guard might be so low there would be no sense of clash to the occasion. Or he might be bitter and vindictive over what, in retrospect, he might now be thinking of as moments of induced weakness. Any one of these contingencies would require a different adjustment on my part. More optimistically, I thought it was possible that Nixon himself might be more candid both about what he had done and—more intriguingly at this stage—why he had done it. Perhaps he might finally be able to help us all examine the mentality of the Nixon White House and how accurately it reflected the suspicions, hatreds and insecurities of the Chief Executive himself.

When he arrived at ten ten Monday, there was indeed a different look about Richard Nixon. Gone was the haunted, embattled appearance of the previous Friday. But neither did he have that confident stride, that "primed to fight" demeanor of the first seven sessions. Rather, Nixon appeared mellow, relaxed and almost relieved, like a man who had endured the worst, yet had still come through it. Having revealed far more of himself than he had planned or than we had expected, he seemed pleasantly surprised that we had not been repelled by what we had seen.

I began the questioning by reminding Nixon that his Plumbers

Unit had been formed shortly after Daniel Ellsberg's release of the Pentagon Papers. And I wondered what he had wanted the new group to do with respect to Mr. Ellsberg.

Nixon broadened his answer to include other leaks as well. And he was ready with statistics. There had been 40 national-security leaks in 1969 and 71 in 1970. But by mid-1971 alone the number had shot up to 82. So the mandate of the Plumbers was to deal with the greater problem.

But Nixon quickly came back to Ellsberg himself. He said he had instructed Bud Krogh of the Plumbers to find out what other papers Ellsberg had, whether anyone else was in cahoots with him and whether he had access to other, more sensitive, material which he might also decide to leak.

Almost as an afterthought, Nixon added that "there was another reason . . . that he also be discredited, which, of course, you'll also want to pursue in your questions."

Nixon was becoming rather thoughtful, I noted, breaking the ice on some tough areas that I would otherwise have had to broach myself. With so willing a subject, it seemed appropriate to move quickly into that area.

It was Kissinger, Nixon said, who was most concerned in the days initially following the Ellsberg leak. He recalled his national-security adviser entering the Oval Office with cables from Canada, Australia and Romania, the cables expressing concern about confidential communications involving the United States and wondering whether they too would be made public.

"We are living actually in a revolutionary period," Nixon recalled Kissinger saying. "We have got to stop this in any way we can. We must discourage it."

But a reminder to Nixon did seem called for that not all of those inside the White House had considered the Ellsberg matter on quite so lofty a plane. I recalled for him Colson's description of the President's instructions at the time he made his own guilty plea. Nixon had urged his team to disseminate damaging information about Ellsberg, his attorney and others. Nixon did not deny it.

"I urged not only Colson, but I urged, I urged the ah . . . the

. . . Krogh and the others and so forth to obtain information which would discredit Ellsberg. As I said, not Ellsberg as a man, not for the purpose of getting him convicted at a trial, but that would discourage this kind of activity."

I asked him how much he recalled of the sequence of events surrounding the Plumbers' break-in at the offices of Ellsberg's psychiatrist, Dr. Fielding. He replied that he recalled very little, not even discussions of the psychological profile the group asked the C.I.A. to prepare, and, when it proved "superficial," to re-write it in a way that would prove far more embarrassing to Mr. Ellsberg.

"But in the actual period before the Fielding break-in, in August, I think, Mr. Ehrlichman has said that he talked to you about the fact that Hunt and Liddy had to go operational . . . had to go to California to find information. How much did he tell you at that time?"

"I do not recall a conversation with Ehrlichman on that," Nixon replied. He did acknowledge that Ehrlichman had testified to that effect, but also that he had himself not known about the break-in in advance. "He has also testified that he did not inform me, since he, of course, did not know . . ."

That was not true. I reminded Nixon that investigators had found a memorandum signed by Ehrlichman approving a "covert opera-tion" to examine the Ellsberg psychiatric files.

"Now we have a situation," replied Nixon, "where he—where the question is whether Ehrlichman informed me that these two men were going to California. He may well have. And, if he had, I would have said, 'Go right ahead.' But I recall no conversation whatever with Ehrlichman about their going to California for the purpose of what was called a 'covert operation' or for the purpose of determining whether Ellsberg's psychiatrist might furnish informa-tion. I have no recollection whatever of that." He added, "I think if Mr. Ehrlichman did have a recollection of ever having informed me of that sort of thing, he would have and should have revealed it in his trial, because it would have been a pretty good defense for him, and he didn't."

Ehrlichman had, of course, been tried in June 1974, a moment when the Nixon presidency was ebbing fast but when Ehrlichman was operating on the assumption that whatever verdict the jury returned he could count on a full Nixon pardon. Not only, then, would that defense—of authorization by the President—have been tough for Ehrlichman to win with, it would probably have meant instant death for the Nixon presidency and a severe falling out with the man who could guarantee, and had actually promised to guarantee, Ehrlichman's freedom.

But I was pressing on with a far more intriguing line of inquiry. I was struck by Nixon's frequent memory lapses. Even more than ourselves, he had tended to regard these abuse-area sessions as the functional equivalent of a criminal trial. And he simply wasn't making statements which could later be contradicted by the testimony of others, or more enticingly, by publication of the tape transcripts now at issue before the Supreme Court.

> FROST: And after the event, when he got filled in on the fact that they had done the job and found very little in this—
> NIXON: Nothing—
> FROST: —illegal break-in . . . nothing—
> NIXON: —dry hole—
> FROST: —did he, what did he tell you about it afterward?
> NIXON: Nothing . . . that I can recall. I have no recollection whatever of having been told anything about it afterwards . . .

Nixon said that his first "recollection" was of his March 17, 1973, conversation with Dean.

There was one particular question that we had discussed among ourselves on many occasions, particularly since Nixon had begun these fascinatingly cautious replies. It was destined to remind him again of the time bombs that might be ticking away among the unsubpoenaed tapes, and then to ask what effect the former President thought that such tapes might have upon his recollections of what had taken place. This seemed a perfect moment for the question. It was a long shot, of course, and I wanted to phrase it as delicately as possible.

"But bearing in mind that the tapes and all are in sort of legal limbo at the moment, and that you were very busy at this period, would you say that if the tapes of this period of August, before the break-in, and in September, after the break-in, were ever to become public, it is—just as you forgot for a while the content of that June 23rd conversation—would you say it's a hundred percent impossible that those tapes would ever show there was any discussion like this between you and Ehrlichman over the Fielding break-in? Is it possible that in fact, then, there could have been such a conversation and—as you say—you quite genuinely don't recollect it?"

"Let me say that I would never say that it was impossible," Nixon replied to my utter astonishment. "I can only say that ah . . . I am basing my recollection on what ah . . . others who perhaps did not have as many things on their mind as I did at that particular time have said . . ."

And he again mentioned his having checked with Krogh, in addition to reviewing the Ehrlichman testimony.

"And I am basing my recollection on that . . . now as far as tapes are concerned, let me say the Special Prosecutors, of course, those that prosecuted Ehrlichman have access—ah . . . and we have . . . acceded to because the Supreme Court has so ruled, we have complied with all requests that they have made. And . . . ah . . . ah . . . I ah . . . if they have . . . any tape in that particular period or any reason to expect that there's a conversation in that period they have not found it . . ."

At that moment, almost everyone at Monarch Bay came to the conclusion that Nixon authorized the Fielding break-in in advance or, at the very least, was informed of it after Hunt and Liddy returned from California.

For one thing, there was Nixon's appetite for that sort of thing. Had he heard about the Hunt-Liddy information-gathering trip, he would have said, "Go right ahead." And why not? Having already approved a Huston Plan calling for covert operations, including burglaries and black-bag jobs on a far grander scale, and having expressed the view that the President has extraordinary domestic powers in areas affecting the national security, there is nothing to indicate he would have found the Ellsberg operation in any way repugnant.

Second were, of course, his memory lapses coupled with the highly technical, legalistic nature of his statements on the issue. Not only could he not recall things on his own, but to the extent he remembered anything, his recollection was always "based on" a conversation with Krogh, or Ehrlichman's testimony—exactly the sort of preface one might expect from a witness anxious to skirt a perjury rap.

Finally, there was Nixon's own obfuscation about the tapes. In fact, the Special Prosecutors had subpoenaed none of the tapes from the August–September 1971 period—as Nixon well knew. And for a very good reason. Ehrlichman at his trial made no claim that Nixon authorized the break-in. His defense was that he, Ehrlichman, had not authorized it in conversation with Krogh, Young, Hunt, Liddy or Colson. Thus, whatever conversations he had with Nixon in the Oval Office or elsewhere were utterly irrelevant to the prosecution of the case and there was thus no reason for the prosecution to subpoena the material. Indeed, trying to get it would have done little but delay the Ehrlichman trial, since Nixon was, at the time, resisting subpoenas both from the Special Prosecutor's Office and the House Judiciary Committee. The Supreme Court decision in *U.S. vs. Nixon* was handed down shortly after the Ehrlichman trial was concluded.

By insinuating that the prosecutors had searched the material before finding nothing damaging, Nixon had in fact done little but impeach further his own credibility. He further reinforced our judgment regarding the limited nature of his willingness to accept blame for his conduct during the period. Rather than the total stonewall, Nixon was willing now to come to grips with what we could prove through our own research. He had reached the point where he would volunteer rather candid assessments of his conduct, but not fresh items of wrongdoing. His admissions in the Watergate area had been on the basis of evidence we had advanced and developed, not evidence he had volunteered. His assessment of the mood and atmosphere within his own White House in these other abuse areas would also deal only with the proven matters of record. During the past few days, Nixon had become a cooperative juror. He was, however, still a most reluctant witness. Like a half-reformed Catholic sinner, he willingly came to confession, but still reserved the right to dissemble once he got inside 'the booth.

"What about the proposal to do the fire bombing at the Brookings Institution?" I asked. "As you know, there is word to the effect that that was something on one tape or another—which I have not heard—that you actually specifically asked for that. Not the fire bombing necessarily, but asked for the Brookings Institution to be covertly investigated."

Again the pattern repeated itself.

He spoke first of rumors that Brookings was preparing a study of U.S. policy in Vietnam during the 1969–70 period and that Xeroxing of some of the Pentagon Papers had been done there.

"I have no recollection of authorizing a break-in at Brookings. I, however, would not say that I did not express deep concern about the fact that Brookings might have this and that I did not express a very great interest in trying to obtain those documents from Brookings. Ah . . . get them back in some way if we possibly could."

"Obtain" those documents. Get them back "in some way." Perhaps a stamped self-addressed envelope? The euphemisms were choice. All of this led us on to the mentality of the Nixon White House, the President's own assessment of the hostile environment all about him, his vision of the White House as a stockade in the midst of rebellion and siege. So we turned to the subject of Nixon's September 15, 1972, conversation with Dean and Haldeman, not the part where Watergate was discussed, but the section where, discussing Washington lawyer and D.N.C. treasurer Edward Bennett Williams, Haldeman says, "That's the guy we've got to ruin," and Nixon replies, "Yes, I think we're going to fix the S.O.B., ah, believe me we're going to."

"Isn't there in that whole conversation, a . . . " I began, searching for the best way to characterize what I had quoted.

But Nixon volunteered it for me.

"A paranoiac attitude?"

"Yes," I replied gratefully. The man's choice of words was immaculate.

"Yes, I know," he said. "I understand that. And it gets back to the statement that I made, ah, rather an emotional statement, the day I left office. And I said, 'Don't hate other people, because hatred destroys yourself.' "

Once again Nixon, unable or unwilling to come to grips with individual acts of excess, had, with commendable candor, taken the far more important step of addressing the totality of his conduct. And, in doing so, he was again revealing personal things he would have denied had they been presented to him in an accusatory way. Yes, he had a temper, he agreed. But he had "weaknesses" —a Nixonian choice of words to describe compassion—where "personal factors" are concerned.

"Now let's, let's take the Kennedys now. Did you know that in eight years after Mrs. Nixon and I had served in Washington for eight years, Vice-President—I was Vice-President and she as my wife—we were never invited to the White House, to a dinner or a lunch? I remember Rose Mary Woods, my secretary who made up the invitation list, went out of her mind when I put Hubert Humphrey on the list for White House dinners; ah, when I put, for example, invited Jackie Kennedy and her two children to come up for a private dinner without any publicity so that they could see where their father had, where they'd grown up and all the rest; when Mrs. Nixon had Rose Kennedy over . . . "

When I had asked Nixon, more than a week earlier, whether he had felt like an outsider in Washington, he had laughed nervously and retreated from all that psychological nonsense. Now he had said the same thing more eloquently and with greater pathos than he could have in response to any direct inquiry.

And he went on to reveal other small acts of personal kindness, not, I was convinced, because he felt sorry for himself and wanted to score some cheap melodramatic points with the audience, but because he wanted desperately to be understood as a complete man, a man with grave—perhaps even fatal—weaknesses, but also a man with another side to his character.

He told of a note he sent Teddy Kennedy after the Senator's young son had been stricken with cancer requiring the amputation of a leg, and of a note to Senator Tom Eagleton's son, who was depressed after his dad was driven off the 1972 Democratic presidential ticket. Also of a kind note he had received during his own illness from his journalistic nemesis, Daniel Schorr, enclosing a "get-well greeting" from Schorr's young son.

"Why do I bring this out? What I'm trying to tell you is this whole business of, am I paranoiac about hating people and trying to do them in? And the answer is: at times, yes. I get angry at people. But in human terms, as far as I'm concerned, I believe that an individual must never let hatred ruin him. I . . . Dolores Hope, Bob Hope's wonderful wife, once said something to me when we first came to California after the resignation. She said, 'Remember, Dick, one person who loves you is worth ten who hate you.' And so, there's a love-hate complex in all of us. And I just hope that when they tote 'em all up before you go to St. Peter's, or the other way down, that maybe the, the ledger's going to come out reasonably well in that respect . . . "

But what had caused this hatred, I wanted to know. What had caused a decent religious sort of fellow like Bud Krogh to write, "Those who are against us we will destroy. In fact, those who are not for us, we will destroy"?

It all had to be understood in the context of the times, Nixon replied. "This nation was at war. Men were dying. The people that got us into the war, ah, the brightest and the best, proved to be the worst in this crisis. Because they could—like Rusk and Rostow—have either supported us, or given us a chance to get out of the war that they'd gotten us into. But, on the other hand, they turned totally around, and they stirred up the demonstrators . . . "

He recalled when Kissinger was first told that the 1969 Cambodian bombing leak could have originated with someone on his staff. And, imitating Kissinger's German accent magnificently, Nixon quoted Kissinger saying, "I veel deestroy zem."

"Henry was not a mean man," Nixon said, recalling his having escaped from Nazi Germany. "But he said, 'I will destroy them.' Why do we feel this way? We felt this way because the people on the other side were hypocritical. They were sanctimonious. And they were not serving the best interests of the country."

They were not intending to prolong the war, he continued, but because of their dissent, the war lasted one to two years longer than it otherwise would have.

"This is why, I must say Henry and I felt so strongly about it. And, ah . . . call it paranoia. But paranoia for peace isn't that bad . . . "

That classic line evoked an immediate suggestion from Zelnick. "I think we ought to start a movement of Paranoiacs for Peace," he told Birt. "I always felt that 'Extremism in the defense of liberty is no vice' was a bit long for a button."

Secrecy was also vital, Nixon continued. Without secrecy there would have been no SALT I, no approach to Peking, and no successful negotiated end to the Vietnam War. "And basically, what Ellsberg really boils down to is this . . . I mean, the discrediting and all the rest, what it boils down to. I didn't want to discredit the man as an individual. I couldn't care less about the punk. I wanted to discredit that kind of activity, which was despicable and damaging to the national interest."

How did the Plumbers run afoul so quickly? Why did it all go so rotten so fast?

On the surface, Nixon was at a loss to explain. He didn't know, he said. But there was ample precedent for that too. Martin Luther King had been bugged, L.B.J. had the F.B.I. bug the Mississippi Freedom Democratic Party at the 1964 convention. Goldwater claimed he was bugged in 1964, Bobby Kennedy as Attorney General had reporters awakened at midnight to see what they knew about monopolistic collusion in the steel industry. The sugar interests had their taxes checked by the Kennedys. Nixon did some wrong things. "Some of them were not right. I do say, let's understand them with a single standard. I do say, let us understand them in the context of the times, that we were in wartime . . ."

Of course, I thought, the Plumbers had not really "run afoul" at all. They had done exactly what they had been established to do. They behaved perfectly, given the desires of the Nixon White House and its expectations of them. Nixon, though, had answered the more basic question. He had shown what it was that made his White House unique. Not in terms of arithmetic. Not in terms of the quality of abuse. These matters had been resolved throughout our earlier sessions. By this time, Nixon's own involvement in activities known to be illegal at the time they took place—institutionalized within his White House, kept secret from the Congress, lied about to the public, ideological in character and ruthlessly implemented against persons and groups thought hostile to his goals—had been shown to exceed in scope and design anything which had come before.

But Nixon had told us why. His passions, his hatreds, his recollections of past snubs, his view of the power and prerogatives of his office, his insecurities, the caliber of those closest to him—these had all played a role. So had his penchant for political gut-fighting and demagoguery. Together they made his White House disaster-prone. Yet in another era, he might well have muddled through. The worst might never have come to pass. They needed a catalyst to become really dangerous.

The Vietnam War was that catalyst. There could be no greater mistake on anyone's part than to define it as limited. And here again there is irony. Because the war *was* limited from the standpoint of military commitment and national objectives. But those very constraints turned it into an unlimited internal political struggle from which no theater of national life was remote.

It was an all-encompassing struggle. And Nixon regarded it as such. And he fought it as such. On every front. With every weapon at his disposal. He was not really all that paranoiac. He was—in a sense—right. The demonstrators and other dissenters may not have been as violent as he feared, or as monolithic, or as hypocritical, or as evil-spirited, or even as effective. But they certainly were fighting against his war. And as long as that war required—as it did—a pervasive political commitment on the part of the American people, they were undermining that commitment. They were not only prolonging the war; they were losing it. They were the enemy.

None of this means that Nixon's conduct was in any way excusable. National survival was never at stake in Vietnam. The constitutional protections written into American doctrine must survive this kind of confrontation, or they are worth very little. And, even now, one would be hard pressed to conceive of a single Nixon excess which in any way aided his ability to fight the war as he felt he must.

But for one seeking to understand why it was that the darker Nixon instincts prevailed, why it was that his chilling views of the power of his office found expression in the activities of himself and his surrogates, the answer is simply, the war. "Those who are against us, we will destroy . . ."

Nixon knew who was against him. All he had to do was look outside the gates of his White House. And he wanted to destroy them.

"You know," I said in the car on the way back to the hotel, "we now have our program on the war. But it's war at home *and* abroad. And the progress from one to the other is almost inexorable."

As the tapings drew to a close, we began to realize—almost nostalgically—that we now had our own collection of Nixon conversational memorabilia to call upon. When Jim asked John a question, he replied, "I have no recollection of that. Of course, I am basing my recollection entirely on Bob's handwritten notes."

And when another downbeat tidbit appeared in that ever vigilant Washington gossip column and Bob informed me of the item and asked if it bothered me, it seemed only right to respond with true Nixonian magnanimity, "Well, it drives my family right up the wall. And it's only because it bothers them that it bothers me at all."

"I feel rather sad," I told Nixon, as we took our places on the set for our last session. "I don't know what I'll be doing in the morning."

Nixon chuckled. "You get a letdown. You always do after these things."

"Yes, you do," I agreed.

" 'Cause you think you're going to feel great, but you feel let down for a few days."

"When you have time . . ." I began.

"Then you'll have to start . . . of course you've got to edit."

"Yes, ah . . . that's going to be hard work."

"And I have to get back to the book."

"Yes," I said, "so neither of us are actually going to have a holiday, are we?"

"No way," said Nixon. "Three days."

"Em . . . three days . . . "

"Five seconds," counted Don Clark . . . three . . . two . . .

Our conversation on the subject of the corruption and bribery charges against Vice-President Agnew soon began to take a number of strange turns. Nixon himself had only got into the picture when the investigation had surfaced publicly on August 7. When he met with Agnew on that date, the Vice-President, according to Nixon, had told him the charges were "just a pack of lies." Then, rather than relating any sense of concern or betrayal he may have felt at the time that yet another member of his "law-and-order" administration was about to come to grief—and this one strictly on the basis of personal greed—Nixon instead said he summoned Attorney General Elliot Richardson to the White House, where he warned him to make sure "that he, Richardson, was not in the position where it would look as if this were ah . . . a political motivation on his part. I mean, there was no secret that Richardson and Agnew didn't like each other. There was no secret that Richardson had ambitions to be Vice-President or President in 1976—and earlier, if possible, if somebody had picked him."

On September 25, Richardson and Henry Petersen reported to Nixon that there were some forty charges against Agnew which they felt were sustainable. Later on the 25th of September, Nixon and Agnew met at the Executive Office Building and here Nixon went out of his way to emphasize that there was no acrimony, that reports suggesting "that the roof actually came off the E.O.B.

building" were false. It was at this point that the Nixon and Agnew cases merged. For Agnew requested that Nixon intercede with the Republican leadership in the House of Representatives in order to have the charges against him resolved via an impeachment proceeding rather than a grand-jury indictment and criminal trial. Technically this would have meant simply a delay in the criminal proceedings, since the Constitution expressly states that a public official impeached and removed from office remains liable to criminal charges. But the specter of the House Judiciary Committee tooling up to conduct a major investigation—in the midst of Watergate—on charges of petty corruption committed by the Vice-President during his years as Governor of Maryland, and having those procedures followed by a full-dress trial in the Senate, even today would strike terror into the heart of anyone remotely concerned about the well-being of the American Republic. With the Nixon presidency itself hanging by a slender thread, could the country possibly have endured a situation where the first man in the line of succession was himself subject to a massive constitutional inquiry?

Nixon did not even mention this ghastly prospect. He spoke only of the problems confronting Agnew, making no secret of where his sympathies lay, and he did as Agnew had asked. He called House Minority leader Gerald Ford and asked him to intercede on behalf of Agnew's request for an impeachment probe. Agnew himself paid a visit on House Speaker Carl Albert with the same request.

But both Ford and Albert insisted that support in the House would not be forthcoming unless the Attorney General was willing to state that as a matter of law an incumbent Vice-President was immune to indictment—the very same question constitutional scholars were beginning to debate with respect to a sitting President.

The Attorney General would issue no such opinion. Indeed, it was precisely contrary to the views of Solicitor General Robert P. Bork, who concluded that while the Chief Executive is immune to indictment while in office, no similar immunity attaches to any other member of the executive branch.

Bork's opinion was received on September 28. "When we got this news, then, frankly, Agnew had come to the point—and he realized that he had come to the point—that he had no alternative but to do everything that he possibly could to avoid going into a court, which would be virtually, he thought—and I'm inclined to believe, he's right, under the tremendous pressures that were developing there in the media and the rest—would be a kangaroo court, where he'd have no chance and serve a prison term. [We thought] that he ought to take the steps that would . . . ah . . . ah . . . lead to a settlement of the matter without a prison term. And therefore a resignation option became absolutely indispensable."

To the end, Nixon said, Agnew protested his innocence. Well, if not exactly his innocence, at least the fact that he had precedent on his side. What he did in Maryland—demanding money from contractors who wished to be considered for state contracts—"was common practice in most of the Eastern states and many of the Southern states. It had not yet swept out to the West." Further, while the contributions were a "quid pro quo" for government business, "there was never an instance when a contract did not go to a highly qualified, and, in his view, the most qualified individual. In other words, his point being, that he did not in effect, accept money from somebody who would not have otherwise been entitled to a contract."

This was spectacular narrative, I thought. And I dared not interrupt it with challenges to Nixon's reasoning, or the incredibly warped outlook it reflected. The role of an interviewer is to draw out his subject in the most revealing way possible, and he needs to know when to shut up. This was one of those moments. A few moments later Nixon explained the Agnew philosophy another way. "I do not think for one minute that Spiro Agnew, for example, consciously felt that he was violating the law, and basically, that he was being bribed to do something which was wrong . . . because of a payment." Thus enunciating the remarkable new legal concept of being bribed to do something which was right.

I had asked Nixon whether he had believed Henry Petersen's

summary of the evidence of Spiro Agnew's protestations of innocence.

"I was very pragmatic," he replied. "In my view, it didn't really make any difference." There wasn't any question that Agnew "was going to get it."

"I felt that in his heart, he was a decent man," Nixon continued. "He was an honest man. He was a courageous man. He made mistakes. I made mistakes." He may have bitter feelings about Nixon, but they certainly aren't reciprocated.

Like Nixon himself, Agnew had been the victim of a "double standard." "I would say that because he was conservative, because he was one who took on the press, he got a lot rougher treatment than would have been the case had he been one of the liberals' favorite pinup boys."

"Yes," I interjected, "although, ah, although, there was Dale Anderson just before him and Governor Mandel since, it's, ah, it looks as though—"

"They're not—"

"—they're administering justice fairly evenhandedly."

The two Democrats are not favorite liberal pinup boys either, said Nixon. "When I say the liberals' pinup boys, you know exactly the ones I mean. Those that go down the liberal line and who can see all of the wickedness among the conservatives and when it's on their side, well, ha, ha, ha. Isn't that just fun and games."

In the production trailer, Birt and Zelnick had alternated between bouts of hilarity and incredulity at Nixon's responses. It was not Nixon's treatment of the Agnew matter at the time which they found hard to comprehend. After all, had the House of Representatives taken the bait and gone the impeachment route with Agnew, that could well have insulated Nixon from danger for a considerable period. Representative Rodino and his Judiciary Committee would have been otherwise occupied. And the Senate, going through the ordeal of impeaching a Vice-President, could hardly be expected to have the stomach for a return engagement with Mr. Nixon. Indeed, the very fact that Agnew would have been so visibly under siege for so lengthy a period could well have caused those pursuing the President to move cautiously or back off entirely.

Nor was it hard to explain why Nixon found it impossible to resist taking a few gratuitous swipes at Richardson, whose refusal to fire Archibald Cox trebled the damage of the Saturday-Night Massacre.

But how could Nixon justify defending a man who had misled him so blatantly when confronted with the charges against him? And why would he now—trying to regain a semblance of national respectability—line up behind a man who was literally without a constituent in the country? The most ardent conservative, who may well have applauded Agnew as the scourge of the Eastern liberal establishment, would today have no reason to support a man who had pleaded *nolo contendere* to tax fraud growing out of bribes received from a state contractor.

An hour or two later, as we concluded this final session, Nixon would—rather defensively, I thought—say, "Well, I hope I wasn't too hard on Agnew." And I would reply, "I wouldn't worry about that, Mr. President. I thought he came off a good deal better than Elliot Richardson."

Nixon's explanation was a simple one. "I just didn't want to kick him when he's down."

Well, maybe that was it. True, even in earlier days, Nixon would have had some difficulty condemning a politician who operated "within the system," even if that system happened to run afoul of the law. And true, if he thought Agnew could "tough it out" successfully, he would have been happy to have him stay at his job. He was indeed "very pragmatic" about the whole thing. He had not an ounce of moral reproof. But there was too a certain perverse, almost kamikaze loyalty about Nixon's responses. Agnew had played the game. He had given as well as taken a fair share of lumps. He had lost. Not because he had done anything "morally wrong." Immorality implies a departure from the norm. And Agnew, if nothing else, represented the "norm" in Maryland political life—where he came from, what his prejudices were, how he did his job, even how he earned a little "pocket money." No, Agnew had simply provided his foes with an opening. He gave them a sword. And, as with Nixon, they stuck it in. And they twisted it with relish. And, if he had been in their place, he would probably have done the same thing.

But Nixon was not about to compound his former colleague's pain or their relish by adding insult to injury. He'd stick up for his old buddy. What the hell. If "they" wanted to crucify him for that too, let them. That, as he saw it, was the least of his problems.

We turned back to the abuses that struck closer to home. I read Nixon the quote from his response to the Church committee. "It's quite obvious that there are certain inherently governmental activities which, if undertaken by the sovereign in protection of the interests of the nation's security, are lawful, but which, if undertaken by private persons, are not." What, at root, did he have in mind there? I wanted to know.

Again Nixon invoked the sacred memory of Abraham Lincoln. Lincoln had argued, he said, that actions which otherwise would be unconstitutional could become lawful if undertaken for the purpose of preserving the Constitution and the nation.

"But there was no comparison, was there, between the situation you faced and the situation Lincoln faced, for instance." Thirteen states were not seceding, for example . . .

"This nation was torn apart in an ideological way by the War in Vietnam as much as the Civil War tore apart the nation when Lincoln was President," Nixon replied.

But it was the legal basis of the President's action I was trying to get at, not another debate over the character of dissent. We felt that we had made our points on the facts where facts had been in dispute. We had developed the theory of the White House environment, the mentality of a President who regarded himself as living under siege. Now I wanted to turn to his theories about his country's Constitution, what its framers had in mind when they attempted to define the marriage of governmental authority and the protection of individual rights. I cited for him the well-known opinion of Chief Justice Charles Evans Hughes: "The

greater the importance of safeguarding the community from in-
citements to the overthrow of our institutions by force and violence, the more imperative is the need to preserve inviolate the
constitutional rights of free speech, free press and free assembly
in order to maintain the opportunity for free political discussion
to the end that government may be responsive to the will of the
people."

Bewilderingly, Nixon replied that the period during which
Hughes was writing—the 1930's—was one of little domestic violence
and scant concern about rebellion "because Communist subversion
hadn't reached a very significant level till long after Hughes left
the bench."

I thought that a startlingly tranquil description of the Depression years at home and the growth of Hitler's Nazi Germany
abroad, but I let it pass. What I wanted him to respond to was
his bedrock claim that he, as President, had the right to decide
unilaterally when constitutional protections could apply and when
they could not. In a sense, I suggested, "You were behaving like a
king . . . you were behaving like George III rather than George
Washington."

Alas, that line would eventually find itself on the cutting-room
floor, because Nixon's answer was unusable. He seemed so thoroughly beaten—or "psyched"—on the question of his own abuses
of power that his defense was no longer even credible enough to
stand as a meaningful test of our two positions. In this case he
began with a brief reference to the Black Panthers and the Weathermen, and then went into a long dissertation supporting his belief
in capital punishment.

I tried to come back to the point, "But when you said, as you
said when we were talking about the Huston Plan, that the President orders it . . . that makes it legal, as it were. But is the
President in that sense . . . is there anything in the Constitution
or Bill of Rights that suggests the President is that far of a sovereign . . . that far above the law?"

"No, there isn't," Nixon replied. "There is nothing specific that
the Constitution contemplates in that respect. I haven't read every

word, every jot and every tittle. But I do know this. That it has been, however, argued that as far as a President is concerned, that in wartime a President does have certain extraordinary powers which would make acts that would otherwise be unlawful, lawful, if undertaken for the purpose of preserving the nation and the Constitution, which is essential for the rights we're all talking about."

"And the point that you rest on is that this was a war situation," I said.

"It certainly was. It was not only war abroad . . . but it was a situation of violence at home . . ."

"But why not act, in order not to endanger the system, through the system, through the Congress?"

"That's a possibility which of course certainly occurred to me," said Nixon almost with appreciation, as though I had come up with a possible approach for solving, say, the welfare mess. "It was a situation, however, where in the temper of those times, to move through the Congress would have probably been an impossibility." It was tough enough to keep their support of the war itself, he said, let alone the measures necessary to preserve civil order.

"Look, I appreciate that it would have been difficult to get these things through Congress," I replied. "But does the Constitution and the Bill of Rights give the President the right to say, I can't get it through Congress, so I'll go around Congress, I'll avoid Congress?"

Throughout this part of the discussion, a single word kept repeating itself in my mind: Danger. We had tried to establish the roots of Nixon's view of the dissenters, his attitudes toward political foes, indeed the entire liberal establishment. We had tested his account of the decisions he made in Vietnam, and the legal basis on which he rested his case for the extraordinary steps he took to quash leaks and quiet the threat of violence. We had been all through Watergate and the work of the Plumbers. Yet it all added up to danger. Richard Nixon had been a dangerous President. Dangerous to the values of his system of government. Dangerous to the democratic traditions of his country. Dangerous to the rule of law so painstakingly established, refined and protected over the years. Whatever his psyche, whatever his motives, whatever the political provocations of his opponents, the fact is that Richard Nixon was dangerous. He may not himself have had authoritarian or totalitarian ambitions, but had the precedent he set gone unchallenged, a future despot with a grander view would have had a distinct head start.

So I recalled for Nixon how some of his own actions had struck fear in the hearts of constitutional scholars. And I recalled for him the classic Ervin-committee exchange between Georgia's Senator Herman Talmadge and John Ehrlichman, where Talmadge recalled the English principle that the humblest citizen in the land was protected in his own cottage, even against the King. Ehrlichman had replied, with apparent relish, "There has been considerable erosion of that principle over the years."

"Can you understand people who saw in what you were doing, the danger of an erosion of civil liberty?" I asked.

"Oh, of course I can understand them," Nixon replied. "And I can understand too why they have a totally double standard on it too." They didn't mind Hoover going after the Ku Klux Klan and other right-wing organizations, he complained.

Then, somewhat more convincingly, he added, "Now when we talk about the great period of repression during the so-called Nixon years, who was repressed? My God, was CBS repressed? Was ABC repressed? *The New York Times?* The *Washington Post?* What about the dissenters? Were they repressed? Were they afraid to speak? What is the situation? All it did as far as they were concerned was to build up their lecture fees and so forth and so on, those that claim they were depressed—repressed."

That may be. To the extent Nixon had an inhibiting effect upon the media, that effect was certainly traceable more to political pressures from the White House—the Colson phone calls, the Agnew speeches, a few roundhouse rights delivered by the President himself—than to any of the conduct regarded as abuses of power on his part.

And I suspect that Nixon might not have quieted all the voices of dissent even if he could have. He thrived on combating them. He may have hated looking out of his window and seeing 250,000 peace demonstrators, but their activities and his battle against them won him, he probably felt, more than that many votes among the Silent Majority.

Still, his answer missed the basic point of what his abuses of power were all about. The United States Constitution had survived as a working document through two centuries of peace and war, insurrection and national harmony, prosperity and hard times, largely because the courts have tended to honor—even expand—its guarantees of civil liberties while applying flexibly those clauses dealing with commerce, the foreign-affairs prerogatives of the President and the separation of powers among the three branches of the government. Thus a process of trial and error was possible in such areas as the regulation of industrial conditions, tax and antitrust policy, the conduct of diplomacy and the shifting of influence among the various branches of the federal government and between it and the states. Such experimentation was possible only because civil liberties were assured, basic freedoms were not lost, democratic traditions were not trampled.

Nixon would have changed all that, some of it undoubtedly without specific intent. But if, for example, a President has the right unilaterally to discard the entire panoply of constitutional safeguards written out of existence by the Huston Plan, the next authoritarian down the line can start where his predecessor left off. That is what the Nixon abuse—and usurpation—of power was all about, and, as we moved to other subjects, it was something I feared he would never quite be able to confront or to fully understand.

It was touching all bases now, guarding against the possibility of a major story slipping away just because a question had gone unasked.

I raised the matter of anything Defense Secretary James Schlesinger might have done to check Nixon's power as Commander-in-Chief during those final White House days. Nixon claimed to know nothing about any effort by Schlesinger to limit his military prerogatives. And that "black box" always with the President, what might have happened if he had opened this key communications link with the military at one minute past noon on the afternoon of August 9, 1974?

"Oh, they would have answered and said, ah, 'Wrong number,' " Nixon replied, getting in his best one-liner of the series.

Returning to the less pleasant subject of his relations with Haldeman and Ehrlichman, I asked Nixon whether he had given either of them indications he intended to pardon them, before he was himself forced to leave office.

Once again his countenance turned grim and plagued. Only moments earlier, it had been relaxed as he joked about the black box aboard Air Force One. Never had I seen a man reveal so much of himself simply by the involuntary change of facial demeanor.

Nixon vaguely recalled a conversation with Haldeman in which he suggested he might use his pardon power if either of his top aides got "a bad rap."

"Of course, I had no idea then that I would be leaving office in the way that I was leaving, and before, of course, they were convicted of anything, before they had even been tried." (Apparently the former President's recollection failed him here, because Ehrlichman had been found guilty in the Plumbers case before Nixon was forced to quit.)

In any event, he confirmed reports that on the very eve of his resignation, both Haldeman and Ehrlichman—the latter acting via a call to Julie—had passed on their "strong recommendation" that he pardon both the draft evaders and all of those involved in Watergate. Never was the compassion of these two more in evidence than when they were themselves the beneficiaries.

Nixon declined. He had no stomach for war resisters and would not go back on his campaign pledge not to pardon them. He was more inclined to pardon his Watergate colleagues, except, "I was resigning office for primarily the reason that I wanted to get the whole Watergate obsession, which had then reached fever heat, cooled down. I wanted Ford to start with a new, clean slate. Ah, I felt that if I were . . . as my last act before leaving office and resigning—and the resigning I thought would prick the boil and let the thing cool down—that if my last act was to pardon everybody who was in Watergate, that would inflame the situation and would obviously look like the ultimate cover-up. So, under the circumstances, I did not consider it."

Nixon's pride was at work again. Having been driven from office because of his own role in the cover-up, he was still resisting any public act which would smack of cover-up. So he did not pardon Ehrlichman or Haldeman, nor did he pardon himself, despite that possibility too having been suggested by one of the defense counsel before he left.

"Yes," I said. "Were there any discussions on the subject of pardon, in fact, between you or your representatives and President Ford and his representatives before . . . before you left office?"

"Absolutely not. No. No," Nixon replied. "President Ford has answered that question under oath, and I consider that I'm responding here, in effect, under oath."

With that extraordinary compliment to the seriousness with which he had approached the Interviews, Nixon again denied any preliminary discussion. The matter had been Ford's own initiative, his counsel Philip Buchen contacting Nixon's lawyer, Jack Miller, with the proposal in early September. Miller flew to San Clemente.

"Ah, it was a terribly difficult decision for me," said Nixon. "Almost as difficult as resigning. Because I thought it compounded the whole situation . . ."

He thought too his acceptance of the pardon would be interpreted as an expression of guilt, not only with respect to Watergate, but also about such matters as the boost in milk-price supports, the sale of ambassadorships, the receipt of illegal campaign contributions and other matters of which he believed himself totally innocent. Strangely enough, it was the same list of three that Nixon gave almost every time that he was proclaiming his innocence of charges brought against him.

Miller reasoned with a client who was by now "emotionally drawn, mentally beaten down, physically not up to par." He told him that there is no legal precedent for the acceptance of a pardon being tantamount to acceptance of the truth of the underlying charges. And he argued that in the current political climate a fair trial was impossible.

So the man who declined to pardon his two top aides because it would have looked like the ultimate cover-up was persuaded by the wisdom and justice of accepting the pardon himself, knowing that it would be viewed as the ultimate cover-up.

"And it had exactly the effect that I expected. It exacerbated the issue. It was embarrassing to Ford. It cost him a great deal."

Nixon called the President a few days later to apologize for all the furor. Ford replied, "I don't give a damn about the criticism, I did it because it was right." Nixon denied he had made any offer to give the pardon back; there was no precedent for such an act.

Nixon referred to his feelings of mental depression during the final White House days and in the period immediately following his resignation. At the same time he had recognized that the Ford pardon had created an outcry from a nation which felt he had been dealt with more favorably than others who had been involved in the Watergate affair. There was an interesting juxtaposition here, Nixon feeling totally wiped out at the very moment that the rest of the nation regarded him as luckier than he deserved. In the hope of his recognizing the irony involved, I asked him to describe his state of mental depression following his resignation. His response would be among the most memorable of the interviews.

He had been "emotionally and physically and mentally fagged out," he said. "I know a lot of people—and I can understand it—say, 'Gee whiz, it just isn't fair, you know, for an individual to be . . . ah . . . get off with a pardon simply because he happens to have been President, and when another individual goes to trial and maybe has to serve a prison sentence for it.' I can understand how they feel. I can only say that no one in the world, and no one in our history could know how I felt. No one can know how it feels to resign the presidency of the United States. Is that punishment enough? Oh, probably not. But whether it is or isn't, as I have said earlier in our interview, we have to live with not only the past but the future. And I don't know what the future brings, but whatever it brings, I'll still be fighting."

Those words would be the last on our fourth program. They were spoken with such sincerity, such conviction and such pathos that even Nixon's most skeptical critics would implicitly recognize in their accounts that punishment is not something that lends itself to easy categorization. Who suffered the most from Watergate? Nixon? Perhaps. Mitchell? Maybe. Dean? Probably not. Certainly in his own mind Richard Nixon had suffered and was still suffering as much as any of them. And that, at that particular moment, seemed a pretty good working definition of punishment.

We talked about Nixon's illness. It had begun with an operation to prevent the clots in his leg from reaching the lung. He went through the recovery room and returned to bed. "It was then, as I was . . . just as I was getting into bed and sitting on the side of the bed, that apparently I passed out. And my blood pressure went down to what is called sixty over zero, which is, ah, as low as you can get and still live. And for eight hours I was in shock."

When he saw his doctor, Jack Lundgren, the following morning, he asked when he was going to have the operation.

"You've already had it," Lundgren laughed.

"Good. Where are my clothes?" Nixon asked. "I want to get out of here."

"Dick, we almost lost you last night," said Lundgren. It was then Nixon knew how sick he had been.

He remained on the critical list for four days, and in the hospital for several weeks after that. President Ford came to visit him, but the big glass door to his room didn't work. As the President paced outside, a big Secret Service man had to use a hacksaw on the door to the Nixon intensive-care ward so the President and former President could say hello.

Encouraged by my success at getting Nixon to reveal his private thoughts, I asked him about his views on the traumatic moment of death, but he begged off. He was "not really good when you go into this psychoanalysis."

"You run a mile from that," I smiled.

But I thought we might get to the same point via a slightly different route. And we did. "Did you, in a sense, feel that resignation was worse than death?" I asked.

"In some ways," Nixon replied. Not as the "popular mythologists" of the period might describe it. He had no desire to "fall on a sword" or to "take a gun and shoot myself." No. "I never think in suicidal terms, death wish and all that . . . that's all just . . . just bunk."

Resignation, however, meant "life without purpose," life without the ability to contribute to the causes he believed in, to fight the battles he enjoyed fighting. In that sense, resignation was "almost unbearable, a very shattering experience, which it has been. And, to a certain extent, still is."

Again, the popular misconception of his fate. People might envy his ability to live in a nice house, wear decent colthes, play golf whenever he pleased. "And the answer is, if you don't have those things, then they can mean a great deal. When you do have them, they mean nothing to you . . ."

"To me, the unhappiest people of the world are those in the watering places, the international watering places," Nixon continued. "Like the south coast of France, and Newport, and Palm Springs, and Palm Beach . . . going to parties every night, playing golf every afternoon, then bridge . . . drinking too much, talking too much, thinking too little. Retired. No purpose."

The people who envy that form of existence, "They don't know life. Because what makes life mean something is purpose. A goal. The battle. The struggle. Even if you don't win it."

That's why the resignation and life in retirement is so painful. "When you play a role that you don't want to play, it's then that you become most depressed, most unhappy, and that's my attitude toward the whole business."

There would be more to the session. It was in the nature of things. This was our last day and we wanted to make sure we had left nothing out. So I would ask him again about the eighteen-and-a-half-minute gap, and his taxes, the Hughes money and the Shanghai Communiqué, and more. And he would volunteer corrections in the record, not of our interview, but of the tape transcript either published or written about in the newspapers. He had never called Judge Sirica a "goddamn wop." Nor had he, in another conversation—not January 3—made disparaging references about "Jew boys."

And as the conversation would turn from subject to subject, Nixon's demeanor would change with it. He would be stern and resolute. He would be pensive. He would be haunted by recollections of Watergate and the other abuses. Once again, this man showed the many faces of Richard Nixon. Which the real Nixon was—or even if there was one—we had long since stopped discussing among ourselves. It was an exercise in futility. Just as the Nixons changed from subject to subject, so we had to adapt to whichever Richard Nixon we were confronting. Alas, the American people had no such luxury. They took all the Richard Nixons or they took none at all. In the end, they decided to take none. Given the circumstances, it is hard to fault their choice.

The substance of our talks ended with a brilliant Nixon tour de force on the Soviet leadership of Brezhnev. Unlike his predecessor, Nikita Khrushchev, Brezhnev had no inferiority complex, no need to play the role of the brutal peasant. Khrushchev had once blown up at a reference by Ike to his vacations constantly being interrupted by telephone calls, Khrushchev regarding the remark as a slap at the scarcity of telephones in the Soviet Union. Khrushchev wore dirty collars and buttons on his shirtsleeves. Brezhnev was immaculately attired. He wore cufflinks. He was also more cautious than Khrushchev, less impulsive. There is more government by committee in the Soviet Union than in days past.

Still Brezhnev had his share of "animal magnetism" as opposed to Podgorny, and also Kosygin, "who's rather cold, more aristocratic in bearing."

But they were all followers of Lenin. "Probe with bayonets. If you encounter mush, proceed. If you encounter steel, withdraw."

But Brezhnev appreciated the possibilities of peace. They once took a boat trip in the Black Sea. They were passing Yalta. Brezhnev was showing him where Churchill and Roosevelt had stayed.

"We were sitting in the end of the yacht, in the back of the yacht . . . together as he pointed this out to me. All of a sudden, impulsively, he reached over and grabbed me—he was kind of like Johnson that way . . . he likes to grab people (he and Johnson would have had a lot of fun—they're much alike), and he put his arm around me, and he said, 'You know, my friend, President Nixon,' . . . he said . . . 'I only hope the day will come when every Russian and every American can sit together as we are sitting now and can be friends.' "

We were a little like Russians and Americans ourselves at that particular moment. I said a mental thank you to my team—to John and to Bob and to Jim and all my colleagues who had worked so hard—for I knew that, like Brezhnev, if Richard Nixon had encountered mush, he too would have proceeded with bayonet. But he hadn't, and I was thankful. Anyway, we were finished now.

"Mr. President, we're at the end of our time . . . Is there any question that I haven't asked you that if you'd been me, you would have asked you?"

"Well," said Nixon, "you know I was working so hard preparing for the five hundred or a thousand questions that you might ask that I haven't really given thought to any new ones . . ."

Nixon had a word to add about our staffs as well.

"Generally speaking in politics and in life generally, as a rule . . . you will find some people are competent but not loyal. Other people are loyal but not competent. And when you find one that is both competent and loyal then you've found the rarest of gems."

"Yes," I smiled in agreement. "But until we find that, we'll have to carry on with this lot . . ."

Wednesday, May 4, the day of our first show, was a day of tension for all of us. Bob Zelnick had flown to Washington to host the press screening in the afternoon. We had not been going to have a screening at first. Then we had thought of having it in Los Angeles. But Nixon and the Nixon presidency were Washington stories, and the Washington press corps deserved the opportunity to cover them.

We had insisted on an embargo. We wanted not so much as a word printed in advance of the broadcast, except for the excerpts we had released. The press corps could view the first program at 3 P.M. in order to have adequate time to prepare stories for the 11 P.M. news and the following morning's papers. But we wanted the audience to share the surprise and drama of the program—which was now the Watergate program—just as we had shared it on the set in Monarch Bay. We would place a total "wire embargo" on the material. AP, UPI and Reuters must not even send it over their facilities accompanied by a "hold" until broadcast. They must not transmit the wire story to their client newspapers, until the program was actually being broadcast.

Watergate had become the first program by universal agreement. "War at Home and Abroad" was an equally strong show in many ways but it had become clear throughout the production period that, until the American public had heard Nixon on Watergate, had seen he was prepared to confront that issue, they would be loath to listen to him on anything else.

The editing schedule for the past two weeks had been brutal. Tony Hudz had run a veritable shuttle service between the editing rooms at Don Stern Productions and John Birt's suite at the Hilton, where John and I would view and make new "paper" edits. Jørn Winther and Don were working up to twenty-four-hour shifts, along with Tony. They lived on cold pizza and warm Coke. Jørn had managed five hours of sleep in one seven-day period. "The five computers in Don's setup over here," he told me around midnight one night, "have become the only functioning brains in the place."

The advertising situation had improved. Bristol-Myers had come through, and had booked sixty seconds in all four shows, just as we had hoped. Alpo and Coleco Toys had also booked thirty seconds in all four shows. And Paramount Pictures and Gallo Wine had made individual bookings. We were at break-even. Or theoretically we were at break-even. Because some advertisers had had to be guaranteed a very high audience in terms of the price they would pay, which could then be reduced proportionately; while other advertisers, still fearful of the potential for controversy in the program, had retained the right to withdraw if they were overwhelmed with a flood of complaints. So, in that sense, we still had our fingers crossed.

After examining the project from all sides, both *Time* and *Newsweek* had felt able to write positive stories. So had *TV Guide* and *60 Minutes*. Even the unwelcome leak of some of our early research documents in Washington had at least allowed the *Washington Post* to become aware of the seriousness of our planning. And had triggered off a frantic, general search for more tapes like the ones Jim Reston had discovered, and which we had kept secret for so many months but which had been mentioned in the research documents which fell into the *Post*'s hands.

However, it was now today's reaction that we were all waiting for. Wednesday, May 4. While John and I carried on editing the second and third programs, we waited anxiously for news from Washington.

The atmosphere at the Capitol Hilton in Washington was electric, Bob told us later. About three dozen invitees clustered about two small monitors to watch the Watergate program. Bob Woodward and Carl Bernstein were there, Jim Naughton, Bill Safire, Fred Graham, Carl Stern, Jack Anderson, Larry Spivak and a host of others. Pam Zelnick and Liz Sykes, my secretary from New York, checked credentials at the door. A guard was posted outside.

Bowing to the wish of the wire services, Zelnick, after checking with Marv, had lifted the wire embargo. Many of the smaller dailies in the nation have early deadlines. Unless the material could go out, millions of Americans would be unable to read of the broadcast in their morning newspapers, Zelnick had been told.

One of the monitors failed. The showing started late. Throughout the presentation Zelnick tried to gauge the reaction on the faces of his colleagues. He couldn't read a thing. He was too nervous and they were not particularly communicative.

After the screening, most dashed off to file their stories without telling Bob of their verdict. Carl Bernstein was one exception.

Carl Stern was another. Both, paying their respects to Zelnick, said we had done a fine job.

Zelnick stacked the cassettes and remaining transcripts in cartons. It was four forty-five. He had promised to drop off a transcript at the home of Bruce Herschensohn, a former Nixon staffer, who was that evening scheduled to appear on a Westinghouse panel discussion. Zelnick's car rolled onto Constitution Avenue. It was 5 P.M. His radio was tuned to WTOP, the CBS affiliate in Washington. Douglas Edwards was coming on with the hourly news. "The Associated Press reports that the embargo on the Frost-Nixon Interviews scheduled for broadcast later this evening has been broken and CBS is free to report that . . ."

Zelnick slammed on the brakes. He executed an illegal U-turn and sped up 20th Street toward CBS. In the newsroom, he was informed that the embargo had been broken by the *San Diego Tribune* and that all three networks were going with the dramatic story on their evening news shows. Most Americans would learn the news at 6:30 or 7 P.M., one half hour before our first broadcast.

Totally crushed by the development, Zelnick borrowed a desk and telephone to call me at the Beverly Hilton.

I had already learned from Marv and Don Clark. I was even more devastated than my colleague. The years of work suddenly seemed in jeopardy. Our audience would be cut in half. The networks would broadcast all the most dramatic moments from the transcript and the suspense would be gone.

"Bob, how did this disaster happen?"

"I lifted the wire embargo to accommodate AP and UPI. And some San Diego paper ran with the story, breaking the broadcast embargo."

"Oh, how could you do such a thing? Why didn't you check with me?"

"It seemed a reasonable request. I didn't want the story to be kept from anybody because of early deadlines."

Lesley Stahl, sitting next to Zelnick, was pulling on the phone. "Let me talk to David," she pleaded.

"David."

"Lesley. How are you?"

"Pregnant. How are you?"

"Terrible. Terrible. I can't believe this disaster."

"It's the best thing that could have happened to you, David. It will do nothing but act as a teaser for seventy million people when all three networks lead with the story. Most producers would give their right arm for something like this to happen."

"Do you really think so?"

"Sure I do."

"You're not just saying that to ease the pain, or to save C. Robert Zelnick from a fate worse than death?"

"No. And don't worry about it. I heard you did a terrific job."

"Really?"

"Really. Everybody says the show is a triumph."

My heartbeat rate began to come back to normal. But there was to be one more shock in the day's proceedings. At five o'clock Los Angeles time, when the show had been on the air for half an hour in Washington, there was a phone call from Liz. She was watching the program in a bar in Washington, and was calling to say that a network news crew had suddenly arrived and started filming audience reactions, including zooming into close-ups of the screen. Had I okayed such an activity? I said that I hadn't, and would get into it the next day. But in the meantime, I asked her, how was the program going?

"Absolutely fine," said Liz, adding, almost as an afterthought, "You know, apart from the one and a half minutes of silence at the beginning . . ."

"One and a half minutes of whaaat?"

Liz explained. For the first one and a half minutes of the program the audience all over the East Coast of America could see that I was speaking, introducing the program, but they could not hear it. I could scarcely believe the bad news. For months we had joked about not having an eighteen-and-a-half-minute gap in the program. And after all that, we had had a gap.

I picked up the other phone and rang Metromedia, from whose

studios we were transmitting the program across America. What the hell had happened? It turned out that a technician, who shall be nameless, had pressed the button that sent the picture across the country but had not pressed the button that sent the sound across the country. And since the program was not being broadcast for another three hours in Los Angeles, it could have been several minutes before the mistake had been discovered, but for the fact that Wayne Baruch, of the Robert Wold Company, who had handled the complex business of interconnecting the stations around the country, had a mother in Florida. Luckily, while the technicians were doing their work, he had placed a call to her.

"Well, Mother," he had said proudly. "What do you think of it? You think it looks lovely . . ." Wayne cupped his hand over the phone and yelled to his colleagues, "She thinks it looks lovely." He took his hand off the speaker of the phone. "Anything else you've got to say, Mother? . . . You can't hear anything . . . ?" He froze, and then repeated the words one at a time. "She . . . can't . . . hear . . . anything."

Wayne's mother had saved the day. Or at least probably two vital minutes of it. Which would probably have been the additional time it would have taken stations round the country to contact that control room with that little bombshell of information. The shocks of the day had done no good to my system whatever. But fortunately the Los Angeles feed that evening went off without a hitch. The team joined me at Chasen's for a thank-you supper. Even those who had been present when the interview was taped shared a sense of discovery, as did John and myself. Every time we saw the show, it seemed new, taking place for the first time before our eyes. It was startling and dramatic. I would catch nuances in Nixon's voice, revealing manual and facial gestures that I'd never noticed before. Though I had been through the material perhaps two dozen times now, I half expected Nixon to keep stonewalling it to the end. And when he didn't, I was just as moved as I had been at the time.

EPILOGUE

I ONLY SAW RICHARD NIXON ONCE MORE. IT WAS A LITTLE OVER A week later, just after the second program on foreign policy had been broadcast. The reaction to the Interviews from both press and public had been greater than I could have dreamt possible. John and I had completed the editing of the third and fourth programs, and I was leaving California. Before I left, I drove to San Clemente with Caroline, to say farewell to Richard Nixon.

The law entitles former Presidents one federally financed office at a location of their choice. Nixon decided to use the Coast Guard compound adjacent to the grounds where his home stands. It used to be called the Western White House. The people who answer the phones there still say, "President Nixon's office." When people call for the first time, the words give them a bit of a shock.

The small buildings that house the offices are Spartan, as befits a military base. In the old days, one office was reserved for Henry Kissinger, another for John Ehrlichman, a third for Bob Haldeman and the fourth for the President.

It is quiet there now, but outwardly little has changed. The

313

lawns are still nicely manicured, the buildings meticulously kept, the photographs of Nixon at various meetings with world and national leaders still line the walls. On some days, you may see Rose Mary Woods answering the phones outside the private Nixon office. Ken Khachigian likes to work in shirtsleeves in the office directly across from Nixon's. But when the former President wants to see him, even for a moment, he puts his jacket on and makes sure his tie is straight.

Nixon gets a lot of mail. Most of it is handled by unsalaried volunteers—mainly pleasant, well-dressed, middle-aged ladies who like the thought of serving both history and a President they much admire.

Manolo Sanchez is usually somewhere about. He is a friendly, beaming, physical man with white hair. He often wears a blazer with the presidential seal on the breast pocket.

The Irish setter, King Timahoe, still has the run of the grounds. Manolo pays a lot of attention to him. He likes dogs. When he senses his boss is angry at somebody, he will often call the person in question "son of a whore." He would rather not use the more common expletive "son of a bitch," because he doesn't like defaming animals. Nixon also avoids that expletive when Manolo is around. The ex-President is sensitive about the feelings of people. He hates to offend. He doesn't like to say no. When put on the spot in private conversation, he will usually give in. He regards that as a weakness in himself. When he was President, he would do his best to avoid people who put him on the spot. Haldeman was effective at screening them out before they got to the Oval Office. Too effective.

"Hello, Mr. President," I begin.

"Hello . . . David." It is an affectionate greeting in its way. Never before has he called me by my first name. Four weeks ago I would have predicted that, once the post-Easter interrogation was over, we would have no communication between us, not even the pretense of a relationship. Yet Nixon has told his friends that he regarded the Interviews as "tough but fair," two words that one would have said were mutually exclusive in his vocabulary. He is full of surprises.

The opinion polls and the press that have been so positive about the program have not been as positive about him. I feel I should murmur my condolences. None are in order. He expected nothing better from the media. "You knew they'd crap on that, didn't you?" he asks. The mail coming to San Clemente has been pretty good. And many of his friends and former colleagues have told him he did much to purge the poison of Watergate from his own system, and perhaps the country's.

But it is not about Watergate that Richard Nixon wants to talk this day, or any other day. It is not about the other alleged abuses of his administration. One suspects that he still does not feel he should have been driven from office. The quality of his own deeds differed insubstantially from those of his predecessors, he believes. Others may honestly regard him as dangerous. They may see in his conduct and mind-set the germ of something drastically at odds with the nation's democratic heritage. But Richard Nixon knows his own mind and his own heart better than anyone else. And whatever others say, he knows that undermining our system of government, the constitutional traditions of the American Republic, the rights and freedoms people enjoy was the furthest thing from his mind. That was never his "motive."

Richard Nixon knows that he played tough. He played hard. But his goals were really quite modest, he would add. He wanted to build support for his policies, stay one step ahead of the dissenters and win reelection by a healthy margin. That was all.

He did not want to change the existing system, bring down the old elite or even realign the political forces in the country in anything resembling a fundamental way. God, if he had really wanted to turn the races or the regions or the classes against one another, how easily he could have done it. If he had wanted to shake the foundations of the establishment to the very core, that too would have been a simple trick, can't people see that? If he had cared nothing for the institutions of his country, don't we realize he could have conducted a cover-up worthy of the name? All right, the fact that he did nothing of the sort is interpreted by the critics and the psychiatrists as proof of his "penchant for self-destruction" and that sort of bunk. But that's typical. If he is not being condemned for running the cover-up, he's being condemned for not running it better. That's why he says they'll never leave him alone.

No, Richard Nixon would say, people have a short memory. A conveniently short memory. And the Richard Nixon who appointed Special Prosecutors, and who let his aides testify before the Congress, and who preserved the evidence which later brought him down, and who obeyed the mandates of the Supreme Court, and who left office voluntarily rather than fight a long impeachment trial in the Senate, was the same Richard Nixon who in 1960 conceded the election of John F. Kennedy rather than testing allegations of electoral fraud in the courts. The presidency in Richard Nixon's eyes is worth fighting for, but only when it is not destroyed in the fight itself. If you believe that—and Richard Nixon believes he believes that—then even the toughest of fighters must know when to quit. And that, to his dying day, Richard Nixon will proclaim that he knew, if nothing else.

But it is painful to talk about that kind of thing now, painful even to think about it. And not really worth it. He has had his say, and that's it. But his country, the world—that is something else again. And that Richard Nixon wants very much to talk about.

In its own way he finds it a more depressing situation than his own downfall. He is pessimistic, almost apocalyptic in his view of the United States and where it is heading. He talks freely about the "end of the American era," perhaps even of Western civilization. Time is running out. The West has dominated the world for the past hundred years. Now, perhaps, for another hundred years, it will be the turn of the Communist states.

He is not one to argue the need for mammoth defense budgets, the ability to outstrip the Soviets in the nuclear race. That is not where the challenge lies, he believes. He sees no likelihood of America losing a great war, no likelihood of one even being fought. He feels that like ancient Rome, we are more likely to suffer a failure of nerve, a breakdown in national will. We are vulnerable to barbarians as much as to superpowers.

Nixon's observations are clinical, not theoretical. The loss of Vietnam was evidence of America's unwillingness to continue in its role as a world leader. The failure to come to the aid of our forces in Angola was similar evidence. The success of the Arab oil embargo during his own administration was a danger sign. Our refusal to come to the aid of Zaire in its recent battle against insurgency also boded ill.

And that Harris poll. That Harris poll. Americans unwilling to fight for Germany, for France, for Israel. Unthinkable. Unimaginable. A clear, indeed an indelible signal to aggressive foes that we have lost the guts for greatness. And why do we proclaim it so loudly? Why do we brandish our weakness with as much apparent pride as we used to brandish our strength? When our leaders say we would not intervene were the Soviet Union to attack the People's Republic of China, we are not just telling the Soviet Union that China is vulnerable, but that we are vulnerable.

"Keep 'em guessing," Nixon says. "A certain unpredictability is an element of strength." He does not have to recall that the Communists attacked South Korea when we said it was outside the perimeters of what we would defend. One knows that example is on his mind. He has spoken about it often in the past.

It isn't the way it was two hundred years ago when Jefferson made the statement that America is the hope of the world. It wasn't yet true then. It is now. America's strength is indispensable. It's much easier for totalitarian regimes. They don't have to deal with dissenters and opinion polls. Totalitarian regimes can do what they want. Democracies have a problem. They tend to get bogged down in narrow domestic self-interest. That's why we may be on the verge of that period of domination by the Communist states.

There are globes in Richard Nixon's house and globes in his office. He looks at them often, studies them, cradles them with his hands as a gypsy fortune-teller does her crystal ball. There is a certain mysticism about it all. It seems the closest he comes to the formal practice of religion.

And his is a proselytizing cult. It has to be, by definition. For the End of Our World may be At Hand. "Now I must talk to you like a father. No, a brother—my daughter Tricia says I look as young as you on camera! You are a communicator. You can set up a worldwide network. You have a responsibility to talk about these things, these threats. A greater responsibility than others."

He adds a postscript. "The most important thing I said in the Interviews you've probably cut out," he says, gently, resignedly.

"What's that?"

"About where power lies today. In the media. With no checks and balances. You've probably cut that out."

"Well, I have half passed the test," I say. "We're including it in the fifth show."

He looks pleasantly surprised. "Well, anyway, take two months before you decide anything. But then talk about these things."

I promise him I'll talk about them. It is not difficult to understand the sources of his concern. His is the classic view of national power. It is not the sort of view that easily accommodates the so-called new realities. It is not a view that reads very much into votes at the United Nations, other than the extent to which such votes tend to symbolize our own decline. It is not a view that pays much attention to the internal processes of other nations. They are with us, against us or neutral. They are Communist or non-Communist. They threaten their neighbors or they don't.

Nor does his view of the world easily accommodate vacuums. They are there to be filled, if not by us then by someone else. It is nice to think of 150 nations going their separate, independent ways, nice to think of zones where there is little ideological competition, where the vital interests of the Great Powers are remote, where purely local destinies will be shaped by purely local conditions. Nice, but fuzzy-headed. Nice, but unrealistic. Nice, but ultimately dangerous.

Because the guys on the other side don't think that way. They don't play by those rules. They don't sit back and wait while Americans toy with macrobiotic diets and try to adjust to the post-Vietnam, post-Watergate morality.

And not only do the guys on the other side not think that way, no power in the history of the world has ever thought that way, or acted that way, or conducted diplomacy that way, or waged war that way.

Order is the essential ingredient for world peace just as it is for the peace of a neighborhood. And order is maintained through strength, moral strength, physical strength, strength of character and strength of will.

I look at Richard Nixon and I see the face of tragedy. He is a smart man, in many ways an incredibly able man. He thinks clearly and he speaks well. He is a man to whom history has relevance. He has a sophisticated understanding of world affairs, a nice touch for dealing with other leaders. He might have made a good Secretary of State. Perhaps a great one.

Yet of all the strengths he has talked about, the one he has ignored strikes me as the most critical. And that is the strength that comes from a nation's belief in the essential rightness of its own cause, in the integrity of its own vision, in the justice of its own ends, in the basic goodness of its own deeds. And that is the strength that was undermined, the faith that was shaken, by Vietnam abroad and by the Watergate era at home. When Richard Nixon talks so sincerely, so articulately, of the developments that he fears and deplores—an American reluctance to assume its global responsibilities as he defines them, and a weakened presidency that makes it more difficult to shake the nation out of its global lethargy—he is talking, in part at least, of his own legacy.

But that part of our conversation is over. And once again he confounds the caricatures of himself. He takes Caroline by the hand, firmly, warmly—this man supposedly so uncomfortable with women. He takes her to the window. "Out there is China," he tells her, pointing and gazing in a dreamy way. "Let me show you the garden . . . " and he leads her out onto the patio. "Brezhnev slept in that room," he tells her. "A great swordsman. The Russians are, you know. Have you read Tolstoy? *Anna Karenina*, very romantic . . . "

They return. For a moment, the usually somber cloud has lifted.

Manolo brings some more Blanc de Blancs. "Get the caviar the Shah sent us for Christmas, Manolo." Manolo is requested to do his favorite imitation: of Henry Kissinger biting his nails, clutching his files, and losing his toothbrush. There is a moment of genuine gaiety. And then the spell is broken. The more somber tone returns. But for a moment it was there. And I had not expected it. Any more than four weeks ago I would have expected him to touch me as he had in our Watergate sessions. To break down, as he had, the barriers to intimacy that he had erected so painstakingly through the years.

But we have trespassed upon his solitude for long enough. It is time to go. We leave him standing by the window, gazing towards the ocean. He has made us feel at home. This man normally so ill at ease with people. Perhaps even more ill at ease with himself. A good mind, with a thirst for nobility. A sad man, who so wanted to be great.

As we drive away, I look back and I wish him peace at the center.